Northwest Historical Series
III

MAJOR OSBORNE CROSS
From an original photograph by the U.S. army signal corps

THE MARCH OF

THE MOUNTED RIFLEMEN

First United States Military Expedition
to travel the full length of the Oregon Trail from
Fort Leavenworth to Fort Vancouver
May to October, 1849

as recorded in the journals of
MAJOR OSBORNE CROSS and GEORGE GIBBS
and the official report of Colonel Loring

edited by
RAYMOND W. SETTLE

THE ARTHUR H. CLARK COMPANY
Glendale, California, U.S.A.
1940

Contents

Illustrations

Preface

The march of the Mounted Riflemen from Fort Leavenworth to Fort Vancouver in 1849 is well known to students of western history and the Oregon trail; yet the primary accounts of this expedition have not hitherto been collected nor presented in a form available to the public. It was with the desire to place these valuable and interesting documents within the reach of all that the work of editing them was undertaken.

The official journal of Major Osborne Cross, quartermaster of the expedition, has been known to a few special students, but on account of the scarcity of the original government document in which it appears, it is available in but a few of the larger libraries.

The two installments of the diary of George Gibbs, a civilian artist and naturalist who accompanied the expedition, have been virtually unknown. Published in a contemporary newspaper, this interesting account was completely overlooked, until it was called to the attention of Henry R. Wagner, as stated in the last edition of his *Bibliography of Original Narratives of Travel and Adventure*.

Colonel Loring's official report of this expedition has never been published separately before.

In the introduction and footnotes the editor has added much new material from family papers and from research in various archives. The full text of the documents has been retained, the editorial work being restricted almost exclusively to simplifying the grammatical structure of the long and involved sentences so popular in the mid-nineteenth century.

The preparation of this work was made possible by the cooperation of many whose names cannot be mentioned here; to them I am deeply indebted. Especially am I indebted to the Librarian of Congress, Colonel C. R. Bennett, Q.M.C., Mr. P. M. Hamer of the National Archives, Mr. Paul North Rice of the New York public library, Miss Louise F. Kampf of Colorado college library, Miss Opal Carlin of William Jewell college library; the state historical societies of Kansas, Missouri, Nebraska, Utah, Idaho, and Oregon; John G. Clemson, John Osborne Clemson, and Charles O. Clemson, grandsons of Major Cross; and to my wife, Mary Lund Settle, for help in research and in the preparation of the manuscript.

RAYMOND W. SETTLE

Lamar, Colorado
June 4, 1940

Introduction

On may 19, 1846 the congress of the United States
authorized the establishment of military posts along
the road to Oregon, appropriated three thousand dollars
to defray the expenses of each, two thousand dollars
each to purchase the right to occupy the ground from
the Indians, and seventy-six thousand five hundred
dollars for mounting and equipping a regiment of
Mounted Riflemen to consist of ten companies of sixty-
four privates each.[1] Persifor F. Smith was appointed
as colonel, and among the captains was William Wing
Loring, later commander of the regiment on its historic
march from Fort Leavenworth to Fort Vancouver in
1849.

This new regiment was recruited in Pennsylvania,
Maryland, Virginia, Texas, Tennessee, Kentucky,
Ohio, Indiana, Illinois, and Missouri. All of the companies were assembled at Jefferson barracks, St. Louis,
Missouri, with the exception of companies C and F,
which were brought together at Fort McHenry, Maryland, and company I at New Orleans.[2]

Regardless of the fact that the regiment was authorized for the specific purpose of garrisoning posts along
the road to Oregon the administration ordered it to the
seat of war in Mexico in november 1846. The diversion
of the Mounted Riflemen made necessary the raising of
a substitute unit to do its work. Consequently, the "Oregon battalion of mounted volunteers" was recruited in

---

[1] *U. S. Statutes at large,* IX, 13; Bancroft, *History of Nevada, Colorado,
and Wyoming,* 688.

[2] Deibert, *History of third United States cavalry,* 4.

Missouri in the summer of 1847 upon requisition by President Polk. The troops were mustered into service at Fort Leavenworth and Ludwell E. Powell was commissioned as colonel. Instead of proceeding at once to Grand island on the Platte river, which had been chosen as the site for one of the new posts, the battalion marched to Table creek, a few miles below present Nebraska City, Nebraska, erected sixty or seventy log cabins with slab, dirt, and straw roofs and spent the winter there. This place was called Camp or Fort Kearny in honor of General Stephen W. Kearny. In the spring of 1848 Colonel Powell marched his command to Grand island where he began work on the new post, which was called Fort Childs in honor of General Thomas Childs. He occupied the place during the summer and was relieved by companies G and I of the Mounted Riflemen under Brevet-major Charles F. Ruff on october 28, 1848. Ruff proceeded to build winter quarters under the severest of handicaps, and on december 30 of that year the name of the place was officially changed to Fort Kearny.[3]

While Colonel Powell and his "Oregon battalion" were occupying the post at Grand island the Mounted Riflemen were engaged in the Mexican war. Proceeding to New Orleans they embarked for Point Isabel, Texas, and from thence to Lobos island, which was General Winfield Scott's base for a campaign against Vera Cruz. Here they were joined by their commander, Colonel Persifor F. Smith, who was soon assigned to command the First brigade of General D. E. Twiggs's division. Vera Cruz was taken march 27, 1847, and the march to Mexico City begun.[4]

From the capture of Vera Cruz to the fall of Mexico

---

[3] *Ibid.*, 6; Nebraska state historical society *publications*, XVI, 237, 239, 241, XX, 176, 177, 184, 185.

[4] Deibert, *History of third United States cavalry*, 6-8.

City the Mounted Riflemen bore their full share of marching, fighting, and hardship. They distinguished themselves at Cerro Gordo, Contreras, Churubusco, and Molino del Rey. At Chapultepec, september 13, 1847, Lieutenant B. S. Roberts led the storming party which opened the attack and planted the first American flag on the Mexican position. Captain Loring lost an arm at the Garita; Captains J. B. Backenstos and S. S. Tucker, and Lieutenants I. N. Palmer and J. G. Walker were also wounded. The flag Roberts planted upon the Mexican position was displayed over the National palace, and while reviewing the Mounted Riflemen september 14, General Scott said, "Brave rifles! Veterans! You have been baptized in fire and have come out steel!" These words were immediately adopted as the regimental motto and have been retained by the organization, now the Third United States cavalry, to the present day.[5]

With the fall of Mexico City the Mounted Riflemen did provost and police duty for the remainder of the war. They fought at Huamantla, Puebla, Matamoros, Galaxara, and Santa Fe. On july 7, 1848, under command of Lieutenant-colonel William W. Loring, they embarked at Vera Cruz for Jefferson barracks, where they arrived on the twenty-fourth of the same month. Their record of honors and achievements was a splendid one. In the eighteen engagements in which the regiment participated fourteen of the officers won brevets and eleven men from the ranks were advanced to higher grades. Their casualties were: killed in action, four officers and forty-five men; wounded, thirteen officers and one hundred eighty men; died, one officer and two hundred eighty men. On august 7, 1848 the men were mustered out of service and the reorganization of the

[5] *Ibid.*, 8-9, 10, 12.

regiment begun. It was now assigned to its original task of establishing and garrisoning posts along the road to Oregon.[6]

About the beginning of the year 1849 preparations for the departure of the Mounted Riflemen from Jefferson barracks began in earnest. An estimate of supplies calling for over half a million pounds of freight, four hundred twenty-nine wagons, and seventeen hundred sixteen mules to draw them was prepared by the regimental quartermaster, Lieutenant D. M. Frost, and forwarded to Major-general D. E. Twiggs, commandant of the Sixth military district at St. Louis, Missouri. Officers on recruiting duty were ordered to close their stations and proceed to Jefferson barracks and may 1 to 15 set as the time for departure from Fort Leavenworth. Early in january Captain Michael E. Van Buren with company A marched for that place, and about the middle of february Captain Noah Newton and company B followed. These companies marched overland, the Missouri river being closed to navigation by ice, and suffered many hardships on the way.[7]

By the latter part of march the remainder of the regiment had been transported upriver on steamboats and was established at Camp Sumner about five miles west of Fort Leavenworth. Here Brevet-colonel Loring drilled his men and assembled his train, which, when ready to march, consisted of seven hundred horses, twelve hundred mules, a number of oxen, and one hundred seventy-one wagons. Since the Mounted Riflemen would be the first military unit to travel the entire length of the Oregon trail Brevet-major-general

[6] Ibid., 10, 11; Jones, Circular letter, july 14, 1848; Nebraska state historical society publications, XX, 246.

[7] U.S. Senate. Executive documents, 31 cong., 2 sess., no. 1, pt. 2, 77-78; Loring to Twiggs, january 12, 1849; Loring to Jones, january 13, 15, february 2, 1849; Twiggs, order no. 8, february 9, 1849; Packwood, "Reminiscences," 42-43; Nebraska state historical society publications, xxi, 220, 227, 228.

Twiggs and Colonel Aeneas Mackay, deputy quarter-master general, came up from St. Louis to see them off. On the morning of may 10 five companies were reviewed and General Twiggs himself gave the order which pointed them toward Oregon. The route they took was that to Table creek and Council Bluffs. Following a course which led them north and west they crossed the Big Nemaha river in southeastern Richardson county, Nebraska, then swung to the northwest along the dividing ridge between that stream and the Little Nemaha. Crossing the north fork of the Big Nemaha they followed a westerly course until they struck Sandy creek in western Jefferson county, Nebraska. Here the road they were traveling joined the main Oregon road from Independence, Missouri. They arrived at Fort Kearny may 19, where Major Osborne Cross joined them and relieved Major James Belger. Under instructions from Major-general Thomas S. Jesup, quartermaster general, Cross kept a journal of the march, which was prepared for publication in Philadelphia, Pennsylvania, after his return from Oregon in 1850. It was included in the report of the secretary of war for that year and a privately printed edition, of which only a few copies are known, was brought out by C. Sherman of Philadelphia in 1850.[8]

Following the Mexican war and the acquisition of California, the Pacific division of the United States army was created and the Mounted Riflemen's old commander, now Brevet-major-general Persifor F. Smith, was placed in command with headquarters at San Francisco. He set out for his new post on november 24, 1848 by way of New Orleans and the isthmus of Panama and arrived at Monterey february 23, 1849. About the same

[8] Packwood, "Reminiscences," 43; Mackay to Jesup, may 17, 1849; U.S. Senate. *Executive documents,* 31 cong., 2 sess., no. 1, pt. 2, 128-231; also U. S. House. *Executive documents,* 31 cong., 2 sess., but without plates.

time Brevet-major J. S. Hatheway, with two companies of the First artillery, sailed from New York for Fort Vancouver, where he arrived may 7 of the next year. One company was quartered in the rear of Fort Vancouver and the other, under Captain B. H. Hill was first sent to Astoria, then to Nisqually on Puget sound for the purpose of establishing a fort.[9]

Osborne Cross was born in Prince George county, Maryland, in 1803. His mother was a cousin of General Zachary Taylor, president of the United States. He graduated from the United States military academy in 1825 and was assigned to the First infantry as brevet-second-lieutenant. On july 1 of the same year he was transferred to the Fourth infantry, with which he served until september 29, 1827, when he was transferred back to the First infantry as first-lieutenant. His first wife, whom he married in New Orleans about 1830, was a daughter of Colonel Bartholomew von Schaumberg and a lineal descendant of one of the Delaware chiefs who sold a portion of Pennsylvania to William Penn. The children of this marriage were Edmund, who died young, Julia Louise, who married John Clemson, and Annette, who married Captain Grove Porter. Mrs. Cross died january 11, 1862, and he married Mrs. Mary B. Dix, widow of Lieutenant-colonel R. S. Dix of Pennsylvania, on july 8 of the same year.[10]

During the years preceding the Mexican war the First regiment was stationed at various points on the western frontier. From 1825 to 1831 it was at Jefferson barracks, Baton Rouge, Forts Wood and Pike, in

9 Bancroft, *History of Oregon*, II, 68-69; Hatheway to Jones, november 5, 1848.

10 John G. Clemson to editor, march 9, 1939; Heitman, *Historical register*, I, 341; *American state papers*, military affairs, III, 625; Hughes-Hallet, letter, n.d.; Kepler to editor, february 23, 1939; Cross file, Pension bureau.

Louisiana, and Cantonments Brooke, Clinch, and King in Florida. From 1831 to 1836 it was in the northwest and distributed among Forts Snelling, Crawford, and Winnebago. Upon the outbreak of the Seminole war in Florida in 1836, it was ordered to that region under Colonel Zachary Taylor. At this time Cross was listed as first-lieutenant with the duties of assistant quartermaster. After the close of the war he seems to have remained in New Orleans, possibly on departmental duties. The First regiment was sent back to the west and northwest where it remained until the outbreak of the Mexican war.[11]

When the conflict with Mexico began, the First regiment, with the exception of three companies which were assigned to Forts Snelling, Scott, and Leavenworth, was ordered to San Antonio, Texas, where it was incorporated with General John E. Wool's "central division of the army of Mexico." Cross, who now held the rank of captain, was made chief quartermaster of the division and upon him rested the responsibility for organizing the great train for the long march into Mexico. He served in this capacity until the close of the war, when he was appointed to dispose of surplus quartermaster's supplies with headquarters at Vera Cruz. This duty was accomplished through private sale rather than by auction, for which he was severely criticised by traders but highly commended by the department. Late in the summer of 1848 he returned to the United States, but what he did during the next six months is not known.[12]

On april 25, 1849, General Jesup ordered Cross to report to Colonel Mackay at St. Louis, Missouri, for service with the Mounted Riflemen. His duty was to

[11] *American state papers,* military affairs, IV, 666, 725, V, 638, VII, 933; U.S. House. *Report of committees,* 31 cong., no. 1, january 29, 1852.

[12] U.S. House. *Executive documents,* 30 cong., 2 sess., no. 1, 192-93, 204-208.

command the supply train and provide quarters for the regiment upon its arrival in Oregon. Having made the journey and discharged the duties assigned him he returned to the United States in february 1850. His activities during the next eighteen months are not known. In 1852 he was back on the Pacific coast as chief quartermaster of the Pacific division with headquarters at San Francisco. Four years later he still held that position, and it is presumed that he continued to do so until the beginning of the Civil war. In the early part of january 1862 he was ordered to relieve Colonel Thomas Swords as chief quartermaster of General George B. McClellan's division. From 1863 to the close of the war he was stationed at Pittsburgh, Pennsylvania, in the capacity of deputy quartermaster general. On march 13, 1865, he was breveted brigadier-general for faithful and meritorious service during the war, and on july 29, 1866, he was promoted to the rank of colonel and retired. He died at Roosevelt hospital, New York City, july 15, 1876, and was buried in the Catholic cemetery, Libertytown, Maryland.[13]

The Cross family made generous contribution of its sons to the army and navy of the United States. In addition to Osborne two older brothers also served in the army. One of these, Trueman, was assistant quartermaster general under Colonel Zachary Taylor in the Seminole war in Florida. Upon the outbreak of the war with Mexico he was assigned to Taylor's division as deputy quartermaster general and was killed by a party of Mexicans near present Fort Brown, Texas, on april 21, 1846. The other brother to enter the army was Howerton, who became a second-lieutenant in the Forty-

13 U.S. Senate. *Executive documents,* 31 cong., 2 sess., no. 1, pt. 2, 126; 34 cong., 3 sess., no. 534, 172; *War of the rebellion,* series 1, VII, 531, 548, xxv, 373, XLVII, pt. 2, 127, 244; Heitman, *Historical register,* I, 341, John G. Clemson to editor, march 9, 1939.

second infantry august 14, 1813, first-lieutenant may 1, 1814, and was honorably discharged june 15, 1815. Joseph Cross entered the navy as midshipman june 9, 1811. During the war of 1812 he served on board the frigate "Constitution" and participated in the battle between that vessel and the British man-of-war "Guerriere." He died at Bladensburg, Maryland, february 10, 1834.[14]

From the very beginning of the march of the Mounted Riflemen desertions on the part of soldiers and teamsters were of frequent occurrence. At Fort Laramie Colonel Loring reported forty, and upon reaching Independence rock he offered a reward of two hundred dollars for the arrest and return of any deserter. This, together with the capture of a number of them, effectively stopped desertions on the route. No sooner had the troops arrived in Oregon, however, than the spirit of dissatisfaction reasserted itself, intensified by reports that laborers were paid from five to ten dollars a day in California and that gold had been discovered on the Rogue and Klamath rivers. By march 1, 1850, about one hundred deserters had passed up the Willamette valley to a predetermined rendezvous in the Calapooya mountains, one hundred sixty miles south of Oregon City. On march 12 Colonel Loring set out in pursuit of them with thirteen officers and eighty men, crossed the Calapooya mountains and seized fifty-six in the Umpqua river valley. Here he was met by Governor Joseph Lane, who was also in the field with a volunteer force of citizens for the purpose of taking the deserters. Colonel Loring turned his prisoners over to Lane and pushed on to the Klamath river, where he captured seventeen more and returned to Oregon City

14 Powell, *List of officers*, 265; Heitman, *Historical register*, 1, 341; Service record, Lieutenant Joseph Cross.

about the first of may. Thirty-five succeeded in building a canoe and making good their escape.[15]

Sometime in april 1850 the headquarters of the Eleventh military district, of which Colonel Loring was now commandant, were removed from Oregon City to Fort Vancouver and the troops established at a place called Camp Talcott. The people of Oregon City, to whom the Mounted Riflemen had been most obnoxious because of drunkenness and disorderly conduct, celebrated their departure by burning down the buildings they had occupied. Upon arriving at Fort Vancouver the troops were put to work building quarters, which were called Columbia barracks. The headquarters staff of the district moved into these buildings november 11, 1850. On may 13 Brevet-major S. S. Tucker was ordered to the Dalles with two companies to establish a post at that place. In may 1851 what was left of the regiment was ordered to return to Jefferson barracks, where the men were mustered out and the regiment reorganized for the third time in five years. Here we leave it, although its subsequent history, under the name of the Third United States cavalry, in the west, in the Civil war, the Spanish-American war, and the World war was a brilliant one. Its present headquarters are at Fort Meyer, Virginia.[16]

George Gibbs, whose incomplete journal appears in this volume, was born july 17, 1815, and was descended from a long line of distinguished forbears. His maternal great-great-grandfather, Roger Wolcott, was deputy governor of Connecticut in 1741, major-general of militia 1745, and governor of Connecticut 1750-1754.

---

[15] Loring to Jones, june 22, october 15, 1849, march 6, april 28, 1850; Loring, proclamation, july 8, 1849; *Oregon spectator*, february 21, 1850; Lane to Nesmith, march 5, 1850; Ruff to Ford, february 26, 1850.

[16] Frost to Loring, may 30, 1850; Bancroft, *History of Oregon*, II, 89, 91, 100; Loring to Jones, november 12, 1850; Oregon historical society *quarterly*, XXX, 333; Deibert, *History of the third United States cavalry*, 17.

Another distinction with which he may be credited is that of having written the first book of poetry published in the colony.[17]

Oliver Wolcott, great-grandfather of Gibbs, graduated from Yale college, studied medicine, and settled at Litchfield, Connecticut, where he filled the office of sheriff for twenty years. In 1775 the Connecticut assembly sent him to interview General Gage in Boston and in the same year appointed him to serve as one of the commissioners to treat with the Six Nations and other Indian tribes. He was a delegate to the first Continental congress and signed the Declaration of Independence. In 1776 he was brigadier-general of the Fourteenth regiment and two years later major-general of the Connecticut troops. He was lieutenant-governor of the state in 1787 and became governor upon the death of Governor Samuel Huntington in 1796. Later he filled the same office by election.[18]

Gibbs's grandfather, Oliver Wolcott, also graduated from Yale college, studied law, and served in two minor revolutionary campaigns in 1777 and 1779. In 1788 he was selected as comptroller of public accounts and successfully reorganized the finances of Connecticut. Appointed auditor of the federal treasury in 1789, he worked under Alexander Hamilton. He was appointed comptroller by Washington in 1791, succeeded Hamilton as secretary of the treasury in 1795, and filled the same office under President John Adams. He was governor of Connecticut 1817 to 1827.[19]

On his father's side the Gibbs line ran back to James Gibbs, who emigrated from England to Bristol, Rhode Island, about 1670. His father, George Gibbs, who by courtesy was called "colonel," married Laura, daughter

---

[17] *Dictionary of American biography*, xx, 445-46.

[18] *Ibid.*, 442-43.

[19] *Ibid.*, 443-45.

of Oliver Wolcott. Having a natural bent toward the sciences, especially that of mineralogy, he brought together, while on a trip abroad in 1805, what was then the largest and most valuable collection of minerals in the United States. In 1810 he loaned this to Yale college and ten years later sold it to that institution for twenty thousand dollars.[20] The Gibbs family lived at Sunswick Farms, near the village of Astoria on Long island.

George was intended for the army, but the necessary appointment to the United States military academy was not obtained. In lieu of this he traveled and studied two years in Europe, during which time he undoubtedly gave attention to drawing. Returning to the United States in 1834 he entered Harvard college and studied law. Upon graduating four years later he entered the office of Prescott Hall in New York. In the same year that he entered college he published *The Judicial Chronicle; a list of the judges of the common law and chancery in England and America*. In 1846 he published *The memoirs of the administration of Washington and Adams,* which was based largely upon letters to and from his grandfather, Oliver Wolcott, while he was secretary of the treasury.[21]

Along with a love for literature Gibbs was possessed of a passion for outdoor life. Hunting and fishing were his chief amusements, to which was added a deep interest in natural history and geology. He mounted a large collection of birds and assembled a considerable mineralogical cabinet which he added to his father's collection at Yale college. When the excitement over the discovery of gold in California swept the country he abandoned his law practice, in which he had little real interest, hurried to Fort Leavenworth, and attached himself to the regiment of Mounted Riflemen.[22] On the

---

[20] *Ibid.,* 445-46; Stevens, *Memorial to George Gibbs,* 1-2.

[21] *Ibid.,* 5-9; *Dictionary of American biography,* VII, 245.

[22] Stevens, *Memorial to George Gibbs,* 6-9.

march to Oregon he made numerous drawings of scenes along the way and kept a journal. The first installment of this was sent back from Fort Kearny to the daily *Journal of Commerce,* New York, july 25, 1849. The second installment, sent back from Fort Laramie, was published in the same paper september 1. These were reprinted in the New York *Mercury and weekly journal of commerce* july 26 and september 6, 1849. His intention was to complete it, but the remainder, for some unknown reason, was never published. The files of these newspapers were searched to 1852, but no additional installments were found.

As an artist Gibbs exhibited considerable talent, both in sketching outdoor scenes and in drawing from life. He made what was perhaps the first drawing of Shoshone falls, and sketched various scenes in eastern Oregon, on the Columbia river, and while crossing the Cascade mountains from the Dalles to Oregon City. In 1850 he was appointed deputy collector of the port of Astoria and in 1851 was associated with Governor John P. Gaines in the making of treaties whereby the Calapooya Indians surrendered their lands in the Willamette river valley. While engaged in this work he made many drawings. In the latter part of the same year he was a member of the Redick M'Kee expedition to northeastern California. While on this journey, which ended in San Francisco the latter part of december, he made numerous drawings.[23] Immediately upon coming into contact with the aboriginal peoples of the northwest Gibbs became intensely interested in their customs, languages, and mode of living. During his service with Governor Gaines he prepared a vocabulary of the Calapooya language, and while with the M'Kee party he did the same for the language of the inhabitants of the regions about Clear lake and the Klamath,

[23] Bushnell, *Drawings by George Gibbs,* 1-28; Bancroft, *History of Oregon,* II, 81.

Trinity, and Salmon rivers. In addition he began assembling a collection of articles illustrating their handiwork, which was sent to the Smithsonian institution in Washington.[24]

After his journey with M'Kee he took up his residence on a ranch or farm near Fort Steilacoom, Washington territory, where he continued his Indian studies. In 1853 he was associated with Governor Isaac I. Stevens in the survey of the western portion of the Northern Pacific railroad route. Next year he was again with Governor Stevens and made a number of maps which are preserved in the Washington state historical society. During 1855 he assisted in the making of treaties with various Indian tribes, and 1857 he served as astronomer and ethnologist on the northwest boundary commission. He made an elaborate report on the natural history and geology of the country through which he traveled and wrote "Tribes of western Washington and northwestern Oregon," which was published in *Contributions to North American Ethnology, United States geographical and geological survey of the Rocky mountain region,* I, part 2.[25]

In 1860 Gibbs returned to New York for what he meant as a temporary visit, but he never returned to the northwest. Upon the outbreak of the Civil war he went to Washington where he served as a volunteer guard for the capital in april 1861. Not being physically qualified for military service he became an active member of the Loyal National league and the Loyal Publication society. Despite the turmoil of war he found time to continue his Indian studies. In 1862 he published, in collaboration with J. G. Shea, a *Grammar and dictionary*

24 Bushnell, *Drawings by George Gibbs*, 1-28.

25 Bancroft, *Washington, Idaho, and Montana*, 71, 383; Bonney to editor, march 24, 1939; Tilden to editor, february 15, 1940; Stevens, *Memorial to George Gibbs*, 10-11; *Dictionary of American biography*, VII, 245.

of the Yakima language, and a year later *Alphabetical vocabularies of the Clallam and Lummi, Alphabetical vocabulary of the Chinook language, A dictionary of the Chinook jargon, or trade language of Oregon,* and *Instructions for research relative to the ethnology and philology of America.* In 1867 he prepared his *Notes on the Timneh or Chippewyn Indians of British and Russian America.* All these were published by the Smithsonian institution. In 1871 he married his cousin, Mary Kane Gibbs, and moved to New Haven, Connecticut, where he died april 9, 1873.[26]

Oliver and Albert, younger brothers of George, ably carried on the family tradition for achievement. The former occupied a professorship at Harvard college from 1853 to 1887. He was one of the founders of the National academy of sciences and associate editor of the *American journal of science.* Albert received appointment to the United States military academy, from which he graduated in 1846. He was a member of the Mounted Riflemen during the war with Mexico and fought at Cerro Gordo and Garita de Belen. During the Civil war he became a major-general.[27]

In addition to George Gibbs, another artist, by the name of William Henry Tappan, accompanied the Mounted Riflemen to Oregon. He was the fourth son of Colonel Ebenezer Tappan, and was born at Manchester, Massachusetts, october 30, 1821. When about eighteen or twenty years of age he went to Boston, where he was associated with George C. Smith in the business of engraving photographs in mezzotint. About the same time he also engraved some line plates in conjunction with Joseph Anderson of the same city. Later he was engaged as draughtsman in the United States

[26] Stevens, *Memorial to George Gibbs,* 12-13; *Dictionary of American biography,* VII, 246.

[27] *Ibid.,* VII, 245-46; Heitman, *Historical register,* I, 452-53.

mint at Philadelphia. In 1848 he was a member of Professor Louis Agassiz's exploring party to the Lake Superior region and visited the Platte river, where he made a large portfolio of drawings. This journey evidently fired him with enthusiasm for that kind of work, for the next year he sought and obtained permission to accompany the Mounted Riflemen on their march to Oregon in order to "make such drawings and collections as will illustrate the geological features, the zoological and botanical products of the country." [28]

Presumably Tappan accompanied a detachment of troops under Major John S. Simonson which left Fort Leavenworth ahead of the regiment. These were transported to Table creek by steamer, from whence they marched to Fort Kearny. A set of fifty drawings in the possession of the Wisconsin historical society, made by an unnamed artist who evidently accompanied this detachment, contains drawings of scenes along the Missouri river above Fort Leavenworth, on the Nodaway river, of old Fort Kearny at Table creek, and of an apparently deserted Pawnee village on the Platte river below Fort Kearny. From this latter place, which was also drawn, the sketches are frequent and the dates noted upon them coincide fairly well with the movements of the regiment. The probability is that Tappan made part or all of these drawings, since in addition to strong circumstantial evidence, the handwriting on some of the sketches bears a striking resemblance to his. [29]

Upon arriving at his destination Tappan located in Washington territory, where he assisted in laying out the town of St. Helen's in the early part of 1851. He

---

[28] Tappan, *Tappan-Toppan genealogy,* 49-50; Wheaton to editor, february 4, 1940; Fielding, *Dictionary of American painters,* 361; William H. Tappan to Charles Tappan, february 15, 1849; Charles Tappan to Greely jr., march 19, 1849; Lunt to Crawford, march 21, 1849; Crawford to commanding officer Mounted Riflemen, march 28, 1849; Winthrop to Crawford, april 6, 1849.

[29] Mackay to Jesup, may 17, 1849.

lived here a number of years, and was elected to the first Washington territorial legislature in january 1854. Having a desire to see as much as possible of the Indian tribes of the interior he resigned at the close of the first session to accept an appointment as special Indian agent for the Columbia river district. In the spring of 1855 he accompanied Governor Isaac I. Stevens to Fort Walla Walla for the purpose of making treaties with the various Indian tribes. About 1859 he went to Colorado with his brother Lewis N. and engaged in the mercantile business at Denver, Golden, and Central City. He returned to Massachusetts in 1876, and was elected to the legislature of that state the following year, and was a member of the state senate 1885-1886. He married Margaret Anderson, april 7, 1857, who died april 11, 1867. On april 2, 1881, he married Augusta E. Wheaton of Manchester, Massachusetts. There were no children by either marriage. He died january 22, 1907.[30]

The question as to who made the thirty-six drawings accompanying Major Cross's journal in the senate edition of the report of the secretary of war for 1850 has not been conclusively answered. Certainly Cross did not make them himself, and either Gibbs or Tappan could have done so. Since the latter accompanied the regiment for the express purpose of making drawings, the presumption that Cross availed himself of them is both reasonable and strong.

A table of distances was kept by Dr. Israel Moses, one of the surgeons accompanying the regiment, and is included in this volume. This table is reproduced from the original manuscript preserved in the National Archives.

[30] Bancroft, *History of Oregon*, II, 251; Talbot, *Journals*, 100, 138; Bancroft, *History of Washington, Idaho, and Montana*, 71, 73, 94; William H. Tappan to Steele, october 8, november 30, 1852; to Prosser, february 12, 1898; to Mason, june 19, 1854; Tappan, *Tappan-Toppan genealogy*, 49-50.

The two journals reproduced herein contain much valuable material on the Oregon trail and the great emigration of 1849. While Cross at times writes as though bored by daily routine, Gibbs seems thrilled by new scenes and experiences. Since the regiment of Mounted Riflemen was the first military unit to traverse the entire length of the Oregon trail these journals assume added importance as the only complete narratives of the long march. Colonel Loring's report is necessarily brief, yet it adds much to the story. When these and the letters, reports, etc., written by Cross, Loring, and other officers are combined the full story of a magnificent achievement is revealed. The chronicle of daily events, comments by the journalists, letter writers, references to conditions encountered, descriptions of natural scenery, and the recital of the experiences of the thousands of emigrants seen on the way, provides much to interest both the student of history and of military undertakings.

The Journal of
Major Osborne Cross

March to Fort Kearny

Philadelphia, May 20, 1850

GENERAL:[31] The order which I have here annexed will show the duty assigned to me by you. In compliance with it I took my departure from Washington City on the twenty-fifth of april [1849] for Fort Leavenworth, Missouri.[32] Here the rifle regiment had been directed to assemble and make such preparations as a march like the one contemplated might call for.

I arrived at St. Louis on the eighth of may, and finding the cholera prevailing to an alarming extent [33] left

31 Thomas Sidney Jesup. Born in Virginia december 16, 1788; died june 10, 1860. Entered the army of the United States may 3, 1808, and served in the war of 1812 on the staff of General William Hull. Rose to the rank of brigadier-general, and commanded troops in the Florida Indian wars, 1836-1838. His long service as quartermaster-general of the army, over forty-two years, has never been equaled by the head of any other department or corps.

32 On may 8, 1827, Colonel Henry Leavenworth, being under orders to establish a cantonment on the Missouri river near the mouth of the Platte river, pitched his camp on the site of the present institution which bears his name. In the spring of 1829, because of malarial fever among the troops, the place was abandoned, the troops transferred to Jefferson barracks, and the buildings occupied by Kickapoo Indians. Six months later Colonel Leavenworth again took over the cantonment. General order no. 11, by the war department, changed the name from Cantonment Leavenworth to Fort Leavenworth. It has never been unoccupied since the summer of 1829. Until the organization of Kansas territory in 1854, certain laws of Missouri extended to the unsettled region west of that state. Hence that territory was commonly, though not officially, spoken of as "Missouri territory." Colonel E. V. Sumner was in command at Fort Leavenworth when the Mounted Riflemen started on their journey. Their first camp was named in his honor.

33 The Asiatic cholera first appeared in the western United States in 1832 by way of the St. Lawrence river through emigrants from Ireland. It spread across the Great lakes, to the troops at Rock island, and down the Mississippi river to Jefferson barracks. It appeared among the Sac and Fox Indians of Missouri that year, but does not seem to have ascended the Missouri river. Reappearing again in 1833, it reached St. Louis in may, where by the latter

on the tenth on board the steamer "San Francisco," [34] after making a hasty outfit there. It will not be out of place to remark here that the cholera was not only in St. Louis, but had spread through every town on the Missouri river. In many instances [it] had raged with great violence on board several steamers, one of which, after losing nearly thirty passengers, was entirely abandoned and left tied to the shore.[35] We were more fortunate on board our boat, having but one case, which may be principally attributed to the untiring efforts of Captain Keneth [Mortimer Kennett], her commander, who spared no pains to keep his boat in excellent police and make his passengers comfortable.

The troops had just passed up the river, and with so great a number it could hardly be expected that they would not be more or less affected by the epidemic. I was therefore exceedingly anxious to reach Fort Leavenworth to ascertain what effect a pure atmosphere would have in dispelling a disease with which all who traveled the Missouri river were in some degree threatened. I was much pleased when I landed [at Fort Leavenworth] on the nineteenth instant after a passage of nine days from St. Louis.

It was expected that the regiment [36] would be in read-

part of the summer sixty of the best citizens had died of it. It was introduced from Canada and Europe in 1834, and from Cuba in 1835. After an interim of ten years, it again appeared in St. Louis in april 1849. During may and june the mortality was excessive. Fifty-two hundred eighty-five deaths in the city were ascribed to it that year. The number of deaths from this disease along the Oregon trail in 1849, while not definitely known, has been estimated at from four to five thousand.

34 One of the five steamers burned at the St. Louis wharf in the great fire of july 29, 1849.

35 On may 22, 1849, the St. Louis *daily republican* reported that the steamer "James Monroe" was laid up at Jefferson City, Missouri, on account of being practically deserted by officers, passengers, and crew, who had fled because of an outbreak of cholera on board. After lying there several months the vessel was taken to St. Louis. No doubt this was the vessel to which Cross refers.

36 The Mounted Riflemen consisted of ten companies, five of which began

iness to take to the field by the first of may,[37] but it was
not prepared to do so for several reasons until the tenth.
To organize properly a train and make all necessary
arrangements incidental to a journey of two thousand
miles required much more time than was at first anticipated. The officers were to make an outfit for a per-
manency in Oregon. They were to be separated from the
civilized world for some time, with their families,[38] and
it was by no means an easy task to make all proper arrangements even for their comfort while on this long
march. In addition to this, the spring had not advanced
sufficiently to justify an earlier move.

On inquiring at the fort I learned that the troops
were ten days in advance of me, which was a very long
start, as my mode of traveling was the same as that of
the regiment. If I could have been fortunate enough to
have procured a few pack mules in place of wagons it
would have greatly facilitated my movements, as I
could have traveled much more rapidly. Not being able

the march from Fort Leavenworth on may 10, 1849. Companies G and I under
Brevet-major Charles F. Ruff had been at Fort Kearny since october 28, 1848.
Major John S. Simonson and a party had been transported to Table creek by
steamer some time before, from whence they marched overland to Fort
Kearny. Company B, under Captain Noah Newton, was already on the way,
and company C, under Brevet-lieutenant-colonel Benjamin S. Roberts, remained at Fort Leavenworth to escort the supply train to Fort Laramie july 1.
Company E, commanded by Major W. F. Sanderson, left at the same time,
but seems to have been under orders to march independently of the regiment.
Loring to Jones, may 10, 1849; to Freeman, october 15, 1849; Mackay to Jesup,
may 17, 1849; for further information concerning officers of the regiment see
notes 280-88, pages 275-77.

[37] The date of departure was set between the first and fifteenth of may
1849. A backward spring, difficulty in securing bids for transporting supplies
and teamsters due to the gold rush to California delayed the march until the
tenth. Twiggs, order no. 8, february 9, 1849; Mackay to Jesup, may 17, 1849.

[38] At least four officers, among whom were Brevet-major Ruff, Captain
Llewellyn Jones, and Lieutenant Charles F. Denman took their families with
them. They had large spring wagons, accommodating five passengers besides
the driver, made in St. Louis. These were so constructed that the seats could
be made into beds and were drawn by four mules. "Notes by Frederica Jones"
in Swift, Personal memoirs.

to do so I had no time to lose, and on sunday may 20 [1849] at two p.m. I left for Fort Kearny [39] after a short stay of twenty-four hours at this place.

Last evening was very pleasant, and the sun, in setting, left behind a bright sky. [This] was indicative of a fair morning, but contrary to our expectations it became cold and commenced to rain during the night, [which] made it extremely disagreeable for our party, whose only shelter was a common tent. As they had to come to it sooner or later, everyone took it quietly and made themselves as comfortable as their means would permit. Many of them were unaccustomed to a life of this kind, and the scenes they were about to pass through, as well as the toil and hardships which they would be required to endure would be a new life to them, of which in reality they knew but very little.

It had been threatening to rain all the morning and continued cold. The sky was becoming overcast by heavy clouds that were rising rapidly in the southwest, and it began to rain very hard before reaching the base of a hill over which our road led. Here we began to realize the labor and trouble which were in store for us. The evening was one of the most unpleasant I had ever experienced. The rain poured down in torrents as if the clouds had been rent asunder by the heavy thunder, which seemed to increase as the vivid lightning flashed incessantly around us. The whole sky was at moments wrapt in one dark canopy, while at others it presented one glare of lightning. Having reached the base of the hill, we found it necessary, from the weak condition of our mules, to attach twelve of them to one wagon to pull up about twelve hundred pounds. With the assistance of all hands at the wheels we succeeded, after two

---

[39] Although Cross consistently spelled this as "Kearney" the editor has changed it to "Kearny" to conform to the decision of the United States Board of Geographic Names.

hours work, in reaching the top of the hill in the midst of the storm. We continued our march after sundown, which brought us to a small stream about four miles from the garrison, where we made our encampment for the night.

It continued to rain very hard. As wood was scarce and we had no means of kindling a fire, the party placed themselves under cover as soon as possible, without having eaten anything since morning. As for myself, I was completely overcome by fatigue and much harassed at the gloomy prospects before me. Every stitch of clothing I had on was thoroughly drenched. In this condition I was taken with a fever, which lasted several hours. During the night it passed off, and in the morning I was much gratified to find myself able to resume my journey.

My outfit was as indifferent a one as ever left for any station, much less the Rocky mountains. The mules were poor, unbroken, and by no means calculated for such a march as we had to perform. The drivers were not only stupid, but totally ignorant of their duty, as they had never been employed in this capacity before. [They] seemed to have no other object in view than to reach the gold region with the least possible expense or trouble to themselves. They were, however, the best among those left at [Fort] Leavenworth by the regiment, and I had no alternative but to take them. They had been hired at fifteen dollars per month and were without the least knowledge of the duty of a teamster or any capacity to learn. I had men of this description with me in Mexico, who generally made out to destroy more public property from gross ignorance than would have hired double the number of good teamsters. From the system that is now observed, it will always be difficult to remedy the evil. It is a laborious life and the sum of fifteen dollars per month will never bring into the service good and efficient men who are calculated for such duty. It is to be regretted that some plan cannot be adopted to supply the department with experienced drivers who are so indispensably necessary upon long marches like the present one. I have been in favor for some time of enlisting men who are particularly qualified for this duty and I regret that the plan you have for so long recommended has not yet been adopted.

MAY 21. The teamsters commenced their labors at daybreak, but the unbroken condition of the mules was such that the greater part of the morning was consumed in bridling and harnessing them. Because of this we were not prepared to commence our journey until half-past eight o'clock. Whoever has witnessed the scene of preparing unbroken Mexican mules for the road will not be at a loss to imagine the position of one with men who had hardly ever taken a whip in their hands and now had charge of such teams. This, in a word, was our condition and I had witnessed enough yesterday to warn me of what might be realized before arriving at Oregon, or even Fort Kearny. The display this morning had not tended to lessen my conviction in the least. This was the beginning of a long and hazardous journey, filled with difficulty and labor. We were soon to find ourselves on a desert waste, cut off from all resources except those we might have with us, and it certainly was no time or place for experimenting.

I sent back for an entire outfit this morning. The post teams, being considered by far too valuable to be spared for such service, were withheld, probably because it was thought I was on the same footing with the balance of the outfit of the regiment. If so, I could have no cause to complain. Be this as it may. To this subject I shall again take occasion to refer before completing this journal.

This day may be noted as the commencement of our march. The morning, although cloudy, gave every indication of a pleasant day, which we stood much in need of after the cold rain of yesterday afternoon and last night. It still continued cold today, which greatly facilitated our traveling.

The road lay over a prairie which was skirted with timber, and at five p.m. we came to a steep hill, somewhat difficult to descend, but [we] succeeded in reaching the bottom without much trouble. While some attended to the mules others held on to ropes attached to the wagons, which brought them to the base without any accident. The broken tongues, hounds, and other parts of wagons showed plainly the trouble which the command had met with at this place. As the evening was drawing to a close, we made our encampment for the night on the banks of a small stream [40] which was running at the base of the hill. Here we found plenty of good water and wood for our use and fine grazing for the animals, [of] which they stood greatly in need. We had not more time before sunset than would suffice for the arranging of our meals and making a few alterations which were required before leaving in the morning. Our tents were scarcely pitched and all things properly prepared for the night before it began to hail. [It] continued until nearly sundown, when it cleared off and became very cold, making a fire quite comfortable.

MAY 22. The morning was clear, and we left our encampment at five o'clock. The road passed over a rolling prairie and across several small streams, which were well wooded, as is generally the case in this vicinity. Towards the close of the day the country became very broken, as we were still near the great Missouri [river] valley. But our trail began to diverge a little, [and] was soon to carry us from it. The beauties of woodland

---

[40] Walnut creek, about fifteen miles northwest of Fort Leavenworth.

scenery were to give place to an endless prairie country, which strikes one as being very beautiful at first sight but becomes tiresome beyond any description after the novelty wears off. It could hardly be expected to be otherwise, when you see nothing from day to day but the broad canopy of heaven above and the greensward below.

We arrived at Wolf creek [41] at half-past five o'clock in the evening, having made a march of twenty-two miles today. I had thrown away nearly all of the two loads when starting yesterday morning, so that we had but little more than our trunks to transport, which could be easily packed.

The country was not the least interesting in this day's journey. It was much more broken than yesterday, which made it very fatiguing to teams that were entirely unaccustomed to traveling. The weather moderated through the day, which made the evening delightful. It was the first pleasant weather we had experienced since the nineteenth, and it appeared to give new life to the whole party. We certainly stood greatly in need of a change. It was also very favorable for our mules, which had suffered much from the cold rains since starting. The thermometer had at six p.m. ranged at 70°, and we had every prospect for a fine day tomorrow.

Since leaving Fort Leavenworth we had met with no one, and our two days' march was very tiresome and monotonous. This evening our camp was visited by a Sac Indian,[42] who was dressed, as is customary among that tribe, with a red blanket and head ornamented with feathers. He soon presented me a paper which had been

[41] In southeast Brown county, Kansas.

[42] In 1837 the government moved the Iowa, Fox, and Sac Indians from the Platte Purchase in northwest Missouri to their new home lying west of the Missouri river, south of the Great Nemaha, and north of the fortieth parallel. Cross overlooks the fact that the passage of thousands of wagons, animals, and people through this region worked hardships upon the Indians.

given him by the sub-agent, the purport of which was to request emigrants passing this way to make these Indians a small present for the use of their wood, which they had complained of having been destroyed by the emigrants. He also made quite a talk about the grass which the animals consumed, and appeared to be fully impressed with the idea that they were entitled to some compensation for it. We gave him something to eat and sent him off very soon after, evidently disappointed and much displeased at not receiving money. He had doubtless made up his mind on having a fine frolic on his next visit to St. Joseph and Weston, places which are frequently visited by them for that purpose, much to the annoyance of the inhabitants.

It is surprising why those employed with Indian tribes are disposed to humor them, as is often the case, with erroneous impressions. Here, for instance, was an Indian furnished with a paper to receive tribute from all who passed. If he should become displeased by not receiving some compensation the tribe was likely to annoy everyone by stealing horses or in some other way. If these people really deserved compensation for the wood used, which was of itself too absurd to think of for a moment, it was a proper subject to lay before the Indian department. To get rid of them these papers are furnished, which can have no other tendency than to annoy travelers and endanger their property.

MAY 23. We commenced making preparation at half-past three o'clock this morning and started as soon as it was light enough to see the road. It was a cold, misty morning. The thermometer was as low as 48° at sunrise, making a difference of 22° during the night. The country began to rise, and with the exception of the distant wood on the borders of several small streams and the valley of the Missouri river, nothing could be seen but a high rolling prairie.

We had been traveling for the last three days on a trail made partly by the Oregon expedition,[43] but had not proceeded very far this morning before a new scene broke suddenly upon our view. We here came into a road as large as any public highway in the United States, leading from St. Joseph and Weston. Large trains were coming in from all points of the Missouri river on trails intersecting this great highway,[44] which would lead them, after endless toil and much suffering, to the gold region. All these trails followed ridges, which placed the wagons frequently in such positions that they seemed to be crossing the prairie in every direction.[45] As their covers were well trimmed, they looked at a distance not unlike vessels on the wide ocean steering for different parts of the globe. For the first time we passed one or two wagons today that had broken down, and also several persons returning who had already lost their cattle, which they were ready, of course, to attribute to the Indians and not to their own neglect. The truth was, they had become discouraged, and were

---

[43] In his order directing Cross to join the Mounted Riflemen, General Jesup spoke of it as "the Oregon expedition." Jesup to Cross, april 25, 1849; U.S. Senate, *Executive documents*, 31 cong., 2 sess., no. 1, pt. 2, 8, 263.

[44] What was known as the "north branch of the Oregon trail" entered present Kansas opposite St. Joseph, Missouri, and ran west through Doniphan, Brown, Nemaha, and Marshall counties and joined the main branch at Marysville, Kansas. This latter route began at Westport, Missouri, ran along the south side of the Kaw river to the site of present Topeka, Kansas, where it crossed and followed a northwesterly course to Marysville. The point where Cross struck the "north branch" was in eastern Brown county, Kansas.

[45] The movement of emigrants westward in the spring of 1849 was phenomenal. The *Daily Missouri republican* reported as follows: april 11—about one thousand emigrants from every state except Delaware and Texas were camped at Independence; may 11—about three thousand emigrants for California had arrived at St. Joseph, and roads in every direction were lined with wagons; may 12—two ferry boats running day and night at St. Joseph could not accommodate the emigrants, and two steamboats entered the ferrying business; may 17—at least fourteen thousand persons were reported as being at the various places of rendezvous along the western border of Missouri, ready to depart. Nebraska state historical society *publications*, xx, 190, 191.

willing to make any excuse to return rather than to continue the journey.

In this day's march I overtook Captain Granger [46] of the rifle regiment, whom I passed. About six o'clock in the evening [I] made my encampment on the prairie, where I found a small stream which was entirely destitute of wood, there being only three solitary trees to be seen. The day was very fine, and the distance traveled was about twenty-five miles. At this encampment our horses found an abundance of grass. The evening was very pleasant, and the thermometer at six p.m. stood at 62°. I learned today that the command was not over seventy miles in advance of me. They had met with much difficulty with many of their teams [47] since leaving Fort Leavenworth, which had given us the opportunity of gaining already considerably on them.

MAY 24. The bugle sounded at three o'clock this morning, when all hands were immediately up and soon prepared for breakfast. At half-past four o'clock we

---

[46] Gordon Granger. New York. Brevet-second-lieutenant Second infantry july 1, 1845; transferred to Mounted Riflemen july 17, 1846; second-lieutenant may 29, 1847; brevet-first-lieutenant august 20, 1847 for meritorious conduct in the battles of Contreras and Churubusco, Mexico; captain september 13, 1847 for gallant and meritorious conduct in the battle of Chapultepec, Mexico; major august 10, 1861 for gallant and meritorious service at the battle of Wilson's creek, Missouri; colonel Second Michigan cavalry september 2, 1861; brigadier-general of volunteers, september 17, 1862; major-general volunteers september 17, 1862; lieutenant-colonel september 20, 1863, for gallant and meritorious service at the battle of Chickamauga, Georgia; colonel november 24, 1863, for gallant and meritorius service at the battle of Chattanooga, Tennessee; brigadier-general march 13, 1865, for gallant and meritorius service at the capture of Mobile, Alabama; major-general march 13, 1865, for distinguished gallantry and good conduct at the capture of Forts Gaines and Morgan, Alabama; mustered out of volunteer service january 15, 1866; colonel Twenty-fifth infantry july 28, 1866; unassigned march 15, 1869; assigned to Fourteenth infantry december 15, 1870; transferred to Fifteenth infantry december 20, 1870; died january 10, 1876. Heitman, *Historical register*, 1, 469. He was engaged in measuring the distance from Fort Leavenworth to Fort Kearny with an odometer.

[47] For the experience of the regiment with its teams see Gibbs's account, pages 282-83.

were ready to commence our march, the thermometer standing at 60°. The day was extremely fine for traveling. We arrived on the Nemaha [48] at eleven o'clock, where we made a halt for an hour to rest the teams. This is a pretty little stream, about sixty feet wide, and is a tributary to the Missouri [river]. Wood is to be found in abundance on its banks, consisting of oak, hickory, walnut, ash, elm, and cottonwood. I judged the soil to be good from its dark appearance, and no doubt [it] would be productive. We continued our journey some distance farther, leaving many emigrants at this stream and [at] the several water-holes in the vicinity of the road, as the cholera had prevented many of them from traveling. One or two families whom I overtook at the Nemaha passed us at Fort Kearny, and by good management were able to keep with the command, which generally traveled faster than the body of emigrants.

The cholera now began to make its appearance along this route, and the number who had died with it was sufficient evidence that the emigrants were suffering greatly from its effects. They are truly to be pitied, as no aid in any way could be afforded them. On the contrary, they were often compelled to travel when it was almost death to them to be moved. The country along here is high, and in fair weather very dry. [There was] nothing to aggravate the disease, as the atmosphere was as pure as the mountain air, and not the least decomposition of vegetable matter to engender it. Still the cholera continued to prevail among the emigrating parties. With every care they resorted to, it remained among them until they crossed the North Platte [river] in the month of july. In many instances [it] raged with such violence as to carry off nearly whole parties.

[48] South fork of the Nemaha in Nemaha county, Kansas. Apparently Cross left the route followed by the regiment in the neighborhood of present Atchison, Kansas, and cut across the country toward the junction of the Little Blue river and Sandy creek.

I arrived this evening on a small stream such as are frequently found among the hills near the Missouri [river]. There were many emigrating families here, who were necessarily compelled to stop in consequence of the prevailing epidemic. The evening was cloudy, and it began to rain very hard soon after our tents were pitched. The rainy season had now commenced. We would be compelled to endure [it] until our daily marches carried us to a section of country where rain seldom falls during the summer, which is generally the case with that section found between the North Platte, the Sweetwater,[49] and [the] Snake river[s]. On the prairie between Forts Leavenworth and Kearny it commences as early as may and seldom stops until the latter part of june.

MAY 25. The rain fell in torrents through the night and was accompanied by sharp lightning and heavy thunder. The bottoms of our tents were partly under water, particularly those that were not protected by an embankment, which should always be made, whether the evening is clear or cloudy. Little calculation is to be made upon the weather during the rainy season in this country.

When the call sounded at four o'clock this morning one of my teamsters was absent. This man, finding that he knew nothing of his duty and having exhausted the patience of all who endeavored to teach him, thought it the safest plan to relinquish his situation as teamster to the Oregon expedition. [He] had run off during the night, leaving us the wagons and but one teamster to get on [in] the most convenient way that could be devised by the party. The corporal of the escort scoured the country without being successful in finding him. We afterwards learned that he had returned to Fort Leaven-

---

49 Though Cross consistently spelled this as "Sweet Water," the editor has changed it throughout to Sweetwater to conform to modern usage.

worth, satisfied, no doubt, that he was not destined to reach the gold region in the capacity of teamster and would wait for a more favorable opportunity.

The morning was very unpleasant. The thermometer at five o'clock stood at 52°. It cleared off towards the middle of the day however, after a drizzling rain all the morning, and the remainder of the day was extremely pleasant. During the day I met two wagons returning to the Missouri [river]. These people were already discouraged, and thought it more advisable to return than to attempt a journey of two thousand miles and run the risk of never reaching their place of destination. Many of them had started very unprepared, while others were entirely unacquainted with prairie life and little calculated to accomplish a journey fraught with so many obstacles as this certainly is. This day's march carried us over a high prairie, very much like that we had already traveled over, and brought us within five miles of a stream called the Big Vermilion.[50]

MAY 26. It was cold and rainy this morning, which prevented us from leaving as early as usual. We left our encampment at half-past seven, and soon came to the banks of the Vermilion, a stream which is about one hundred feet wide, quite rapid, and barely fordable at this time. From this point the road commenced to ascend gradually. The ground was firm and the wagons were able to move rapidly through the day. The country was not so rolling as heretofore, but presented a series of plains rising one above another. This day's march brought me to a stream having on its banks cottonwood and scrub oak in small quantities. The soil bore much the appearance of that on the streams we had already passed. From the great exposure which the

---

50 Now known as Black Vermilion.

party had been subjected to, a teamster was taken with pleurisy, while one of the escort was seized with the cholera. Having no medical aid along, our situation was certainly a very unpleasant one. We however administered to them such medicine as we had with us, and rendered them all the assistance in our power. Being compelled to continue our march, it was impossible to make them the least [bit] comfortable.

It would be useless to attempt to enumerate the deaths that had occurred among the emigrants. The graves along the road too plainly told us that the cholera was prevailing to an alarming extent. At this point we were one hundred thirty-eight miles from Fort Leavenworth, one hundred seventy-two miles from Fort Kearny, [and] entirely cut off from all assistance or the possible means of getting any relief. It was out of the question to lie by. Being in the rear, we were compelled to move rapidly on to overtake the command. It was a serious subject to think of, and I know of no danger that I would not sooner be exposed to, than again suffer the uneasiness of mind which I experienced at this time. We had not only full proof of the prevalence of this dreadful scourge along the road, but were actually carrying it with us in our wagons.

If I were to enumerate all the sufferings of the emigrants and enter into a minute description of our critical situation it would take more time and space than would be proper for me to devote to this subject. I feel that it is necessary to touch upon it, so as to give the department some idea of the peculiar position in which we were placed and the grave risk everyone ran who traveled this route. When we arose in the morning it was a question among us as to who might fall a victim to it before another sun.

We met at our encampment this evening two men

who were returning to their homes in Tennessee, having
heard of the death of some of their relatives, which required them to retrace their steps. This presented a
favorable opportunity to us to send letters back to our
friends, who, hearing of the existence of the cholera
along our route, would doubtless feel great solicitude
for us and be much relieved on hearing of our safety
thus far.

The distance passed over today was about thirty
miles. Having a good road and traveling quite late in
the evening enabled us to make a very long march, but
it was somewhat necessary as water was scarce upon the
route. I hired an emigrant last evening to drive one of
my wagons as far as Fort Kearny in place of the teamster who had so unceremoniously deserted us. I found
him a very efficient man who earned well his dollar a
day, which I was compelled to give him while in my
employment.

MAY 27. The bugle this morning called us at half-
past four o'clock. The usual preparations for breakfast having been made, we were ready at half-past five
to resume our march. The morning was clear and
bracing. The thermometer, at six a.m., was as low as
54°. The road lay over a flat prairie all day, which was
very muddy and difficult to pass in bad weather. We
overtook at least one hundred wagons and met one man
and his family returning to the states. Many of these
people were from Illinois. They had crossed the Mississippi [river] at Palmyra and struck the Missouri at
St. Joseph and Weston.[51] Those destined for Santa Fe

---

[51] In 1849 there were two main land routes across Missouri for emigrants.
One began at St. Louis and followed the Boonslick road to Howard county,
where it crossed the Missouri river at Franklin, Arrow Rock, or Glasgow
and took the Santa Fe trail to Independence and Westport. The other began
at the Mississippi river in the neighborhood of Palmyra (Marion county)
and ran west across the state to St. Joseph. Many emigrants to California and
Oregon outfitted at Liberty (Clay county), then either crossed the Missouri

generally stopped at Independence and Liberty, which are below the mouth of the Kansas river.[52]

We crossed today two streams, one about ninety feet wide. In rainy weather it would be difficult to pass, but at this time the water was lying in holes and very indifferent to drink. Our teams were kept back by the number of trains we overtook today and did not reach our encamping ground on the Big Sandy [53] until nearly the close of evening. We found a large number of emigrants on this stream who were seen in every direction, above and below the crossing. A great number were also passed at the several water-holes along the road. It being the Sabbath, many of them had stopped to rest – some no doubt from religious scruples, while others believed it indispensably necessary to lie by one day in seven for the purpose of resting their animals. It is a very good plan and should be resorted to whenever time will permit.

Towards the close of the evening very little was heard but the cracking of whips and a general talking among the parties coming in as to where their encampments were to be made and whether grass and water could be found contiguous to each other. They relished but little the idea of driving their cattle any distance from camp, where they would be compelled to guard them during the night.

Doctor Browne, of St. Louis, was kind enough to visit the sick this evening and prescribe for them, but pronounced one of their cases to be a very hopeless one. He rendered them every assistance in his power and

river to take the main branch of the Oregon trail or traveled northwest to Weston or St. Joseph to take the "north branch" of the Oregon trail.

[52] Independence (Jackson county) was the main outfitting point for travelers and traders to Santa Fe, but other western Missouri river towns, such as Lexington (Lafayette county), Liberty, and Westport enjoyed more or less of the business.

[53] Tributary of the Little Blue river in southeastern Nebraska.

visited them again this morning before our departure.

Since leaving Fort Leavenworth I had seen no game of any importance, although this is a region where deer and buffalo are generally found in the greatest abundance. At this season herds of buffalo are always seen on the Little Blue, a stream which we were fast approaching, but the immense emigration that had already gone on would no doubt drive them from the vicinity of the road and cause them to become very wild. The few deer I had met with thus far were extremely shy and showed the effect the emigration had produced already in passing this spring. The distance traveled today was about twenty miles. The grazing at our encampment was very good, as I had generally found it since leaving Fort Leavenworth.

MAY 28. Wood being scarce on the Big Sandy we did not succeed in getting our breakfast before a late hour. It consisted, as usual, of nothing more than fried ham, stale bread, and bad coffee. It was, therefore, after six o'clock before we commenced our march. The land on the Big Sandy is of a light soil and poor. The wood on this stream is very scarce, consisting principally of cottonwood. The road today led over a prairie somewhat level, though much better than that of yesterday. It brought us on the Little Blue [river] where the road passes along its valley for at least forty miles.

Among the multiplicity of troubles which we had met with since leaving, one of the wagons today broke down and was abandoned in consequence of having neither timber to substitute nor mechanics to repair it. The sick, together with a part of the escort, were left with it. I was not with the wagon when the accident occurred, and this arrangement was made by a person in charge of the teams. It greatly annoyed me, and although near sundown when they came into camp, I

directed them to unload and return for the party they
had left behind. This was accomplished, and they returned to camp about twelve o'clock at night.

By this time the man who had the cholera became
entirely deranged and required the strength of one person to keep him in the wagon. His sufferings were very
great and his cries most distressing, particularly as it
was not in our power to render him any assistance or
relief. The condition of the sick, as well as the general
indisposition among the party, rendered it necessary
to reach Fort Kearny as soon as possible or it would
become necessary to lie by. I was now reduced to one
wagon to transport the sick, my own outfit and that of
the party, as well as the luggage of the escort. I determined, therefore, to leave all the stores that were not
absolutely necessary for us for the next two days, hoping
by that time to arrive at the fort or overtake the command.

MAY 29. The morning was clear and pleasant after a
rainy night. I did not leave the camp until seven
o'clock, for the loss of one of our wagons had greatly
deranged our movements and compelled me to make
entirely new arrangements. Beds, boxes, and all bulky
articles were left behind, and having a heavy load I
attached eight mules to it, with two of the drivers,
who succeeded in getting them along much better than
anyone anticipated. The remainder of the animals were
driven by the escort and gave us much trouble. Being
wild, they greatly preferred the prairie to being driven
quietly along.

The road here passed along the valley of the [Little]
Blue [river], except in one bend, where it crosses a
high, level prairie about six miles wide, which I found
very muddy. In wet weather [it] is extremely difficult
to travel on. This is generally the case on all parts of the

road where the prairie is not sufficiently rolling to carry off the water. The ground in this state becomes saturated, making the sward easy to cut through. [This lets] the wheels sink and causes the hauling to be extremely fatiguing.

Wagons, as usual, were to be seen at every bend of the road and along the banks of the river.[54] Having made a late start this morning we were necessarily thrown behind large trains that had started before us and compelled to travel much slower than usual. I therefore found it a better plan to make early starts in the morning, as the emigrants seldom move before sunrise. By reaching some spot in the evening where there were none [we] would [be] able to keep clear of them during the day.

It is not frequently the case that you meet on the prairie mountaineers returning with their peltry, but today I met with a Frenchman who left Fort Laramie [55] with two wagons loaded with buffalo skins. [He] had been twenty-three days from that place. Although he gave the cheering news that the regiment was only one day's march in advance, which was the first correct information I had received since leaving Fort Leavenworth, he was the harbinger of unpleasant information relative to the country over which he had traveled for the last three weeks. He stated that there had been much

---

54 See Gibbs's account, pages 298 and 301.

55 The first fort built here, called Fort William, was erected by William Sublette and Robert Campbell on the left bank of Laramie creek in 1834. It consisted of a palisade fifteen feet high, with log bastions at diagonal corners and a log blockhouse over the main gate. It was sold to Thomas Fitzpatrick, Milton Sublette, and James Bridger in 1835. The following year the new owners sold it to the American Fur company, which rebuilt it at a cost of about ten thousand dollars and called it Fort John. The name, however, did not take, and it was soon known as Fort Laramie. On june 26, 1849, Lieutenant Daniel P. Woodbury, acting for the United States government, purchased it for four thousand dollars. Hafen and Young, *Fort Laramie*, 27, 31, 44, 70, 142.

rain between Forts Laramie and Kearny this spring, which had swollen the Platte river and made the trail very heavy. There was [therefore] every probability that it would be too high to cross on our arrival. From his statement, several thousand wagons were already ahead of us. Many of them had passed Fort Laramie, and at all the convenient places for stopping the grass had been pretty much consumed. The Platte [river] valley, which in dry weather is generally very fine to travel over, had been so cut up by the immense emigration that he found much trouble in traveling. It was highly probable that we would find it but little better. The only hope was that it would cease raining, and in that case a few clear days would make it passable. It was extremely gratifying, however, to know that we were so near the command. [This] would enable me, should I overtake them, to get clear of the sick, who in my present condition had become a great burden.

We stopped today at two o'clock to graze our animals, which had become very tired and were near giving out. This was not very surprising, when we reflected upon their condition when we started and the distance they had traveled. I would recommend by all means [that] small parties stop in the middle of the day and particularly those with pack-mules, as the loads are easily adjusted and but little time lost. [By this] your animals become greatly relieved. With large trains there is much trouble and but very little advantage [in the mid-day stop] unless you are driving oxen. [These] never require more than a few minutes to turn loose and are equally as easy to prepare for the road again.

I here began to discover that the grazing had changed very materially on the [Little] Blue, which was caused not only by the number of cattle that had been grazing on it for some time, but the cold weather had considerably impeded its growth. [This] confirmed me in the opinion that the first of may is too soon to leave the Missouri river unless you contemplate a rest after arriving on the borders of the Platte river. In that case, if you have the means to carry along a small quantity of grain, which can always be done, instead of the many surplus articles that often encumber your loads to but very little purpose, the earlier you start the better. A rest of a week or ten days has a great tendency to prepare your animals for a long journey, which they would not have by being kept constantly on the march.

The day was pleasant, but our late start and the difficulty of passing trains along the route brought us into camp after sundown. We did not accomplish more than twenty-four miles during the day. The thermometer this morning at six o'clock stood at 54°, and this evening, at the same hour, it was as high as 76°. Since striking the [Little] Blue I have not met with any buffalo, as the passing of the emigrants this spring has driven them entirely off. Not more than half a dozen have been seen within the last ten days. Deer are equally as scarce, and you seldom meet with either without traveling some distance on the prairie back from the river.

MAY 30. We left our encampment at five o'clock this morning and continued up the [Little] Blue about four miles, where the road turns off across the prairie to the Platte river. The night was threatening, it commenced raining early in the morning and continued until ten o'clock. Then it cleared off, and the remainder of the day was more pleasant. We pursued our journey through the day until we came in sight of the hills which form a small range that divides the prairie from the valley of the Platte, where I encamped for the night.

My encampment was upon the borders of a pond of water, or what is more generally called a water-hole,

which is often found on the prairies. It was half-past
seven o'clock before my wagons arrived and some time
after sundown before we made ourselves comfortable
for the night. The evening being damp and windy, the
cold was felt very sensibly. The thermometer in the
morning stood at 62°, and [at] half-past seven o'clock
this evening at 56°. We met here another family returning to the Missouri river, already surfeited with gold-
hunting, which had cost them much labor and deprived
them of the many comforts of life. Having staked out
our animals and taken a scanty meal, we retired to rest,
being very much gratified with the pleasing reflection
that the march in the morning would bring us to Fort
Kearny.

The distance of our journey today was twenty-one
miles. We passed a stream about eight miles before we
reached our encampment that was extremely boggy and
difficult to get through. The prairie from the [Little]
Blue, over which we had traveled today, is very high
and level. The road being filled with wagons, we had
much trouble and detention in passing them.

MAY 31. We left our encampment at five o'clock this
morning for the fort, the distance being about ten miles
over a sandy road, and reached it at ten o'clock simul-
taneously with the rifle regiment. It rained during the
day, which made it very cold for the season. The regiment made its encampment about two miles above the
fort, intending to remain until the whole train was examined, reorganized, and put in a condition to renew
the march.

Fort Kearny is situated on the right bank of the Platte
river, at the head of Grand island. It is garrisoned by
a troop of the First regiment of dragoons [56] and a com-

---

[56] This troop consisted of two companies, one of which, under Major R. H.
Chilton, arrived may 23 and the other under Lieutenant Thomas O. Davis on
the twenty-eighth. See page 302.

pany of the Sixth infantry.[57] This post was located here as a substitute for the one formerly at the mouth of the Platte,[58] being more on the direct route from Fort Leavenworth to Fort Laramie, as well as from the small towns on the Missouri river from whence emigrants generally take their departure. It is very well located to keep in check the Pawnee and Sioux nations and is also a great protection to the emigrants who travel this route to California and Oregon.

The smallpox,[59] as well as other diseases, has greatly diminished the Pawnee nation. A few years back they were looked upon as a large and powerful tribe, but they have dwindled away so rapidly of late years that they are no longer feared by the neighboring tribes. The Sioux are fast encroaching on them, and frequently make war on them successfully.[60]

[57] Company D, Sixth infantry, under Lieutenant Levi C. Bootes, which arrived may 29. This company, although first ordered to constitute a part of the garrison at Fort Kearny, was sent to Fort Laramie, where it arrived august 12, 1849. Twiggs, order no. 8, february 9, 1849; Bancroft, *History of Nevada, Colorado and Wyoming,* 691 footnote.

[58] "Old" Fort Kearny at Table creek.

[59] This scourge appeared among the plains Indians as early as 1837. In the spring of that year it broke out among the negro deck crew of the Missouri river steamboat "St. Peter," as she was on her way up that stream to the mountains. Runners were sent forward to warn the Indians to keep away from the river banks, but notwithstanding this precaution the disease was communicated to every tribe between the Missouri river and the Rocky mountains. The fatality among the Indians, who were ignorant as to how to treat the disease, was appalling. Nebraska state historical society *publications,* xx, 70-76.

[60] The establishment of missions among the Pawnees at Bellevue and the village of the Grand Pawnees on the Platte river by the Rev. John B. Dunbar and Samuel Allis in 1834 aroused the jealousy of the Dakotas or Sioux so that they began a long and deadly series of forays and raids against the Pawnees. In 1846 a large war party of Sioux fell upon the Pawnee village on the Loup fork, killed sixty-seven warriors, burned twenty out of the forty-one lodges of which the village consisted, seized two hundred horses, and took a number of women and children captive. This completely unsettled the Pawnees who became marauding rovers, always subject to attacks by the Sioux. Adams, "Biography of John Brown Dunbar," in Kansas state historical society *collections,* x, 103.

The site for this post is not a very pleasing one, having nothing to recommend it in the way of beauty.[61] The valley of the Platte is entirely destitute of wood in this vicinity, besides being low. It has the muddy Platte river on one side, which gives to the Missouri much of its color. A chain of unprepossessing sand-hills are seen on this side, which forms a dividing ridge between the valley and the country back. [This] is the commencement of the first highland that ranges along the river, which gradually rises until it becomes a bluff of considerable height.

What few buildings were inhabited, I observed, were made of sward, cut in the form of adobes.[62] The hospital was the only building which was being erected. These buildings were under the direction of an officer of the engineer corps,[63] who for want of proper materials, was unable to progress very rapidly with them.

Wood can be obtained on Grand island, which is about thirty miles in length, and about five miles wide. Lumber for building is extremely scarce. Cottonwood is the principal timber found on the island and is considered very inferior for building. The stream is not

61 For Gibbs's opinion of the location for Fort Kearny, see page 299.

62 Stansbury, who left here june 21, said, "The post at present consists of a number of long, low buildings, constructed principally of adobe or sun-dried bricks, with nearly flat roofs; a large hospital tent; two or three workshops, enclosed by canvas walls; storehouses constructed in the same manner; one or two long adobe stables, with roofs of brush; and tents for the accommodation of officers and men. *Exploration and survey,* 30.

63 Lieutenant Daniel P. Woodbury. On december 7, 1848, he reported that "during the last month the adobe storehouse was finished. One building 20 by 50 feet and another 20 by 35 feet put up, two sod buildings 48 by 38 feet finished and two temporary stables for 48 horses each erected. The officers and men are in tolerable quarters." On june 2, 1849, he reported that "the buildings which I hope may be erected here this season are the hospital, two double blocks of officers' quarters, and one block of soldiers' quarters." By september 7 a bakery 20 by 16 feet had been erected and another building 80 by 24 feet was nearly completed. Willman, "History of Fort Kearny," in Nebraska state historical society *publications,* XXI, 257, 259, 262.

very wide between the mainland and the island and is seldom more than five feet deep. The bottom is very uneven and filled with quicksand like other parts of this stream.

In the partial cultivation of the soil it has been discovered not to be productive. Gardens have been started,[64] but to little purpose except that the experiment had partly convinced them that it was only labor lost. Still, I am of the opinion [that] when time has been allowed to find out its qualities better, that not only vegetables may be raised in abundance, but grain of every description.

Grazing for our animals in the vicinity of this post is extremely good, but I apprehend that grass for hay is very difficult to procure in the fall. The emigrants had not been permitted to encamp immediately around the fort, which gave our animals a fine field to range over during the time they remained. They stood greatly in need of it.

This day's journey had not only brought me to the regiment, which I had been pursuing with all possible speed for ten days, but also to Fort Kearny, a distance of three hundred ten miles from Fort Leavenworth. I now considered that I had fairly reached the point where my duties were to commence. The march from Fort Leavenworth was a very severe one. The rainy season having set in it rained nearly every day from the commencement of our journey to our arrival at Fort Kearny. If we were fortunate enough to be blest with one bright morning we were certain to have a shower either in the

---

[64] These were planted by the garrison. Gibbs noticed actual attempts at settlement; see page 304. Evidently this was not a success, for on february 14, 1850, Lieutenant Woodbury remarked in his report to General R. Jones that "no one has yet been found willing to settle in the neighborhood as a farmer though I believe that moderate crops may be raised here." Willman, "History of Fort Kearny," in Nebraska state historical society *publications,* XXI, 265.

evening or during the night. Among persons totally ignorant of a life like this, whose avocations have unfitted them for such labor as is incidental to a prairie life, the experience which they had already gained by the journey thus far would teach them at least that it would require a great deal of philosophy and patience to surmount the obstacles and endure the hardships that were still to be met with before reaching Oregon.

The entire route from Fort Leavenworth to Fort Kearny passes over an undulating prairie which is of a dark vegetable mould. Many parts might be productive if cultivated, particularly on the large streams. In rainy weather the whole route becomes extremely muddy and very difficult to travel over, but in this respect it does not differ from any of the prairies of the west. When the season is dry the ground becomes very firm and as there are no hills to impede traveling nothing can prevent trains of any size from moving over it with much ease and great rapidity. The few obstructions met with are found in crossing some of the streams, which could be removed with very little labor. It is in the power of the government to make it one of the best public highways in the western country. There are many small streams on this route, such as Wolf creek, the Big and Little Nemaha, the Vermilion, Big Sandy, and the Little Blue, besides many others which may be looked upon as drains to the prairie. There are waterholes off the road which may be known by mots or small groves of timber. [These] added to the streams afford an abundance of water.

This is a part of that great prairie country which ranges from the Red river of the north to the Rio Grande and can be traversed throughout the whole distance without the least difficulty. As far back as 1828 cattle were driven from Independence, Missouri, to the

St. Peter's river, which empties into the Mississippi river a little below latitude 45°. [About that time] it was not infrequent for sheep to be carried as far as the settlement on Red river in British territory.[65] From Lake Qui Parle [66] to the Yellowstone [river] it was commonly the route taken by the traders to carry their goods instead of ascending the Missouri river. There is nothing to prevent this whole range from being traveled as far as the Rio Grande except the danger of encountering hostile Indians who are frequently met with between Independence and Santa Fe, particularly the Comanche tribe, who are constantly ranging between the Arkansas [river] and the southern boundary of Texas. Game of every description is found on this prairie; buffalo, elk, and antelope are seen in great numbers. This year very few have been met with, owing, doubtless, to the great emigration passing this way, which has driven them farther south.

While at Fort Kearny I had occasion to converse frequently with Colonel Bonneville,[67] the commander of the post. [He] had been many years ago among the Indians in the Rocky mountains and had obtained while there much valuable information which he freely imparted to me. I found it, in more than one instance before reaching the Columbia river, [to be] of great importance.

---

[65] Founded in 1812 by Lord Selkirk on the site of present Winnipeg, Canada.

[66] A widening of the Minnesota river in southwestern Minnesota.

[67] Benjamin L. E. Bonneville. Born in France about 1795, and died at Fort Smith, Arkansas, june 12, 1878. Graduated from the United States military academy in 1815 and led an exploring party to Oregon in 1832. He fought with conspicuous gallantry in the war with Mexico and commanded the Gila expedition in 1857. He was retired in 1861. His journal and other papers relating to his journeys in the west were edited by Washington Irving. He was commandant at Fort Kearny from may 29 to july 16, 1849.

March from Fort Kearny to Fort Laramie

JUNE 1, 1849. The whole outfit was carefully examined today, that it might be put in as good a condition as our time and means would permit. It required but little experience to see that the condition of the mules was not such as to justify the command leaving for the Columbia river with any certainty of arriving there without accident. The mules were principally those brought from the Rio Grande in the fall of 1848, and were wintered in the vicinity of Fort Leavenworth by contract. They had been badly taken care of, and when the spring commenced there was not sufficient time to put them in a proper condition for the march. Many of them were partly broken down by former hard service.[68] Others were wild, and it seemed almost impossible to break them to harness. They had just completed a journey of three hundred ten miles in very unpleasant weather. The citizen and soldier teamsters were entirely incapable of driving, with the exception of a few of the former who had been in Mexico. With all this combined, it had greatly impaired the condition of many of them.

---

[68] "The train started from Fort Leavenworth in a condition wholly incompetent to perform the service required of it. The teams were very poor, feeble and small, having just passed a winter in which hundreds had perished. As an evidence of the condition of the mules, I would merely state that I was obliged to call in the aid of men to assist teams in starting off the CAMP GROUND on a level road, and these teams were to perform a journey of two thousand miles, unrelieved, and WITHOUT THE AID OF A SINGLE EXTRA MULE. The wagons were so insufficiently supplied with extra tongues, hounds, etc., that we were obliged to send back for an additional supply before we had traveled fifty miles . . . the harness was bad, many of the hames being of cottonwood." Frost to Cross, october 26, 1849.

The responsibility which was about to devolve on me to transport the troops safely to the Columbia river, whether much or little was expected by the department, determined me not to take the charge on myself without letting it know the condition, at least, in which I found things. Although I did not consider that anyone was to blame since the march commenced, I preferred calling for a board of survey, and it was convened in compliance with the letter here annexed. The board inspected the animals, and passed their opinion upon them, and out of the whole number condemned one-third, as I was officially informed. Although this was their opinion, I never was able to obtain a copy of the report, as they committed an informality, which caused the proceedings to be annulled. This was the aspect of affairs when I took charge of the department and relieved the officer who had accompanied the troops to Fort Kearny.[69]

JUNE 2. This day was passed in making out papers and arranging the train.[70] The command moved four miles above to change their encampment, get better grazing, and be nearer to the water. An order was issued by Colonel Loring [71] separating the command into three

---

[69] Major James Belger. He remained at Fort Kearny until about june 12 when he set out for Fort Leavenworth with an escort. Stansbury, *Exploration and survey*, 27.

[70] Owing to the weakness of the teams a part of the extra supplies were left at Fort Kearny. Loring to Freeman, october 15, 1849.

[71] William Wing Loring. Born at Wilmington, Delaware, december 4, 1818; fought in the Florida Indian wars as member of the Second Florida volunteers and was commissioned second-lieutenant at nineteen years of age; studied law at Georgetown college, practiced law in Florida, and was a member of the Florida legislature; appointed captain in the Mounted Riflemen may 27, 1846; major february 16, 1847; brevet-lieutenant-colonel august 20, 1847 for gallant and meritorious service at the battles of Contreras and Chapultepec where he lost an arm; lieutenant-colonel march 15, 1848; brevet-colonel 1849; commandant Eleventh military district 1849-1851; colonel december 30, 1856; served in Utah under General A. S. Johnston 1858-1859; year's leave of absence traveling in Europe 1859; commandant department of

divisions of two companies each.[72] They were to march at an interval of five miles between the first and third divisions, and encamp in the same order until otherwise changed. This necessarily separated me from the greater portion of the command and confined me to a division, changing from one to the other as my services were most required.

Having only Lieutenant Frost [73] with me as acting assistant quartermaster, who was in charge of the regimental train and similarly situated, I was compelled to trust much to the agents.[74] [This] greatly increased my responsibilities, as it was expected that I would not only see that the property was taken care of, but the troops properly transported. This plan was decided on before I took charge of the department, and no views of mine, founded on former experience, could alter it. If it had been absolutely necessary to cause the divisions to march several days apart, from the great scarcity of

New Mexico 1860-61; resigned to join Confederate army may 20, 1861; brigadier-general may 20, 1861; major-general february 1862; corps commander in Georgia, Mississippi, Tennessee, and Carolinas where he surrendered to General W. T. Sherman april 1865; lived in New York until 1869 when he and other Confederate officers entered the service of the Khedive of Egypt; assumed command of all Egyptian coast defenses 1870; took part in Egyptian campaign against Abyssinia 1875-1876; promoted to general of division, elevated to the rank of Pasha, and decorated with the Egyptian orders of Osmanli and Medjidie; died New York City 1896. *Dictionary of American biography*, XI, 420-21.

[72] For the personnel of these divisions see page 304.

[73] Daniel Marsh Frost. New York. Brevet-second-lieutenant First artillery july 1, 1844; transferred to Mounted Riflemen july 17, 1846; second-lieutenant february 16, 1847; regimental quartermaster march 18, 1847 to november 4, 1851; brevet-first-lieutenant april 18, 1847, for gallantry and meritorious service in the battle of Cerro Gordo, Mexico; first lieutenant november 30, 1850; resigned may 31, 1853; brigadier-general Confederate army march 1861-1865; died october 29, 1900. Heitman, *Historical register*, I, 438.

[74] At this time the commissary and quartermaster's departments hired agents, wagonmasters, and teamsters. The agents commanded trains, wagonmasters superintended the details of the route, and teamsters handled the teams.

grass, the plan would have been a very good one. This was not the case, and [the plan] increased the COM-MANDERS when I found ONE amply sufficient. I saw no good reason for it, and having no officer of the department to receipt for the property in the several divisions and superintend their movements my position became a very unenviable one, increasing my labors threefold, both bodily and mentally.

JUNE 3. It became necessary before leaving Fort Kearny to increase the subsistence stores, which called for additional means of transportation. I was, therefore, compelled to resort to ox-teams, [these] being the only transportation that could be obtained at the post, and we were very fortunate even to get this. I placed them under charge of a wagonmaster, [with orders] to proceed directly to Fort Laramie in company with the emigrants, without being governed by the movements of the expedition. We were required to make short marches in consequence of the delay of the beef contractor,[75] and the delay would enable them to get considerably the start of us.

JUNE 4. We left this morning at seven o'clock and arrived on Plum creek early in the evening, where the third division made its encampment for the night. This is a very small stream, which rises among the bluffs and empties into the Platte [river] a few miles below where the road crossed it. My tent was pitched on the banks of the Platte for the first time this evening. [It] was swollen and extremely muddy from the heavy rains that had recently fallen, which gave us much apprehension that the information recently received would prove true. In its present stage it was very doubtful if we were not detained on reaching the crossing of the South fork.

75 M. L. Young, Platte county, Missouri. He contracted to deliver about five hundred head of beef cattle to the regiment may 15, 1849, at Fort Kearny. Bennett to editor, january 27, 1939.

When we look at the width of this river, its muddy water and rapid current, we are greatly reminded of the striking resemblance it bears to the Missouri [river], of which it is one of its principal tributaries. When we reflect that there is only a short portion of the year that it is not too high to prevent you from fording it, we are impressed with its total uselessness and insignificance when compared with the smallest of navigable rivers in our country. Although it is large, it is but a drain for the melting snows from the mountains, and can only be remarkable for possessing more sandbars, less depth of water, and more islands half covered with useless timber than any other stream of its size in the country. It is not navigable, nor can it be made so, and [from] a commercial point of view has very little to recommend it.[76]

This river is formed by the North and South Platte, which, after passing through the western prairies from the mountains several hundred miles, come together eighty miles above Fort Kearny. The South fork we were soon to cross, when our route would lie along the North fork for nearly four hundred miles, until it turns to the south, where it rises in the mountains west of the Medicine Bow range, at least two and a half degrees from where the Oregon and California trails leave it.

The valley of the Platte being as destitute of a tree as the adjacent prairie, or that which we had passed over, we found wood very difficult to procure at our encampment this evening. What little was used by the troops they brought on their shoulders from an island, which they reached by wading.

---

[76] This opinion of the Platte river was common. A correspondent with General W. S. Harney's expedition, 1855, said, "In truth this Platte river is a humbug. It is about dry, and a person can cross it dry-shod. . . From one hundred miles east of Fort Kearny to the foot of the Rocky mountains the land is unproductive and uninhabited." Nebraska state historical society *publications*, xx, 278; see also page 306.

The mode adopted for the arrangement of the three camps was the same. Each division or squadron occupied two sides of a rectangle, the tents pitched sufficiently far apart to make room on the other two sides for the supply train. This generally made sufficient space to contain all the horses and mules. The wagons are driven sufficiently close to allow the tongue of one to reach the hind wheels of the other, which is called corralling a train. [This] makes a very formidable defense either against foot or mounted troops. When it is desirable to leave the camp open the train is generally parked in several lines, making them as compact as the nature of the ground will admit.

At the end of a day's journey the horses and mules of the division are staked out until sundown, then brought into the corral and there kept until morning. Each animal is made fast to a lasso about twenty feet long, which is attached to an iron pin of about fifteen inches in length. At the head [is] a ring that works on a pivot which allows the horse to move around without disturbing the pin. About four o'clock in the morning they are all taken out and allowed to remain until five, when they are prepared for the march. All being ready, the squadron moves off, followed by the baggage train. Next comes the supply train, which has an agent whose duty it is to examine his train throughout the day, making such alterations as might be deemed necessary to facilitate its movement. The train is divided into sections of a certain number of wagons [and] placed under a wagonmaster, who is responsible to the agent for the good order of that particular part of the train. I generally found that twenty wagons were as many as one man could properly superintend, particularly when the teamsters were indifferent and the roads very bad. On this march it was not infrequently the case to require his services at several points at the same time. In that case, I never found that I had too many in my employment. I will take this occasion to remark that the number employed did not render my own situation a sinecure. Being always at the head of my own train, I often FOUND MYSELF, as well as my clerks, with OUR SHOULDERS literally to the wheel working as hard, as it is well known, as any laborer along. I found it necessary to do so to enable us to accomplish our march. This was the course adopted and continued through the route. As the baggage train was necessarily required to be in camp early, it was under the direction of the acting quartermaster,[77] who was responsible for its order, as the property was under his charge. The supply train, not being required to reach camp so early, generally moved less rapidly and in consequence came in less fatigued and in much better order.[78]

JUNE 5. Large trains could be seen this morning wending their way along both sides of the Platte. The river here is nearly three miles wide [and] interspersed with islands, some of which are thinly covered with very small cottonwood and willow. In many instances they are entirely bare. It rained a little before we left camp, which made it muddy, but as it remained cloudy it was pleasant for traveling and rather facilitated our movements.

Our march was eleven miles today. We have done little more than change encamping grounds since leaving Fort Kearny, it being necessary to wait for the [beef] contractor who was hourly expected. This gave the mules and horses an opportunity of recovering from their march from Fort Leavenworth. Having arrived in camp early today, I overhauled the wagons which

---

[77] Lieutenant D. M. Frost.
[78] This train was in charge of Cross himself.

contained the lumber intended for such repairs as we might require on the route, and found that we had but very little along with us, there being but four pairs of hounds and eleven tongues. This was a scanty allowance for the repairs of one hundred and sixty wagons that were to pass over rough roads for two thousand miles. I had no desire to send back for timber, which had been done previous to my arrival. [I] rather preferr[ed] to trust to a good trail and the improvement of the teams and teamsters.

JUNE 6. It rained very hard last night and continued [to do so] this morning. The dark clouds, accompanied with wind, were fast covering the heavens. The lightning was very severe, and it rained and hailed very hard. We left our encampment at half past nine o'clock and traveled ten miles today. The march being short, nothing occurred worthy of note. The evening cleared off beautifully after the rain, and the mules bid fair to be well prepared by morning for a good day's journey, as they were up to their eyes in grass.

While quietly wending our way along the Platte today I saw an antelope for the first time, and was somewhat disappointed in its appearance. There was not that beauty [in its] form that I had expected to find from the descriptions so often given of the "swift-footed antelope" when compared with the deer. I consider it by no means as handsome or as delicately proportioned. At a distance, however, it is much the same. The head of this animal is very much like that of a sheep. The body appears shorter than that of the deer, with hair much coarser and longer. It stands very erect and leaps with much quickness, gathering its feet apparently at the same time immediately under it. Its curiosity exceeds [that of] any animal I have ever seen, except the mountain goat. When it first saw me it approached almost within gunshot, when, stopping for a few minutes, it ran off for a short distance, then it turned again apparently to satisfy its curiosity. It ran parallel to the road, sometimes getting ahead, and then returning. If I stopped suddenly, or there was anything seen to attract its attention still more, it would run directly towards me until its curiosity was fully satisfied. Then it would bound off with great rapidity until out of sight. It is much lighter in color than the deer, particularly on its sides, breast, and hindquarters. This, with a black stripe which it has about the eyes, gives it a striking appearance, though it does not add much to its beauty.

Desertion at this time was rapidly increasing, [but] whether from the alarm of the cholera or a distaste for soldiering, I am unable to say. Four men ran off last night, taking a complete outfit with them. This was not very unexpected to us when we considered the material of which the regiment was composed. [Many men] merely enlisted, it is well known, for the purpose of getting comfortably transported to California at the expense of the government, and not from any partiality for the profession of a soldier.

JUNE 7. The command got under way a quarter before seven o'clock this morning. The rain of last evening made it very muddy and the hauling along the valley very heavy. The day was quite warm. The thermometer at six a.m. stood at 52°, and at twelve noon it ranged as high as 80°.

Today buffalo were seen for the first time, which created no little excitement. We had been hoping for several days to be gratified with a sight of them, for the road was entirely destitute of interest, and we were much pleased on hearing the news that game was so near us. We were now getting into a section of country where it is generally found abundantly in the spring, and looked forward to something in the way of sport to divert us from our monotonous life for a time. A journey over a prairie affords no pleasure except that of hunting, and when that cannot be found any other scenery is far more preferable.

After arriving in camp, which we reached early in the day, having traveled but twelve miles, Mr. Wilcox [79] and myself ascended the bluffs and continued for a short distance back into the country. Here the prairie was very much broken, forming deep ravines [which] appeared to continue for a long distance, and rising at the same time quite high. The ground was so much broken as to make it difficult to travel on horseback on these ridges. Nothing could be seen but large buffalo trails.[80] The deep ravines were much trodden and torn up, forming what are generally called buffalo wallows, which are resorted to by them when these places are partially filled with water. We expected to have been successful in finding game beyond the bluffs, but were compelled to return after sundown without seeing one buffalo. A large hawk was the only thing killed. It measured four feet ten inches from the tip of one wing to the other, and was quite remarkable in other respects. Today the [beef] contractor arrived. [He] had been looked for with much anxiety, and [his arrival] would enable us in a few days to increase our daily marches. The grazing at this encampment was much the same as had been met with for the last few days.

JUNE 8. We left our encampment at seven this morning and traveled about three hours, making about six miles, when we halted for the day. The road was extremely heavy from constant rains. It was very pleasant. The thermometer, at seven o'clock in the evening, was ranging at 75°.

---

[79] One of the guides.

[80] For a good description of these see Gibbs's account, page 310.

Today a buffalo was killed by Mr. Leech,[81] one of the train agents, and it was the first time I had ever tasted the meat of one. The hump is considered a great delicacy, but for my part I did not consider it anything to compare with beef. It was unfortunately an old bull. The young cows are doubtless much finer, but we had just been feasting on fine Missouri beef and were therefore ready by comparison to condemn the wild beef of the prairie. I think if we had been pinched by hunger it would have been unanimously pronounced to be the best of the two.

The command stood greatly in need of wood, for we had reached a region of country entirely destitute of it, where a tree might be looked on as a curiosity. We were therefore compelled to resort to the *vache de bois* [buffalo chips], which is a fine substitute when you get used to it. It is always used by hunters, who never think of the scarcity of wood when this can be obtained.

Grazing along the river banks was becoming very indifferent. [This] made it necessary to encamp nearer the bluffs, which often made it difficult to procure water. It probably was better in some respects, as the Platte river water was thought to have greatly increased the cholera symptoms since we first commenced to use it.[82]

JUNE 9. It rained a little last night and had much the appearance of it this morning. The thermometer at six o'clock was at 64°. We got under way at half-past six o'clock this morning. The day being fine, it enabled us to make a long march, and at half-past two o'clock we arrived at camp, having traveled nineteen miles. Here we pitched our tents on a small branch about half a mile from the Platte river, and made ourselves as comfort-

---

81 James B. Leech, agent and wagonmaster, first division. Bennett to editor, january 27, 1939.

82 For an opposite view see Gibbs's account, page 322.

able as circumstances would permit for the night. It continued cloudy during the day and became quite cool in the evening. The thermometer stood at sundown at 55°, making a difference of 9° since the morning.

The bluffs about this point begin to approach the river very near.[83] They have varied heretofore from two to four miles from the banks of the Platte. Our encampment was made within five miles of the junction of the North and South forks of the Platte. [This was] sixteen miles from where the emigrants make their first crossing of the South fork, commonly called the lower crossing,[84] which, I believe, is generally considered the best. [This] being a fine section of the country for buffalo and antelope, Mr. Wilcox went over the bluffs last evening on a hunting excursion. He returned, after traveling twenty miles on the prairie, without being successful, a disappointment seldom known to a hunter along the Platte before this spring.

This valley has been heretofore a great range for game of all kinds. Herds of buffalo, consisting of thousands, have been seen grazing at one time a few years since. Such has been the effect produced on them by the immense emigration this spring that [they have been driven] far beyond the bluffs. The buffalo seldom return to the river except when forced to do so for want of water, and then in small numbers. Their range is now on the headwaters of the Blue and Kansas [rivers], and from thence to the Arkansas. I have no doubt [that] if the emigration continues a few years more as large as it is this year not one will be found along the borders of the Platte or near Fort Kearny, where they have been

[83] O'Fallon's bluffs.

[84] There were three principal crossings of the South fork of the Platte river; the lower, near Hershey, Nebraska, the middle, five miles below Ogallala, Nebraska, and the upper or "California crossing," seven miles below Big Spring, Nebraska.

known to approach the out-buildings, apparently for shelter in the winter.

We had the unpleasant duty today of passing along the road many graves of the unfortunate emigrants. Among them was the grave of a man who had died at the age of sixty-four years from general debility. One would suppose, with a man who had arrived nearly at the age of three score and ten, that his thoughts would have been on anything else than the treasures of this earth, but such is the charm in wealth that on this route it was not unusual to overtake men and women who were scarcely able to walk from age, all destined for the gold diggings.

I had not proceeded very far beyond this place before I came to the resting spot of Captain P. S. Gray, of Texas, who had served in the Mexican war. I could not help thinking, as I passed, that he had traveled far to find a solitary grave, so distant from relatives and in a spot where the prints of the white man's [feet] were never seen until within the last few years. His comrades, however, had performed the last act of kindness by decently interring him in this lonely spot and placing at the head of his grave a well-cut slab with the date of his death, name, age, and the disease with which he died, being cholera.

On the right of the road, and not far distant, we passed the encampment of a party of Cherokees [85] who

---

[85] News of the discovery of gold in California stirred the Cherokee Indians living in Indian territory, many of whom had been miners in the gold fields of northern Georgia before their removal from that state. In the spring of 1849 what was known as the Cherokee, Washington county, or Evans company was formed and a rendezvous appointed at the Grand Saline for april 21. One hundred twenty-four persons, including Cherokees and white men from Washington, Benton, and Madison counties, Arkansas, assembled, elected Lewis Evans as captain and set out on the twenty-fourth. They broke a new trail between the branches of the Verdigris river and reached the Santa Fe trail which they followed to Pueblo, Colorado. A party of Cher-

had broken up their [original] party, [a practice] which had become very general among the emigrants since leaving Fort Kearny. A few days ago it consisted of fourteen persons. Since yesterday six had died with the cholera, one was dying at the time they were visited, and the remainder were too ill to assist in burying the dead. Among the whole of this party there was but one man who really was able to render any assistance to the others. This was a sad spectacle to behold. These people had left homes where many of them were no doubt comfortable and happy, and [where they had] perhaps never been required to labor for their daily bread half as hard as they had on this march. The gold mania had, however, spread far and near. Being seized with it, they had abandoned comfortable homes, blinded with the belief that fortunes were soon to be realized, which in a great degree was imaginary. They, like many others similarly situated, found their graves in this wild and lonely region.

Much fear was entertained that the cholera would increase. We certainly had every reason to suppose so, from the many deaths among the emigrants along the road and their present helpless condition. Within the last four days the command had lost several men by cholera, and it had every indication of increasing among them. On the fourth two men died,[86] one on the

okees, under Dr. Jeter L. Thompson, either detached itself from the main party, or what is more probable, organized independently, and went by way of Fort Scott to Westport and Independence, Missouri. Dennis W. Bushyhead, formerly clerk of the Cherokee national assembly and principal chief of the Cherokee nation, 1879-1887, was a member of this party. From Westport they followed the Oregon trail to the Platte river, where they were attacked by cholera. Bushyhead was the one man able to render assistance to the sick. Hafen, "Gold-seekers in Colorado, 1849-1850," in *Colorado magazine,* xv, 101-109; Bushyhead, "Autobiography," 1; Eloise Butler Bushyhead, statement to Grant Foreman, january 23, 1939; Ballenger, *Around Tahlequah council fires,* 26-28.

86 Privates Jacob Shaffer and Aeneas Foulke. Previous to this date the fol-

seventh, and Doctors Moses and Smith were seriously attacked by it. They were the only two physicians along with us to attend the three divisions that were required to travel some distance apart.[87] I had seen so much of it between Forts Leavenworth and Kearny that I did hope the command would, before our reaching it, be entirely clear. It seemed [however] to move as the emigrants did, and we were destined to keep it among us in spite of every precaution until our arrival in Oregon.

I think it was about this place that a man was found near the bluffs who had entirely lost his reason. He had been abandoned by the company to which he belonged,[88] either to starve or to be picked up by some emigrating party who might possess more humanity for him than was shown by them. He was taken to Fort Laramie by the troops, and there left under the care of the physician of that post.

The road today was much cut up by gullies, which are the natural drains from the highlands to the river. In many places they were so broken as to render it necessary to cut down the banks and make other improvements before we could pass them, without which it would have been very fatiguing to the teams. The road thus far along the valley of the Platte was good, and with the exception of the mud, which made it very heavy, it could hardly be surpassed by any I have ever traveled over. It reminded me very much of the roads

lowing men died; Private William Boyd, may 15; Private Joseph C. Lyons, may 17; Private Hiram C. Hitt, may 18; Private Patrick Caldwell, farrier of company F, may 26; Sergeant William H. Snyder, may 29; Privates Jacob Goss and Charles Kallensback, june 1; Private John C. Smith, june 3; Corporal Norman C. Michael, june 5. Monthly returns, Mounted Riflemen.

87 "In consequence of the division of the command . . . it has been found necessary to employ a citizen surgeon. I was fortunate enough to secure the services of a gentlemen of high reputation in the state of Missouri." Loring to Jones, june 22, 1849. The surgeon was Dr. Thomas J. White of St. Louis, Missouri.

88 See Gibbs's account of this man, pages 304-305.

in the Mississippi bottom, which are always fine in good weather, but are the reverse whenever the rainy season sets in.

The valley of the Platte is very level and uninteresting, and but little better beyond the bluffs. There you find a little undergrowth of dwarf oak and elder in the ravines. The wild gooseberry and currant are the only fruits to be met about here and are very inferior in taste when compared with those cultivated. They can be made palatable when properly served up and afford a little variety to those who are compelled to resort to salt food, which is so very deleterious to health when constantly used on a long march like this.

JUNE 10. Today being the Sabbath, it was a day of general rest among the emigrants. As the command had been considerably delayed since leaving Fort Kearny it became necessary to make up for lost time. Therefore [we] did not follow the good example set by our fellow-travelers, deeming it more prudent to rest toward the end of our journey, if time would permit us, than at the commencement of it. I think, however, one day in the week should be taken for that purpose. It relieves the teams and prepares them anew for their labor. The morning was cloudy and disagreeable. The thermometer at five o'clock was at 58°. Each division marched off about the hour of six, the third division having fallen some four or five miles in the rear of the second, which was some distance behind the first.

I ascended the bluffs this morning and could easily discover where the two forks of the Platte river came together. It was not immediately below the lower crossing of the South fork, but at least sixteen miles [farther down] and a short distance above where our encampment was made last night.

Today five buffalo were seen. When first discovered

they were running from the river across our road and
making toward the bluffs. It created, as might have
been expected, a very great excitement. From the highest to the lowest all seemed to be desirous of joining in
the chase, and it was with some difficulty that they were
prevented [from doing so]. Several of the officers, with
some of the men, gave chase and soon came up with
them. Then the firing commenced. One of the buffalo
was singled out, [which], taking a circuitous route,
received an additional fire as he passed toward the rear.
Before being brought to bay there was a small troop in
pursuit of him. He at last came to a stand, and although
writhing with pain, he would now and then make at
the nearest horseman who was disposed to approach
him. One of the soldiers, it may be truly said, attacked
him sword in hand, giving him a blow over the head,
as if he really thought any impression could be made
upon him.

I think I counted sixteen men after this poor animal,
who kept up a regular fire with revolvers. All seemed
to be eager to have the satisfaction of saying they had
shot at a buffalo, [even] if they were not successful
enough to kill one. Lieutenant Lindsay [89] at last brought
him to the ground and had the credit of being the victor.
The other four were all disposed of. Lieutenant Frost
killed one, but the most successful of the hunters was
Captain Rhett [90] who, being mounted upon a fine, swift,

[89] Andrew Jackson Lindsay. Alabama. First-lieutenant Mounted Riflemen
may 27, 1846; captain october 31, 1848; resigned may 5, 1861; colonel Mississippi cavalry, Confederate army 1861-1865; died june 3, 1895. Heitman,
Historical register, I, 633.

[90] Thomas Grimke Rhett. South Carolina. Brevet-second-lieutenant july 1,
1845; second-lieutenant Mounted Riflemen may 27, 1846; first-lieutenant april
18, 1847; brevet-captain october 12, 1847 for gallant and meritorious service
in the defense of Puebla, Mexico; captain september 16, 1853; major, paymaster, june 14, 1858; resigned april 1, 1861; major, assistant adjutant-general, Confederate army, 1861-1865; died july 28, 1878. Heitman, *Historical
register,* I, 826.

and extremely active [horse], was well prepared for a good chase. Singling out an old bull he was determined to kill him without the assistance of anyone. His horse, being very fleet, soon brought him alongside of the buffalo. He had not run very far before he was able, with his six-shooter, to place a ball in a vital part of the animal. The horse appeared to enter as much into the spirit of it as the rider, and being very manageable, could be placed wherever required.

Having amused himself by riding sometimes alongside, and then [being] chased for a short distance by the animal, he at last put an end to his sufferings. In true hunter style, taking such portions as are considered most delicate, they took what they wished and left the rest to be devoured by the wolves, which are found in numbers prowling about the prairie, and particularly the buffalo range. Mr. Leech was not in the last hunt. He killed another, making his second since we left Fort Kearny.

We met this morning a man from the Salt lake, who informed us that he had been robbed by a party of Crow Indians, who took from him his horse.[91] He also gave us the unpleasant information that grass was extremely scarce beyond Fort Laramie. [This was] caused by the immense emigration which had already passed the fort, [it] having started early in the season. By him we were able to send off letters. Such opportunities were very seldom met with, and we were glad to seize upon any, and particularly one so favorable as this.

---

[91] On may 23, 1849, Bruce Husband, in charge of Fort Laramie in the absence of Major Andrew Drips, wrote Drips a letter saying that three Mormons had arrived the day before from Salt lake. They had been plundered by the Crows in the neighborhood of the Mormon ferry on the Platte river. He bought four inferior horses from them and gave them a canoe in which to descend the Platte river. They arrived in Council Bluffs the latter part of june and reported their loss. The identity of these men is not known, but evidently the man Cross mentions was one of them. Hafen and Young, *Fort Laramie*, 133; *Frontier guardian* (Kanesville, Iowa), june 27, 1849.

We soon came to the lower crossing of the South fork, where we found a number of wagons on both sides of the river. Some had crossed, not without much difficulty, others were crossing, but with much trouble, for the rains had greatly swollen the river, so as to endanger their stores as well as running the risk of losing their wagons. Many were on this side waiting for a more favorable opportunity to get across.

The banks of the South Platte seemed to be lined with large trains on both sides of the river and over the divide which separates the North and South forks. They could be seen as far as the eye extended. To look at them it would seem impossible that grazing could be found for such an immense number of cattle that must necessarily be thrown together when it sometimes becomes necessary to stop for water. As the emigrants passed Fort Kearny this spring the wagons were counted by the guard daily. On the first day of june better than four thousand had passed, not reckoning those that were on the left bank of the river [which] could not be seen from the fort. While on the journey to Oregon I had a good opportunity of ascertaining the number of persons with each wagon, and it was a small average to estimate four to each one, which would make, at this time, nearly twenty thousand persons ahead of us. The number of oxen were very seldom less than ten to each wagon and more frequently twelve. With this number, together with the many outriders, as well as the cattle which were driven along, the number of animals in advance of the regiment could not have been less than fifty thousand. From this statement it will not be difficult to calculate the number of emigrants who went to California, as but few, comparatively speaking, were destined for Oregon. To this number add those who took the Santa Fe route, also those that were still in the rear of us, and it will not fall short of thirty-five thousand souls. I feel confident in saying that on this trail there were not less than from eight to ten thousand wagons passed during the season, with animals in proportion.

There were with the command about twelve hundred mules. The horses belonging to the whole regiment amounted in all to about seven hundred – a pretty round number to provide for daily for a period of five months. On the prairie, where one million buffalo have been seen scattered over the hills and valleys, it may be thought that the animals ahead of us were of but little importance, but when you think of this number stopping on the borders of some convenient stream to be adjacent to water and kept within a short distance of camp it will strike one with surprise how we ever got through the country beyond this, where grazing is always bad, without some great disaster. When I reflect upon the past it often seems astonishing to me how we ever reached the Columbia river without losing half of our teams.

Colonel Loring concluded to ascend the river from this camp, hoping to find a better crossing. We continued our march a few miles farther, where the second division encamped among the hills and their horses were taken to an island to graze for the night. The first division stopped about five miles ahead of us, and the third in the bottom near the lower crossing, which we had passed during the afternoon. The distance traveled today was twenty-five miles. The road being excellent and the day pleasant our teams came into camp much less fatigued than usual.

JUNE 11. We did not get off before six this morning. The storm of last night scattered our mules and much time was lost in hunting them. The wind blew a perfect hurricane, knocking down our tents and blowing off the wagon covers. The rain fell in torrents, as if it would deluge the valley below us, and it was very fortunate that we had encamped among the hills.

I do not know when I have experienced such vivid lightning. So great was the glare that the whole camp was at moments perfectly visible. The braying of mules, lowing of cattle, and the racing of horses through the camp gave an additional excitement to the scene. Very little rest was enjoyed by anyone through the night. The storm caused a stampede among the horses and mules of the third division. Four belonging to the traveling forge ran off, but [with the exception of one] were overtaken and brought back after having been followed nearly fifteen miles. There was much firing among the hills during the night by the emigrants who were guarding their cattle, the storm having caused a stampede among them. The guard in following them became separated and were only able to find their camps by this means.

On a march of this kind many amusing scenes take place, and seldom occur without being seen and heard of by the whole command. Thrown together as they are while in camp and traveling during the day, every little occurrence that takes place is treasured up for the want of better by those who are always ready to amuse themselves at the expense of others. One of our men wandered out of camp last night in pursuit of his horse. Getting a little confused, [and] his whole mind [being] filled with Indians and the thought of losing his scalp, he lost his self-possession. Doubtless thinking that he had been out longer and had gone much farther than was really the case, he set up a yelling with the hope of bringing someone to his rescue. He made as much noise as if he had been attacked by a band of Indians. The guard found him in this condition, running about the hills with but little knowledge of what he was doing and much less as to where he was going, and relieved him, no doubt much to his satisfaction. Greatly to his surprise he found himself within a few hundred yards of camp. It was soon known this morning, and the poor Dutchman, who had never dreamed of a prairie or an Indian until he came on the march, had but little rest the balance of the journey.

The day was clear, and the road lay over a rolling prairie, which soon became dry and firm. We traveled fifteen miles, reaching camp about five o'clock this afternoon without any difficulty. We had now been several days in the Platte river [valley], on a road not the least rolling, and it was a relief to the troops, as it was to the teams, to get among the hills again. It [was] less severe hauling than on a level road, such as we had traveled over since leaving the fort.

A short time before stopping for the evening we saw on the [other] side of the river an encampment of Sioux, who immediately struck their lodges, proceeded [upstream] and encamped nearly opposite us.[92] A deputation, consisting of the old chief and about eighty of his party came over to see us. This old savage had tried to make himself look as respectable as possible and had given a coloring with a little vermilion to his grey locks, which hung profusely around his shoulders. His only article of dress was a green frock coat, not of the latest cut, that reached to his ankles. On his shoulders were an old pair of epaulets, which looked as if they had seen some service. His leggins, which were of grey cloth, were a substitute for pantaloons. To complete his costume, his cap was made of grizzly bear skin, with a long red feather supported by a brass plate in front. [He wore a] medal suspended from his neck, made in 1809,

---

[92] For additional information concerning this incident see pages 313-15.

with the likeness of President Madison on one side.[93]
To take the whole group together, with him at the head,
would have been a scene for any painter. Of all attempts
at dress this exceeded any I have ever seen among the
Indians. He felt, no doubt, that he was dressed for the
occasion and [that] we should have felt ourselves
highly honored. It did afford us a little amusement.
This was the celebrated Queue de Boeuf,[94] one of the
Sioux chiefs from the plains.

These Indians were very anxious to let us know their
great friendship for the whites and expressed much
pleasure at seeing so many white warriors. They were
very inquisitive, wished to know how far we had come,
where we were going, and how long we would be traveling. [They] ended their visit, as is usual among them,
by asking for provisions and a few presents, which the
colonel gave them. This was a war party, who had been
in pursuit of the Pawnees, and were then returning from
below. We were unfortunate not to have an interpreter
along who could speak the language, as it would have
been well to have explained to them our object. I believe I was the only person in camp who could understand anything they said, and my knowledge of their
language was very limited, having forgotten much since
being stationed among them many years since.

Having obtained for them such things as they seemed
to desire, I returned to the second division, which had
encamped two miles in the rear of the first. I found at
my tent two young warriors, one of whom presented me
with a piece of buffalo meat, which like all Indian gifts

93 On treaty-making occasions medals bearing the likeness of the president
on one side and an appropriate design on the other were frequently given to
the participating chiefs. Treaties with the Sioux were made during President
Madison's administration and undoubtedly this was one of them.

94 Bull Tail, principal chief of the Brulé Sioux. He was present at the council held by Colonel W. S. Harney with the Sioux near Fort Laramie, 1845, and
spoke for his people.

cost me in presents double its value. He commenced by begging for bread, meat, and whiskey. Indeed, he wanted something of everything he saw, and finally concluded that he would like a Mexican blanket I had on my bed, which I declined giving him, and at the same time making him fully understand that it was time to be off. He very soon left, but not without getting a little whiskey, which he coolly put into the tripe of a buffalo which he had killed that day, and appeared to be as well satisfied as if it had been placed in a cut-glass decanter. What the taste of it could have been by the time he drank it will not be very difficult to imagine.

Shortly after leaving the Indians at the encampment of the first division quite an excitement occurred among them. It proceeded from a horse being ridden into camp by one of their young warriors, which was recognized and taken by the command. It appeared that the animal had been carried off by a deserter, and as they said, sold to an Indian who, believing himself justly entitled to it, could not be made to understand why it should be taken from him, as he had come honestly by it. When the mark of "U.S." was pointed out to him, and they endeavored to make him comprehend by signs that the horse was the property of the command, it seemed impossible to do so. A shake of the head was all that could be got from him. He either did not or would not understand anything that was said to him. It was, however, made very plain to him that there was more than one owner when he saw his horse led off to one of the companies. The deputation moved off quite incensed at the wrong they conceived had been done one of their party. [They were] too much offended to carry off the provisions that had been given them.

Upon reflection it was thought to be the better plan

to send the horse back to their encampment. The Indian had obtained him in good faith, although the animal was stolen property. [At this] they became quite pleased and expressed much satisfaction. They soon sent for the provisions they had left. It was very well that this course was adopted, for during the night they would have given us much trouble to secure our horses, having it in their power to have annoyed us considerably without the least fear of being punished.

Our encampment was made near the bluffs this evening, the bottom being too wet and low to approach the river any nearer. The mosquitoes were very numerous here, and had annoyed us very much throughout the day. Our horses were frequently covered with them, which made them very restless. [They] had greatly troubled [the animals] since leaving the fort.

JUNE 12. The night was cloudy, and the morning quite chilly. The command left at six o'clock and traveled about twelve miles to another ford,[95] which we found upon examination to be too deep. The bottom was very uneven and filled with quicksand. One squadron crossed after much difficulty. It was thought to be too deep to venture the train, and as the trail led farther up the river, the colonel, with two guides, Lieutenant Frost, and myself followed it about thirteen miles to where it crossed,[96] leaving the command at the middle ford, where they made their encampment for the night. Finding the bottom of the upper ford much more even and [with] less quicksand we determined to cross at this place and returned to camp, which we reached at seven o'clock, [and] in time to get clear of a very severe thunderstorm that was fast gathering.

About a mile from the upper crossing an Indian

95 The middle crossing, five miles below Ogallala, Nebraska.

96 The "California" or upper crossing, seven miles below Big Spring, Nebraska.

lodge was seen standing alone on the prairie, which we took for a medicine lodge or where some chief had probably been buried.[97] It was too late for us to visit it, as the afternoon was drawing to a close, and we were necessarily compelled to postpone it until tomorrow.

For the last two days antelope in great numbers were seen on the prairie, but very few deer. This evening was very rainy and disagreeable. Grazing for the animals at this encampment was very indifferent. The spring being backward in this section of the country the growth of the grass had [been] impeded very much.

JUNE 13. Our tents were left to dry, which prevented us from getting off early this morning. The divisions left at seven, eight, and nine o'clock. We proceeded to the upper crossing, where we found that the river had risen a few inches during the night. This was much against us, [it] being already too high to risk the trains. The colonel's carriage was first sent over and reached the opposite side without much difficulty. We next tried a loaded wagon drawn by six good mules, which was nearly one hour in getting over. The river here is one thousand ninety yards wide, and I began to think at one time that it would not reach the opposite bank in safety. After this I had ten mules attached to each wagon and half the supply train driven in at one time. As long as the leading wagon kept moving the rest followed very well and got across better than anyone supposed. The mules frequently got into the quicksand, but the extra-duty men, being stationed in the river at the worst places, were ready to give immediate assistance. Such was the course adopted, and the trains passed over in safety. Out of one hundred sixty teams we lost but two mules, which were drowned in recrossing the river. Being compelled to return against the

---

97 See Gibbs's account, page 315.

current they often became entangled in their harness.

It was a [matter of] astonishment [to] all that more accidents did not take place. It was not uncommon to see teamsters down in the water at the same time with the mules, and so entangled with the harness that it appeared impossible to extricate them. To make it more disagreeable it rained throughout the evening. The command all got across in safety and encamped on the left bank of the South fork this evening, much to the gratification of everyone, for we [had] dreaded the crossing of this stream more than the balance of the journey.

We had with us four families, who remained in their carriages while passing over. [They] deserved great credit for the firmness and presence of mind they evinced. There was not only great danger, but the looks of the muddy water, the great width, and the rapid current of the river were enough to deter the stoutest hearts. On examining the train I was pleased to find the stores all safe, having suffered but very little damage, although the river was deep enough in places for the water to enter the wagon bodies. The mules, after the labors of the evening, were much the worse for wear, and a day's rest would have been of great advantage to them, as the grazing was very good at this place. Having reported their condition, an order was issued for the second and third squadrons to move on the fifteenth and the first at twelve o'clock tomorrow.

This morning I examined the lodge referred to yesterday. It was of a conical form [and] made of dressed buffalo hides nicely stretched over sixteen cottonwood poles. There were inside the remains of an Indian lying on the ground and covered with a buffalo skin pinned to the ground with small wooden stakes. A small scaffold was erected over the body, supporting what appeared to be a pack and several small trinkets that were formerly worn by the deceased. On the outer side of the lodge, and out of our reach, there were several strands of hair, indicating the number of scalps taken by him. From the great care in which everything was arranged I inferred he was some great chief. The dirt was carefully thrown up around the lodge, and strange as it may seem, the wolves had not in the least disturbed it. An old United States flag was suspended from the top of the lodge, much torn by the effects of the wind against the points of the poles. Some emigrant had cut a small hole about two inches long in the lodge to gratify, no doubt, his prying curiosity. We found [this hole] very convenient for the same purpose.

It is a curious fact that in no instance will one nation disturb the dead of another or anything that may be about them, not even when at war. The Indians deserve great credit for the respect they show their dead. Each tribe has its own peculiar mode of burial, [but] in many respects they are very similar. An order was given that the lodge should not be disturbed, which was very proper, as there might have been some thoughtless person who would not have considered it a very heinous offense to have taken for a curiosity a beautiful pipe, which was lying on a scaffold inside the lodge.

JUNE 14. The second and third squadrons remained here all day, the first leaving at twelve [noon]. Today was passed in unloading, drying, and preparing everything for tomorrow. We had now been out thirty-five days from Fort Leavenworth and much longer than it should have taken, but the mules were poor, and several days were lost in waiting for the beef cattle. We now began to feel as if the journey had really commenced. Having crossed the South fork of the Platte [river], we had no more obstacles between here and Fort Laramie.

JUNE 15. We left our encampment this morning at five o'clock, crossing the "divide" between the two forks. This is a high level prairie until you approach near the Platte where you strike Ash hollow,[98] a deep ravine that runs to [this stream]. [It] is about two miles long. The country about it is very broken, and we were compelled to let the wagons down into it by ropes. In this hollow there are a few ash trees and dwarf cedars. The bluffs are very broken and composed of rotten limestone and sand, which is generally the composition of those along the river.

It rained very hard last night, making the roads heavy until the middle of the day, when it cleared off and became very pleasant. We encamped on the North Platte this afternoon at five o'clock, having marched twenty-two miles. [We accomplished] that distance without any difficulty [and] lost not more than three hours in letting down the wagons. We found the ravine very sandy, as well as the bank of the river equally so.

While crossing the prairie I saw a large herd of buffalo, but valuing my horse much more than the pleasure of the chase, I passed without disturbing them. They were the last met with until arriving at Deer creek.[99]

The country in the vicinity of the North fork is entirely destitute of wood, but in this respect it does not differ from that already passed over. The river is much narrower than the South fork, less muddy, and differs materially in the formation of its bluffs, which in many

---

[98] Opposite Lewellen, Nebraska. The descent into this place was difficult and dangerous. Sometimes the oxen or mules were all unhitched and the wagons let down the steep slope by ropes. Again the wheel-spans were left in, the hind wheels of the wagon double locked and wrapped with log chains to make them cut into the ground while the men held on to anchor ropes. Sometimes oxen or mules were hitched behind the wagon to hold it back. Accidents here were frequent and often serious. Dougherty, "Experiences on the Oregon trail," in *Missouri historical review*, XXIV, 373-74; Clark, "Diary of a journey," *Ibid.*, XXIII, 16-17; Hulbert, *Forty-niners*, 100.

[99] A stream emptying into the North Platte opposite Glenrock, Wyoming.

instances become rugged, steep, and frequently approach near the bank of the river, making the valley in places very narrow. The grass was very scarce this evening, compared with that at the crossing of the South fork.

JUNE 16. The day was very windy and clear, making it a fine day for traveling. The road was extremely sandy, which made the hauling very heavy. We commenced our march at six o'clock in the morning and stopped in the afternoon at five o'clock, having traveled only eighteen miles.

I was called on today to assist an emigrating party, consisting of a woman, her son, daughter, and son-in-law, all of whom were too sick to attend to their wagon. I placed one of the extra-duty men with them for the day, to drive until they were able to hire someone or take charge themselves. We passed many emigrants today who were very much discouraged at their condition. The greater portion were sick, others began to consider it a hopeless undertaking, and many were turning back who brought, as might be expected, discouraging news of the country ahead.

It was evident that out of the immense emigration that had left the Missouri [river] there were a great number who must suffer before they could possibly reach their destination or [a place] where assistance might be given them. As to the little they received from the troops, it was merely temporary. Large numbers required the same, and it was impossible to render them all any material aid. Besides, it would have hazarded the accomplishing of our own journey to have attended to their wants. I shall not here attempt to give any description of the sufferings of these people, as I should be compelled to diverge too much from the narrative which I am required to give of what appertained simply to the command. The public prints, in different parts of the country, have long since given a detailed account of their sufferings. I can only say that they were not at all exaggerated. Our encampment this evening was made between the river and the bluffs. The grazing along here is very indifferent.

JUNE 17. We started at six o'clock this morning. The road lay along the river and passed over much higher and more rolling country than yesterday. After a march of twenty miles we came in sight of the Lone tower [100] and Chimney rock.[101] The former is about six miles from our encampment and to the left of the road. The latter could just be seen and was still one day's march from us, although from the state of the atmosphere it appeared but a very short distance.

Our road today led by a hill where the Indiana company had interred three men, Russell, Judson, and Phillips,[102] who died with the cholera on the fourteenth, fifteenth, and seventeenth of this month while encamping at this place. As this hill is somewhat prominent it will be a landmark hereafter for future travelers who pass this way. The grass for our animals this evening was very good at our encampment, which was on the banks of the Platte river. The evening was delightful, with every prospect of a fine day tomorrow.

100 This was Courthouse rock, which was known by various names, such as "Castle rock," "Solitary tower," etc. Shepard, Diary of a journey, may 25; see also pages 318-19. Located a few miles south of Bridgeport, Nebraska.

101 South of Chimney Rock, Nebraska. Stansbury said "it consists of a conical elevation of about one hundred feet high, its sides forming an angle of about 45° with the horizon; from the apex rises a nearly circular and perpendicular shaft of clay, now from thirty-five to forty feet in height . . . That the shaft has been very much higher than at present, is evident from the corresponding formation of the bluff. . . It is the opinion of Mr. Bridger that it was reduced to its present height by lightning, or some other sudden catastrophe, as he found it broken on his return from one of his trips to St. Louis, though he had passed it uninjured on his way down." Exploration and survey, 51; see also pages 320-21.

102 These graves were opposite and some three miles above Broadwater, Nebraska. Henderson to editor, december 31, 1938.

JUNE 18. The morning was calm and warm. We started at nine o'clock and visited the Lone tower on the route. It is about two hundred feet high and stands alone on the prairie. It has much the appearance of a tower or old ruin as you approach it, and no doubt was once connected with the high range of bluffs that pass the Chimney rock twenty miles from here. At present it stands entirely alone, the range of bluffs not being within two miles of it. A small stream passes its base, which, after winding through a valley about three miles wide, empties into the Platte river near where we encamped last night. We [made camp] this afternoon three miles from Chimney rock on the banks of the Platte, where we found very good grazing after a march of twenty miles.

JUNE 19. I visited Chimney rock this morning as the command wended its way along the river. The column did not appear to be more than fifty feet high, is composed of light clay, which I found to be extremely soft, and [is of] the same composition as that of the bluffs near it and the Lone tower. From the base of the hill on which it stands it is probably over two hundred feet high. There is no reason to doubt that this column of earth once belonged to the bluffs which are very near it. By time and the assistance of the elements [it] has been worn to its present form. It takes a variety of forms when approaching it – sometimes that of an old ruin, then a very sharp cone, but after all, more the shape of a chimney than anything [to which] I can compare it. The variety of forms which are seen proceed from the winding of the road and the position of the bluffs about it. We left the river soon after passing it and reached Scott's bluffs,[103] where we made our encampment for the night, having traveled twenty-three miles.

---

103 A series of bluffs opposite Scottsbluff, Nebraska.

The scenery for the last two days has been very picturesque. The hills are much higher and more broken
than any we have seen on the march and begin to change
the monotony which we have had so constantly since
leaving Fort Kearny. This evening we suffered for
water, having only a small spring for two squadrons.
The water used for the horses came from mud-holes
which we found near camp.[104] Wood as usual was very
scarce, but we obtained enough in the valley for our
use. It had been swept from the hills by the heavy rains
which frequently fall during the summer. What was
found consisted principally of dwarf cedar and pine.
We had but very little for our horses at this encampment, and the grass began to change as rapidly as the
face of the country.

JUNE 20. Previous to reaching our encampment last
evening we had a heavy shower of rain accompanied by
hail, which made it very cool this morning. We got
under way at six o'clock. After passing up the valley
about five miles [we] ascended the first high hill since
leaving Fort Leavenworth. This is partly covered with
cedar, which was the first we had met on the march.
There is also a spring of delightful cold water which
we should have reached last evening, but from want of
proper knowledge by the guide we failed to do so. Here
was a blacksmith shop and trading-house, built in the
true log-cabin style, which made us all feel as if we were
in reality approaching once more a civilized race.

Shortly after ascending the hill we came, for the first
time, in sight of Laramie's peak which belongs to the
range of Black hills.[105] The scenery is very beautiful
from the top of this hill, presenting to view mountains,

---

104 Gibbs explains this lack of water, pages 321-22.

105 Name given the Laramie mountains west of Fort Laramie. Not to be
confused with the Black hills of northeastern Wyoming.

hills, and valleys in every direction, and entirely changing the scenery which we had been so long accustomed to. It convinced us that we were in reality approaching the Rocky mountains so long talked of. I do not know when I have witnessed a more beautiful sight. The road from here began gradually to descend. Towards the close of the evening we arrived on the banks of Horse creek [106] and made our encampment for the night. [Today we traveled] a distance of nineteen miles. It remained cool all day, which made it very pleasant for traveling, and we got on without much difficulty.

One of our teamsters ran off this morning, taking with him a public mule. A party was dispatched in pursuit of him, but finding he was closely followed, he took to the hills and succeeded in escaping. Another mutinied today and threatened to shoot one of the agents. He was placed in close confinement and taken to Fort Laramie, where he was left to be sent back to Fort Leavenworth by the first conveyance. This was the commencement of difficulties with the teamsters, who began to show signs of insubordination. It was feared that many of them would leave us as we approached South pass and Salt lake. For my part, I placed but very little dependence in any of them, and would have not been surprised to have seen them leave at any moment.

JUNE 21. Before arriving in camp last evening we crossed a very miry creek that gave us a great deal of trouble. We were frequently required to haul the mules out of the mud, besides breaking several of the wagons. It weakened the teams more in crossing this stream than the distance traveled since crossing the South Platte. We got off at six o'clock. The morning was fine, but bid fair to be very warm through the day. The bluffs were

---

[106] A stream emptying into the North Platte opposite Morrill, Nebraska.

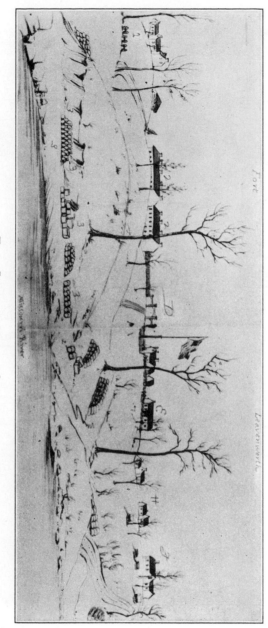

FORT LEAVENWORTH, 1849

From an original drawing in the state historical society of Wisconsin.

The numbered notes are by Gen. Charles King. [1] Guns, 6 or 12 pdrs bronze unlimbered. [2] Barracks. [3] Stores & supplies, flour, bacon, pork—almost everthing. [D] Gate & possibly sentry. [E] Guard house probably. [F] Storehouses Q.M. & commissary, other buildings, adjutants offices, etc. [H] Officers quarters probably.

FORT LARAMIE, 1849

very broken and the road sandy. This proved to be the warmest day experienced since commencing our march. It had rained but very little since crossing the South fork, which made it very dusty. Our road today passed close along under the bluffs, which intercepted the breeze and made it almost suffocating. In addition to this the mosquitoes and buffalo gnats were very annoying to the animals and men.[107] We had been much troubled with them ever since leaving Fort Kearny. We encamped on the Platte this afternoon at three o'clock, having traveled nineteen miles. [This] was a good day's journey, against the heavy, dusty road passed over and the heat we were compelled to support.

It was at this place that we got wood for the first time since the ninth of this month, and the men seemed eager to gather it for fear of a scarcity the next day. Our animals fared badly at this encampment, as they had [done] for the last three days. It was fortunate we were so near Fort Laramie, where it was in contemplation to rest, for our mules were fast giving out and the *cavayard* was daily increasing.

JUNE 22. The morning was fine. Having prepared for the march we left our encampment at six o'clock and arrived at Laramie's creek [108] at two p.m., where the trading-house is located. It was excessively warm and dusty. Although we had a light shower during the night it had but little effect in laying the dust.

Fort Laramie is situated on Laramie's creek, a rapid

---

107 "On the Platte the most detestable thing in creation is the buffalo gnat, a very small, diminutive insect, that, before you are aware of its presence has bitten your face, ears, and neck in a thousand places. My face at one time had the appearance of smallpox, my eyes were swollen so much that I could hardly see, and my ears as thick as my hand." "R. H. D.," correspondent for the *Daily Missouri republican*, august 28, 1850, in Nebraska state historical society *publications*, xx, 226-27.

108 A stream emptying into the North Platte in southwestern Goshen county, Nebraska. Named for Jacques La Ramie, who erected a cabin on it, possibly as early as 1815, and is said to have been killed there by Indians.

stream about sixty yards wide with a firm pebbly bottom. This stream rises among the Black hills to the west and falls into the North Platte about half a mile below the fort.

This fort is built in the form of a quadrangular figure and of unbaked clay or adobes. The wall is about twenty feet high, with a small palisading on a part of it. There are two blockhouses at the corners, diagonally from each other. Over the main entrance, which faces the river, there is also another small blockhouse. The buildings are made inside, the wall forming a part of them. They are very small, and have but few comforts to recommend them.

There are no trees about the fort to protect it from the rays of the sun, which are reflected from the surrounding hills. It is by no means a handsome location, the scenery of the adjacent country being entirely intercepted by small, barren hills which form the valley of Laramie's creek. The hunting at this place has generally been very good and is [its] only attraction. Even this has greatly diminished since the emigrants have made it the great thoroughfare to Oregon and California. There is fine grazing on Laramie's creek, where hay may be gathered in the fall. Wood is scarce immediately in the vicinity of the fort, but pine and cedar may be procured on the hills across the Platte [river] about eight miles above here.

We had now arrived at Fort Laramie, six hundred thirty-nine miles from Fort Leavenworth, where the government has established a military post [and] two companies of the rifle regiment are stationed.[109] [This]

---

109 Brevet-lieutenant-colonel Sanderson arrived here with company E, Mounted Riflemen, june 16. This company comprised five officers and fifty-eight men. Besides Lieutenant-colonel Sanderson the officers were Major S. P. Moore, surgeon, Captain Thomas O. Duncan, and Brevet-captain Thomas G. Rhett. Cross' reference to two companies of the Mounted Riflemen is puzzling,

was to be a resting place for us for a few days. Our train could now be overhauled and repaired, leaving such wagons as might be dispensed with and mules that were broken down and unfit to continue the journey. There was still plenty of time for them to be recruited and sent back to Fort Leavenworth before fall.

Since leaving Fort Kearny we had traveled three hundred twenty-seven miles over a bad road, which in dry weather does not present one obstacle. In the rainy season it is extremely heavy and very severe upon teams. In such weather I think it worse than the road from Fort Leavenworth to Fort Kearny. There are many deep gullies which require repairing, but a small party can always render them passable by being a little ahead. Water is generally to be had through the day, as the river is frequently touched, and is always in striking distance, except at Scott's bluffs, where you leave it and do not strike it again for forty miles.

From the first of june our journey was made very unpleasant by constant rains which made the roads very heavy and the hauling extremely hard. Wood is not to be procured from the time you leave Fort Kearny until you arrive at this place. Nothing is to be seen but the naked valley and boundless prairies in whatever direction the eye is turned. There is a little more variety after arriving on the North Platte river, as I have stated in my daily marches. The high bluffs on the banks of the river, as well as the several broken ranges in the vicinity of Chimney rock and Scott's bluffs, are a little relief after the great monotony which we have so long looked upon.

since Lieutenant-colonel Benjamin S. Roberts did not arrive with company c until july 26. Company d, Sixth infantry, under Lieutenant Levi C. Bootes arrived august 12. Gibbs mentions Colonel Sanderson and company e, but makes no reference to company c. Therefore Cross is evidently in error when he mentions the latter company being there when he passed.

March from Fort Laramie to
Independence rock

JUNE 23 [1849]. The day was fine, and every possible arrangement was being made for a speedy departure. The whole train was overhauled today, and the clerks kept busily engaged until eleven o'clock at night arranging papers, so as to be ready for the march.

I regret to say that the dissatisfaction on the part of the teamsters was becoming more manifest, making it necessary to place another in irons who had openly resisted the authority of those placed over him. Indifferent as I found them, I do not know what we should have done without them, for the soldiers were raw recruits. Some, not speaking the English language, were not capable of taking care of one horse, much less a team of six mules. Although their threats were regarded of no importance, still we were in a country where there was neither law nor order. I therefore left him at Fort Laramie to be sent back, thinking it the better plan to get clear of such disaffected men, as the example which they set did not tend to benefit the others, who in many instances, were disposed to do their duty.

The commanding officer of this post released them a few days after we left, considering, I presume, he had no authority to keep them in confinement. They followed the command and emigrating parties, stealing whenever opportunity afforded. They stole several mules from the command. One of the thieves was taken twice, but the guard not being VIGILANT enough to secure him, he was allowed to escape.

My labors with the command were daily increasing. Both the agents and myself were required constantly to be on the alert. This was done until we were completely worn down, although I was fortunate enough to be blessed with health, which kept me in the saddle from the time I commenced my journey until I arrived at the Dalles [110] on the Columbia river.

JUNE 24. I was agreeably surprised to find that the ox-teams that had started from Fort Kearny with the subsistence stores on the third of june had arrived in very good order. It was not my intention, when they first started, to take them any farther, but their condition was so much better, as compared with the mules, that I determined to push them on to Fort Hall. [111] They crossed Laramie's creek this evening, the wagonmaster having been given orders to move with such emigrants as are regular in their daily marches, and not to be governed by us.

This was a very fine day, although much warmer than heretofore. The clerks worked hard throughout the day and very late tonight to get everything in readiness by the morning, so as to leave. All the stores were overhauled and inventories taken of them. The papers connected with the property [were] left at this place, [and] the report of our march made to the head of the quartermaster's department. I turned over to the acting assistant quartermaster [112] at Fort Laramie twenty

---

[110] The French word *dalle*, meaning trough or canal, was applied to places where the river channel is narrowed between rock walls and rapids are produced. As applied to the Columbia river it describes the geographic features of the stream from the Big eddy on the west to Celilo on the east. The most noted places are, from west to east, Big eddy, Five-mile rapids, formerly known as the "Long narrows," the Great Dalles, and Ten-mile rapids, which were also known as the "Short narrows" or "Les petites Dalles." Barrows, *Columbia river*, 49.

[111] Built by Nathaniel Wyeth on Snake river about seven miles above present Blackfoot, Idaho, in 1834. He sold it to the Hudson's Bay company in 1837.

[112] Lieutenant Thomas G. Rhett.

wagons and one hundred twenty mules, also other property for the use of the post, and reported the train in readiness to move in the morning. Having completed the labors of the day and the writing which was necessary to be done by eleven o'clock at night, we retired to rest pretty well fatigued.

JUNE 25. The squadrons left at six, half-past six, and seven o'clock this morning, all being ready before the first squadron crossed Laramie's creek. This stream was very high and up to the wagon bodies, which damaged a little some of the stores. Having got all across without any accident, it may be said that we had now fairly started again, not to stop before reaching Fort Hall, a distance nearly equal to that which we had traveled, and by far worse, for we were to pass over spurs of mountains, and through broken, hilly country almost destitute of grass. Without overcoming all this our journey could hardly be expected to be accomplished.

We had now commenced a journey over an entirely new country, filled with hills and valleys, and in many places broken and rugged,[113] which was to cause us much labor and fatigue. Our road was a very rough one today. Mountains were to be seen at a distance,[114] rearing their heads far among the clouds, presenting a scene which was beautiful to look upon, and admonished us that what we had still to contend with would not be accomplished without much toil and suffering, not only to ourselves, but more particularly [to] our animals.

We continued our journey among the barren hills until we came to a deep, sandy ravine, through which the heavy rains from among them pass into the North Platte probably eight miles from the fort. On the right

---

[113] For a description of this country see page 233.
[114] Laramie mountains.

side of the road and about three hundred yards below where it crosses the ravine there is a fine spring that breaks from the side of the hill [and] affords an abundance of water.[115] The men made an excavation that collected a sufficient quantity in a few minutes for the whole command. It was very refreshing, being the first we had met with since morning. [It was] by no means warm, although [it was] not as cold as springs generally are among the hills.

The road turns a little to the left and leads through a deep gorge, ascending a high, steep hill covered with cedar and dwarf pine. After reaching the top you again strike the prairie. About three miles from here we took a road to the right, commonly known as the Mormon trail.[116] It had been but a little traveled this year, and there was every prospect of meeting with better grazing for our animals for the next two days than by following the road which leads toward the mountain range, although it was much more rugged than the old trail.

We made our encampment on a small stream in a very broken part of the country, [which had] a little cottonwood on its banks.[117] Before reaching it we had a very heavy rain accompanied by hail, which certainly fell faster than any I have experienced for some time. [This made] a hill which we had to descend very diffi-

---

115 Warm spring.

116 Upon leaving Fort Laramie the trail swung about a mile and a half to the west, then turned northwest about the same distance to Mexican hill. Here it divided. One branch, known as the "river road," which Cross calls "the Mormon trail," followed the windings of the Platte to a point opposite Guernsey, Wyoming, then struck across the hills to Cottonwood creek. The other, known as the "hill road," turned due west at Mexican hill for about eight miles, then north to join the river road some three miles from Cottonwood creek. Henderson, Map of the Oregon trail.

117 Cottonwood creek, sometimes called "Bitter Cottonwood creek." The latter name was used by Dr. I. Moses who kept the table of distances on the march of the Mounted Riflemen. Stansbury calls it "Bitter creek," while Colonel Loring calls it "Bitter Cotton creek."

cult for the train. I doubt if this rain will ever be forgotten by those who were exposed to it, as it was among
the last of any importance until we arrived at Fort
Vancouver [118] on the Columbia river. It lasted but a
short time and was very partial, as the rear division got
none of it. The water came in torrents from the hills.
While crossing the bottom beyond the creek we met it
rolling on, half-leg deep, to the stream below. The ravines, which a few minutes before were dry, soon became filled, and the dry bed of the creek which we had
just passed was made suddenly a large stream.

The evening cleared off and the night was very pleasant. The distance marched today was twenty-one miles.
The mules and horses were very much fatigued, as the
road throughout the day passed over hills and valleys
that were very rough and entirely different from [those
of] any day's march since the commencement of the
journey.

JUNE 26. The road this morning passed along a narrow ridge. After getting under way at the usual hour
Captain Tucker [119] and myself descended a deep valley
entirely surrounded by perpendicular rocks. A small
canyon which led to the river is the outlet [for] the
water which accumulates from a spring at the head of
it. There was very fine grazing in it, sufficient for two
thousand horses, with fine water which came from the
spring running entirely through it. As the view of this

---

[118] The most important fur-trading post on the Pacific coast and headquarters of the Hudson's Bay company in that region. It was situated on the north
bank of the Columbia river, about six miles above the mouth of the Willamette river. It was founded in 1824-1825 by Dr. John McLoughlin, who remained in charge until the fall of 1845, when he resigned from the company
and took up his residence in Oregon City. Peter Skene Ogden, who succeeded
him, was in charge when the Mounted Riflemen arrived in 1849.

[119] Stephen S. Tucker. Arkansas. Captain Mounted Riflemen, may 27, 1847;
brevet-major september 13, 1847, for gallant and meritorious service in the
battle of Chapultepec, Mexico; resigned june 30, 1851. Heitman, *Historical
register*, 1, 973.

place from the road was intercepted by other small hills and ravines there are but few who ever notice it. Here I got possession of a fine pair of elk horns, which, from the size, induced me to carry them to the Columbia river and thence to Washington, as they are probably the largest ever brought from the mountains.

This day's march [of fifteen miles] brought us to Horseshoe creek [and] near Heber's spring,[120] where we procured wood, water, and grass in the greatest plenty. This surpassed any camping ground we had met with since starting on the march. The grazing at Fort Laramie was certainly very excellent, but nothing to compare [with] this. The country, although uneven, was not very hard to travel over today and we completed our journey by two p.m.

I received orders this evening from the commanding officer to fit out Colonel Porter [121] with material to prepare a raft at the Mormon ferry [122] on the North Platte, now eighty-seven miles from us. Although late at night it was complied with, and he left the next morning early for that place.

JUNE 27. This morning was very pleasant, after a slight shower yesterday evening. We proceeded along a level road today until we again struck the river [123] at a grove of cottonwood trees about twelve miles from

120 This stream empties into the North Platte above Glendo, Wyoming. On june 7, 1847, Heber C. Kimball, member of the pioneer Mormon party and counselor to Brigham Young, discovered this spring and named it for himself.

121 Andrew Porter. Pennsylvania. First-lieutenant Mounted Riflemen may 27, 1847; captain may 15, 1847; brevet-major august 20, 1847, for gallant and meritorious service in the battles of Contreras and Churubusco, Mexico; lieutenant-colonel september 13, 1847, for gallant and meritorious service in the battle of Chapultepec, Mexico; colonel Sixteenth infantry may 14, 1861; brigadier-general volunteers may 17, 1861; mustered out of volunteer service april 4, 1864; resigned april 20, 1864; died january 4, 1872. Heitman, Historical register, I, 798.

122 Established by Brigham Young in 1847. There were three ferries in operation here in 1849.

123 At Elkhorn creek.

where we encamped last night. Since leaving Fort Laramie we had traveled but little on the Platte, being separated from it by high rocky cliffs and broken ground along its banks. Trees were lying in every direction at [this] grove, having been cut down by the emigrants the few years previous for food for their animals. It may be thought a poor substitute, but the bark as well as the small limbs are very nutritious and have often been resorted to in this region to sustain animal life for months.

We continued up the valley a few miles, when we left the river, not to strike it again until we came near Deer creek, where we might be required to cross. Our march was now through narrow gorges, winding around hills the whole afternoon until it brought us on a ridge where the country could be seen in different directions for a long distance. Here we made our encampment for the night, although a very poor one, as the grass was very indifferent. Since leaving Fort Laramie we had passed over a fine range of country for game. Elk and antelope abound in great numbers, and if time had permitted us to hunt them they could have been killed without difficulty.

The scenery from the top of the ridge was very picturesque. Laramie's peak and the range of the Black hills, [which] could be very distinctly seen, frequently reminded me of the mountain scenery I had met with in Mexico. I ascended several high hills and had a fine view of the country I traveled along today, but there is nothing to recommend it except the beauty of the scenery. The land is very poor and barren, being of very light soil and covered principally with wild sage.

JUNE 28. The morning was clear and mild. We did not commence our march until seven o'clock. The road led along the ridge for some distance, then pass[ed] into deep ravines and over high hills where our route could be seen for twenty miles ahead. At such places it was very distinctly marked, as the soil is of a reddish cast, being a mixture of red marl and sand.

About the middle of the day we arrived at a rapid stream, called the Bitter Cottonwood,[124] which is about thirty feet wide, and the water very fine. Previous to reaching it the road became very sandy and difficult to get over. There is a fine, cold spring to the right as you enter it which is seldom seen. After crossing the stream the road ran along the left bank for several miles, when it again turned in among the hills and ravines. At the end of our day's journey we arrived at the base of a range of high hills, which might be more properly called a mountain spur, where water could only be had by digging for it. This is commonly called the Spring branch. Here we made our encampment, having traveled twenty-one miles.

After crossing the Bitter Cottonwood and before stopping for the night we came to the base of a hill where we found a large quantity of gypsum, which is very near a stream where the water was lying in holes and of a very inferior quality. There is much bitter cottonwood on the stream we first passed today, from which it takes its name. With the exception of this, we have met with no wood of any importance, the hills and valleys being entirely destitute of anything like vegetation except artemisia.

JUNE 29. Our road today passed over a dreary and uninteresting route – more so than any since leaving Fort Laramie. The hills are not so high as you approach the Platte but [are] entirely barren. Nothing

---

[124] Cross is evidently in error here. This stream was the La Bonte, which empties into the North Platte below Orin, Wyoming. Stansbury saw the same gypsum Cross mentions and placed it on this stream. *Exploration and survey*, 58.

was to be seen but the artemisia or wild sage, which is extremely uninteresting, having neither beauty nor usefulness to recommend it and its odor [is] by no means pleasant. We were destined to travel a very long distance where this shrub was constantly to be seen in greater quantity than had been already met with. It may be truly said that we had just entered it, as it was not very [plentiful] or large, compared with what we afterwards met with on the route. There must be something in the composition of the earth particularly adapted to its growth, for whenever the grass was scarce we invariably found it in great quantities. I have traveled for days before reaching the Columbia river where nothing could be seen on the highlands and plains but the artemisia, which for miles looked as if the whole country had been cleared of all other vegetation to make room for it.

The morning was clear and the day throughout very warm. The command was detained by the hunting of horses and mules, which was usually the case, but more so this morning. With all this we accomplished twenty-six miles. It was necessary to reach the river, we were told, [in order] to get grass for our horses, but we encamped at the mouth of Deer creek. Here grazing was even worse than might have been found at [several] of the streams which we crossed today,[125] one of which was the [La] Bonte, a fine, clear, rapid little stream which came from the Black hills and falls into the Platte about ten miles from where our trail crosses it.

The route today was very well watered by these streams, which was the only recommendation it had, as the soil and face of the country have been the same since leaving the fort. We got in very late this afternoon. Twenty-one miles was a long march as well as a warm

---

[125] On this day's march they crossed La Bonte, Wagonhound, La Prele, and Boxelder creeks.

one. The indifferent grazing for the last two days and the heavy hauling over this uneven country had weakened our animals very much and jaded them considerably. Seven of our teams gave out today, which was very discouraging, but our consolation was that while we were crossing the river it would enable them to become sufficiently rested to pass over the barren region which lies between the Platte and the Sweetwater, where better grass would be obtained. The valley of the Sweetwater has been heretofore noted for it, as well as for its good water.

It was too late in the afternoon, after arriving at camp, to examine the country around us. We therefore staked out the horses and mules to do as well as they could for the night, intending to take them to the base of the mountains seven miles distant in the morning. This will, no doubt, appear a long distance to drive animals to obtain grazing, but such was the state of the country this season that it became necessary to do it to prevent starvation. [This fact] will give some idea of what we were frequently compelled to resort to on this march for the preservation of our horses and mules.

JUNE 30. Although the morning was very pleasant we did not leave camp until half-past seven, as the horses and mules had scattered in every direction among the hills, having got but very little last night. It was our intention to go but a few miles today, where we would be nearer the base of the mountains. Lieutenants Frost and Palmer [126] left camp early to examine the range

126 Innis Newton Palmer. New York. Brevet-second-lieutenant Mounted Riflemen july 1, 1846; second-lieutenant july 20, 1847; brevet-first-lieutenant august 20, 1847, for gallant and meritorious service in the battles of Contreras and Churubusco, Mexico; captain september 13, 1847, for gallant and meritorious service in the battle of Chapultepec; regimental adjutant may 1, 1850 to july 1, 1854; captain Second cavalry march 3, 1855; major april 25, 1861; lieutenant-colonel july 21, 1861, for gallant and meritorious service in the battle of Bull Run; brigadier-general volunteers september 23, 1861; lieu-

and did not overtake us until we arrived at Crooked
Muddy creek,[127] a distance of ten miles from our encampment this morning. We encamped on this creek
and sent the mules and horses about seven miles off
where there was very good pasturage and had them
guarded by teamsters while there. The river presented
a very busy scene. Emigrants were crossing in several
places,[128] while others [were] engaged in constructing
rude rafts of dry logs, which were attached together and
pieces pinned across to confine them. By placing at the
end two oars, which [were] used as sweeps, they [were]
propelled to the opposite side, descending at the same
time partly with the current. After reaching the [far-
ther bank] a yoke of oxen [was] attached to it, and it
[was] carried up the stream sufficiently far that when
let loose it reach[ed] the point from where it originally
started by the force and effect of the current and the
aid of the oars. The wagons were taken apart, and it
generally [took] three trips to carry over one and its
load. This, you will perceive, was very slow work, and
would be still more with a train as large as the one with
us.

JULY 1 [1849]. The command remained here today.
[Although it was] extremely warm this would give us
an opportunity of resting, being the first day we had
stopped since leaving Fort Laramie. I went to the base
of the mountains, accompanied by Mr. [Nathan A. M.]
Dudley and had a very pleasant ride, as the ground be-

tenant-colonel Second cavalry september 23, 1863; major-general volunteers
march 13, 1865, for long and meritorious service in the United States army;
mustered out of volunteer service january 15, 1866; colonel june 9, 1868; retired march 29, 1879; died september 10, 1900. Heitman, *Historical register*, I,
767.

127 About midway between Glenrock and Casper, Wyoming.

128 Clark mentions a "lower Platte ferry," which was near the mouth of
Muddy creek. Next day he crossed at a "new ferry" about eight miles east of
the Mormon ferry. "Diary of a journey," in *Missouri historical review*, XXIII,
21, 22.

tween the river and [the] mountains is very rough. We saw antelope in great numbers and one or two buffalo, which we chased for two or three miles. Being better able to clear the gullies and difficult places than we were, they soon left us out of sight. Although large and apparently unwieldy, they are extremely active. It was in this same chase that I saw [Samuel A.] Miller, one of my wagonmasters, for the last time. He was seized with the cholera after returning to his camp where the mules were grazing, and died in a few hours. He was a very efficient man and a great loss to me. In the morning he was as well as any belonging to the train and had been sent out to take charge of the party who were guarding the mules. Before the sun went down he was no longer among the living, but was resting quietly in his grave. This was the last case of cholera, I believe, which occurred in the command, much to the gratification of everyone, for it was by no means a pleasing reflection to think we were surrounded by a disease which carried off the strongest without a moment's warning.

This range of mountains was thickly covered with cedar and pine, [and] here lumber for public purposes could be easily obtained. There is coal on Deer creek and along the valley. In one of the hills near Crooked Muddy creek I discovered it myself and I have no doubt it may be found in great quantities. Having returned to camp orders were given for the third division to cross at this place,[129] while the first and second should move up the river to the Mormon ferry, where we might attempt to cross on rafts, or use the ferry. It was not far, as the distance was only eleven miles from here.

The colonel and myself left camp at six p.m. for the purpose of reaching Colonel Porter's encampment, and having traveled about eight miles diverged from the

129 At Muddy creek, Clark's "lower Platte ferry." The first and second divisions crossed at the Mormon ferry july 4 and 5.

road toward the base of the mountain. After riding
some time we came to the place he had left that morning. Where to find him we did not know, as the guide
to the camp was completely lost. Having wandered
about for some hours, we again reached the river and
arrived at the Mormon ferry about twelve o'clock at
night. At this place we learned that the party we were
in search of was up the river about four miles. We pursued our journey, and after winding among the cottonwood trees and bends of the river, found them at half-
past one o'clock in the morning. It was a bright moon-
light night, and with the exception of being lost and the
fear of not finding the party before the next morning,
the ride was by no means unpleasant.

JULY 2. The morning was clear and quite cool before
sunrise. The raft was hastily put together, and every
preparation made for crossing the river. It was soon
found, however, that the length of time and the injury
which the property would sustain by exposure would
not justify it, when the Mormon ferry could be hired
for four dollars per wagon and the same guaranteed to
be delivered with its load on the other side of the river
in safety. The raft was therefore abandoned and the
ferry hired.

JULY 3. This evening several wagons of the first
division were crossed, and instructions given by me to
have the mules of the first division swim across early
in the morning, which was accordingly done. The day,
though warm, was very pleasant, but the mornings and
nights were getting quite cool.

JULY 4. Previous to leaving our encampment, which
was about five miles from the ferry, a partial stampede
took place among our horses, created by a general
stampede of those from the first division. They had been
turned loose to cross the river but evinced no disposi-

tion to do so. After making several efforts to get them over they broke through the command, running at full speed in different directions — some toward the base of the mountains and others up the river, passing by our encampment and taking with them a number of our horses. It was in this stampede that one of my riding horses played a conspicuous part. Since he was hobbled by the forelegs, so as to range about camp, [we] believ[ed] him perfectly secure. I was soon convinced that this mode of hobbling horses was no preventive against their running off, for he ran with them several miles and was not very far behind the gang. They were, however, turned and brought back after having run for several hours.

This stampede was very injurious to the horses and they showed the bad effects of it a few days after. My horse was brought back with his legs much cut by the hobbles, and was more injured by it than by the march from Fort Leavenworth. He did not recover throughout the journey. From the time the troops commenced the march the horses and mules had never been allowed to run loose but were staked out at the termination of each day's march. Finding themselves free they were extremely difficult to manage. The proper course would have been to have supplied SIDE-HOBBLES for the horses of each company. By allowing them to range around camp on the prairies, where grazing was not difficult to procure, they would very soon have become used to them and could at any time have been turned out without the fear of their running off. I am compelled here to remark in connection with this subject that there was not one hobble along, nor could I find a bell in the whole train, which is frequently required in herding animals when it becomes necessary from the scarcity of grass to turn them loose.

The hills, or more properly speaking, the range of mountains which are a continuation of the Black hills, approach the river within four miles at this place and are thickly covered with very fine pine and cedar. This is a great place for buffalo and game of every description. It is said that numerous grizzly bears are found here. They were seen and shot at by the emigrants, but none of our command were so fortunate as to come across them here or on any part of the journey. Large herds of buffalo were seen toward the head of Deer creek, but as our time did not justify any delay or that we should waste the strength of our horses, which were already in a poor condition, we had to forego the pleasure of chasing them.

This morning a fine elk came within gunshot of our camp. He was chased by a party of us into the mountains without being successful in killing him, although he was shot at. The black-tailed deer are quite numerous about here, but it was difficult to find them without crossing the range, which would have occupied more time than we could conveniently lose.

The grazing on Deer creek and along the base of the mountains toward the head of Little Muddy creek is extremely good, and there is everything here to recommend it as a pleasant location for a post should the station be changed from Fort Laramie. [This would bring the troops nearer] the South pass, where the Indians on war parties often frequent. [They] probably would be more disposed to commit depredations here than at any other point between Fort Laramie and Bear river. An excursion could be taken by the troops during the summer along the Sweetwater [river], where their horses would have fine grazing. [This] would give them an opportunity of scouring the base of the Wind river mountains,[130] where they would most probably

---

[130] The regiment would cross these at South pass.

meet with the Crow Indians. The emigrants commence crossing about the mouth of Deer creek and along the river for fifteen miles. By establishing a good ferry here the troops could pay for the erection of a post, if the emigration should continue for a few years longer as large as it was this year. The price of crossing the Mormon ferry varies from three to four dollars a wagon.

The morning was fine, but very cold at five o'clock. The temperature of the nights and mornings at this place was sufficiently cold to make it necessary to resort to fires to keep ourselves comfortable, although in the middle of the day it is generally very warm. The first division succeeded in crossing today, and the second moved down to the ferry toward the close of the afternoon and commenced to cross. This was the manner in which the fourth of july was spent by the command, while throughout the country, in every city and hamlet, it was kept as a day of rejoicing. We had tried to reach Independence rock in time to spend it there, but owing to our great detention immediately after leaving Fort Kearny we were unfortunately prevented from doing so by three days.

JULY 5. The second division crossed over five of their wagons last evening. This morning, at a quarter after four o'clock, we commenced to ferry the remainder. We finished at two o'clock, and made our encampment on the hill immediately above the landing, where we remained for the day. An order was issued this morning for the divisions to travel one day apart. The scarcity of grass through the country which we were about to travel over rendered it necessary to adopt some plan of this kind. The face of the country having entirely changed since leaving Fort Laramie, it was only at certain points in our day's marches hereafter that grass could be procured, and even then in limited quantities. The first division commenced its march this morning. Our mules were driven out about three miles from camp, [grass] being far better [there] than on the banks of the river, where they were guarded during the day and kept until the morning.

In crossing the river yesterday we were so unfortunate as to have two men drowned.[131] One of [them], wishing to get something from the opposite side, rode his horse into the river, and being fully equipped for the march, no sooner reached deep water than both man and horse went down. In the other case, one of the rafts was loaded with saddles and men. Upon reaching the middle of the stream an accident occurred [caused] by the breaking of an oar. Being carried down by the current, a panic [arose] among those on board. [They] rush[ed] to one side [and] careened it so as to induce them to think it was sinking. Losing [their] presence of mind, the men jumped overboard and made for the opposite side. [They] all reached [shore] in safety but one. It was astonishing what little forethought and presence of mind the men evinced in many instances on the march. They remind me more of children than persons arrived at the age of maturity.

The river is not over four hundred yards wide at this point and has a very rapid current. To have attempted to cross the whole command on rafts would have caused much delay, as well as the loss of property and lives. No emigrants crossed without losing a portion of their stores and wagons, while others lost their lives. Besides, the state of the country which we were to pass over rendered it necessary to lose no time in getting ahead of the

131 Privates William Taylor and Daniel Zengenfous. Since june 9 the following men had died; Private Francis D. Frennd, june 15; Private George Stillman, june 15; Private James Robey, june 19; Private James French, june 21; Corporal Thomas Mooney, june 27; Corporal William H. Scott, july 1; Bugler Peter Pauli, july 2. Monthly returns, Mounted Riflemen.

great mass of emigrants, who were making every effort to push forward to get better grazing. There is but little timber along the [North] Platte river. The river is almost as destitute as the upper part of the South fork. What there is consists [of] cottonwood found scattered along its banks for about fifteen miles.

Today was extremely warm, the atmosphere dry and sultry. Rains had become less frequent of late, which made the nights cold and the middle of the day suffocating. We [were] now fast leaving the country for game, and a few more days' marches would carry us to the South pass where buffalo and deer are seldom seen now in large numbers. The country between the mountains [is] almost too barren to support them, and the immense emigration [is] driving them from the Sweetwater valley where they [are found] early in the spring in large herds. We were soon to see no more of them after leaving here. Captain Granger informed me that there must have been at least five thousand in one herd on Deer creek. This has always been considered a great range for them, as they were seen [here] in gangs at the time General Kearny returned from California in 1847 [132] to the number of a million.

This evening we observed lights in the mountains, [which were] supposed to be made by deserters as signal fires. Many had left the command and we had every reason to think there was constant communication between them and those who contemplated leaving, and who were doubtless supplied of nights, in many instances, [with] provisions from the command.

JULY 6. The second division commenced the march at half-past six this morning, passing up the river, and

132 In the summer of 1847 General S. W. Kearny marched his command from Sutter's fort in California to Fort Leavenworth, following the Humboldt river route to Fort Hall and from thence to his destination along the Oregon trail.

over a very sandy road for about eight miles, making
the hauling this distance very fatiguing. It became
better during the day. The road leaves the river at this
point and does not touch it again, but passes over a rolling country filled with alkali ponds and artemisia. The
ponds are covered with an incrustation of saleratus and
much of it is deposited at the bottom.

Our march today brought us in sight of the Red
hills,[133] where we made our encampment for the evening about a mile from the road, below an alkali
swamp and [a] mineral spring. The water at this spring
is very cold, and its taste that of stone-coal. There were
other springs also passed [which] were considered very
deleterious, the taste being extremely disagreeable.

This was the first day we observed the cattle of the
emigrants were dying, and it was a lamentable sight to
see these fine animals lying along the road at distances
of not more than a few hundred yards apart. In one
instance I saw where an entire team had been stricken
down where they stood linked together to commence
their daily work. From the Platte [river] they were
constantly met with along the road in large numbers
until we arrived at the valley of Bear river, a distance
of two hundred miles. [Then] they began to diminish,
much to the gratification of the emigrants. The death
of these animals was attributed by many to the drinking
of alkaline water. There were doubtless several causes
combined, to which it might be ascribed, [such as] the
change of atmosphere, which had become dry and sultry since leaving Fort Laramie, and the drinking of
impure water when much heated after a hard day's
drive over a dusty road filled with alkali. As emigrants
along this route commence to increase their marches,

---

133 Variously called "Red buttes" or "Red bluffs." About ten miles southwest of the Mormon ferry.

being often compelled to do so to arrive at the end of their journey before fall, they travel with much more rapidity than the condition of their teams should justify.

Our horses fared very badly this evening for grass, as there was none of any importance. What little they did get was trampled down by the horses of the first division and cattle belonging to emigrants who were still ahead of us. While on the prairie between Forts Leavenworth and Kearny there was no portion of the route but what grazing could be had at any moment, though [it was] much better in some places than at others. Such is the formation of the soil [here] and its extreme sterility that you are compelled to travel sometimes a whole day before getting to a spot where you can find the least quantity, and these places this spring have been so frequented that the grass has been entirely consumed. Our march was eighteen miles over a very dusty road, but we were compelled to stop here or go farther and fare even worse. The camp was pretty well supplied with wood, as we procured as much as we required for the night.

JULY 7. The command left at seven o'clock and struck the main road two miles from our encampment of last night. We continued our journey over a rolling country, entirely barren, having no scenery to interest one in the least until we arrived at the Willow spring.[134] Here we found, for the first time today, a small stream of fine, pure, cold water which came from the head of a small ravine formed by several hills. The spring takes its name from the number of small willows about it and along the gorge where the water passes. A number of emigrants had collected at this place, where some of them had been for several days.

This water was by far better than any the emigrants

---

[134] Thirty miles southwest of the Mormon ferry.

had met with since commencing their journey, and they seemed disposed to make the most of it before moving forward. We found a large number who had encamped and taken their cattle over the hills about four miles to graze, where they represented it to be better than at the last encampment or [at] any since crossing the North Platte. This is not to be taken as any proof of good grazing, for that was not to be found among these hills. Being in the vicinity of good spring water, which seems so highly valued by these people, the grass that was found was better than nothing. In their estimation the want of quantity [of grass] was made up by the quality of the fine, cold stream which gushed from the base of the hills. [It] increase[d] as it pass[ed] through the gorge [and found] its way along the hills and through these dry plains until it reach[ed] the Platte, to which we had now bade adieu for the last time. Our course [led] to the northwest, while [that stream] soon turn[ed] to the south.

After winding up the gorge and ascending a very long hill [135] a new scene broke upon our view. We could easily see the spurs of the mountains that formed the Sweetwater valley, while others ranged to the northeast, forming, with the Wind river mountains still farther north, a large and extensive valley. We had a very fine view of the adjacent country in every direction from this peak.

The Sweetwater valley was beautifully marked out by hills until it reached the Platte. The country to the north [was] interspersed with mountains and valleys, while that to the east presented a broken and uneven country, entirely sterile. The whole was destitute of wood, which is so indispensable to scenery. [Since] it was too early in the afternoon to stop at the spring we

---

135 Prospect hill.

continued on to Greasewood creek,[136] which comes from
the Wind river valley, and encamped for the night.
Several places were passed in the afternoon, but the
water was too impure to encamp. They were nothing but
alkaline bogs. Our horses were taken about three miles
from our encampment to graze for the night and carefully guarded by the teamsters, who were responsible
for their loss. From among them a guard was formed
whose duty it was to keep watch all night under the
direction of the wagonmaster and agents. The extra-
duty men were also required to perform the same duty.
After walking and frequently working pretty hard during the day, to be required to stand watch was sometimes found to be severe duty, and a little more than
they had contracted to perform.

I found in a range of hills a fine specimen of coal,
which I was unfortunate in losing before arriving at
Fort Vancouver on the Columbia river. The country
from Deer creek to the Sweetwater river abounds in
coal in great quantities I have no doubt. It is found on
the left bank of the Platte [river] at the Mormon ferry,
and up to this place the hills bear every sign of it. The
specimen I obtained today showed a very fair quality,
and I think it might be obtained in great quantity here.
The distance traveled over, where coal may be seen in
places, is about forty miles and [it] no doubt continues
entirely across to the Wind river mountains. The train
came in this afternoon in very bad order. Many of the
teams [were] completely worn down and several of the
mules had given out.

In this day's march of twenty-two miles there were
not less than fifty dead oxen passed on the road. The
grass in every ravine was eaten to the ground, and the
earth presented a frosted appearance from the deposits

136 About forty miles southwest of the Mormon ferry.

of alkali. Nothing but wild sage and the greasewood shrub were to be seen all over the country.

The wind blew very hard through the day and the dust was so thick at times as to hide the whole division. Both men and animals suffered very much, particularly the teamsters, who were unable to avoid it. I required the wagons to be kept some distance apart so as to escape as much as possible the heavy clouds of dust that were constantly kept up through the whole day. It was very cold during the day and the wind, sweeping over the snow-capped peaks of the Wind river mountains, which were not far off, made it as unpleasant as if it had been the middle of october. No wood was to be had on this stream but the artemisia and greasewood which were used and answered as a very good substitute.

JULY 8. Last night was very cold and a fire of oak wood would have been very acceptable. The morning was clear and it continued cold. We got off at eight o'clock and after passing along a level, sandy plain for eleven miles arrived at Independence rock [137] which had been the theme of conversation with us since leaving Fort Laramie. It was a spot often spoken of by those who had passed before us, [was] known as a great resting place [and had been made] somewhat noted by emigrants who had been fortunate enough to be there on the fourth of july. We expected to have reached it this year by [that date] but unforseen circumstances prevented [us] from doing so.

It is immediately on the Sweetwater river, leaving only sufficient room for the road to pass. It is of granite, about five hundred yards long, one hundred fifty wide, and forty yards high. It stands entirely isolated at the east end of a small valley formed by it and the adjacent

137 Fifty miles southwest of the Mormon ferry. The United States geological survey in 1870 gave its dimensions as 1550 yards in circumference, 193 feet high at the north end, and 167 at the south.

INDEPENDENCE ROCK, JULY 9, 1849

WIND RIVER MOUNTAINS

hills and mountains. This rock bears the name of almost everyone who can take time to carve or write his name on it. There is nothing very remarkable about it, except that it is not frequently the case you meet with so long a mass of rock without the least vegetation of any kind on it. Its position makes it somewhat remarkable, looking, as it were, like some huge monster rising from the ground.

Our encampment was made about a mile above the rock on the bank of the river where we overtook the first division, which was much exhausted by the very fatiguing march of the last three days. Many of the mules had broken down and [they] were compelled to travel so slow that the second division gained one day since leaving the Platte. This division encamped above us at the Devil's gap [138] until the tenth, when we all moved about five miles up the river and beyond the mountain that makes across the valley. The grazing was pretty good along the base of the mountains. There were several alkaline ponds in this vicinity which by evaporation had become dry, leaving their beds well covered with alkali which had very much the appearance of snow. I procured several specimens and brought them safely home.

This day's journey was extremely disagreeable. The wind seemed to collect between the openings in the mountains [and] came upon us with all its fury, blowing the dust and sand, mixed with alkali, into our faces and eyes, until it became insupportable. Several persons had their eyes very much affected by it. My own suffered very severely and have never recovered from it to this time.

---

[138] About six miles above Independence rock. A narrow, three-hundred-fifty-yard long passage through a range of granite hills. The width in some places was no more than forty feet and the height of the walls was from three to four hundred feet.

The scenery about the valley of Independence rock is very beautiful. The mountains, though not so high, are very picturesque and pleasing to the eye. The valley is about four miles long, made by small ranges of mountains to the north and high hills to the south, [which are] covered with a few dwarf cedar and pine. It has a spur of mountains to the west through which the river passes and small disconnected hills to the left which give a distant view of the scenery beyond. The Sweetwater [river] can be seen quietly running toward the mountain through which it passes with a great deal of violence between perpendicular rocks which are several hundred feet high. Resuming again its natural current [it] quietly flows through the valley until it mingles its crystal waters with the muddy stream of the Nebraska [Platte river].

JULY 9. The day was very pleasant except [for] the wind which, blowing as usual, created a great deal of dust. As we remained here today the first division train was placed in a condition to continue its march. Repairs and alterations were also made to the second division so as to enable it to move with as much ease as possible. The condition of both trains greatly required it. Our march to Fort Hall was to be a long and tedious one, [it] being four hundred miles distant, and the teams [were] becoming weaker every day. In this vicinity game is generally abundant. One of the clerks killed an antelope near our camp this morning, and I found the meat extremely fine. Though much like venison in flavor, I think it even better. This range has been very good for buffalo, but the valley along the Sweetwater being very narrow, they have been driven off by the emigrants and could not be seen without going too long a distance after them. The mountains about here abound in mountain sheep, which are often seen among the high, rocky cliffs, but being extremely shy, are hard to shoot. Several of our party who were acquainted with their habits went into the mountains in pursuit of them, and though unsuccessful, they brought to camp several antelope.

The camps of the emigrants now began to bear evident signs of their condition. Provisions of every description were lying about in piles. All surplus baggage which had impeded their march and assisted in breaking down their teams was now thrown away. Their wagons were broken up to mend others, while some were left along the road. Their loss of cattle was daily increasing and it seemed doubtful whether many of them would ever reach Oregon or California. These people were very fortunate in having got rid of the cholera so early. We had seen no cases since crossing the North Platte, as the last one which occurred among us was at Crooked Muddy creek, eleven miles from the Mormon ferry.

March from Independence rock to Bear river

JULY 10 [1849]. The two divisions were ordered to move at twelve noon. Having made preparations, we crossed the river and took the road which leads over the rising ground and passes between the hills and the terminus of the mountain which forms the Devil's gap. This gap is truly wonderful, being a space not over twenty yards wide and about five hundred feet high, having very much the appearance of being chiselled out by the hand of man rather than the work of nature. It seemed very extraordinary upon examination that there should be so near this great opening a fine wagon road, as the distance from the gap to the terminus of the mountain is not half a mile. Such are the singular freaks of nature that we so often meet with. We encamped this evening about six miles above the Devil's gap, through which we had a fine view of the valley we just left. Our mules were put out to graze and were well guarded by such teamsters and extra-duty men as I could place confidence in.

We saw lights this evening in the mountains, not more than two miles from us, which were evidently made by deserters who kept the disaffected portion of the command aware of their movements. Desertion had become so frequent of late, and the repeated threats of what they intended to do [so numerous], of which we were kept advised, that it became very necessary some course should be adopted to put a stop to their running off.

We had ample proof that many of these men had enlisted for no other purpose than to get the means of
reaching California. There was no portion of this regiment now with it who had served with so much honor
to themselves while in Mexico, as they had been disbanded immediately after the termination of the war.
The regiment at this time was composed of raw recruits,
many of them foreigners who scarcely knew enough of
the English language to understand an order when
given to them.

The colonel issued a proclamation at Independence
rock offering a reward of two hundred dollars for every
deserter that might be brought back.[189] On reaching
Fort Bridger [140] five of these men were turned over to

189 The gravity of the situation here is evidenced by Colonel Loring's report from Fort Laramie, in which he said, "There have been forty desertions
since our departure, several of them within a short distance of the settlements. Many of them have been among the soldiers employed in the quartermaster's department, where during a long march, they have been in a great
measure thrown from proper military restraints, associating with citizens and
doing a duty for which they think they were not enlisted, they become dissat-
isfied. Moreover, the fatality among the emigrants from the cholera and a
consequent scarcity of labor, has led them to hold out great inducements to desert." Loring to Jones, june 22, 1849. "Upon publishing the notice desertions
immediately ceased, and although we passed several roads leading to California few or no attempts were made." Loring to Freeman, october 15, 1849.

140 Built by James Bridger and Louis Vasquez on Black's fork in southwestern Wyoming in 1843 to cater to the trade of emigrants. The first and
second divisions of the regiment turned southwest to this place after crossing
South pass, but the third division, with which Cross was traveling, took Sublette's cut-off to Bear river and did not visit this fort. The first and second
divisions reached here july 21. On the same day Colonel Loring received an
express from Oregon City bearing letters from General Persifor F. Smith,
Major Hatheway, and Lieutenant Hawkins. Those from General Smith dealt
with the establishment of posts, Major Hatheway gave advice as to routes
from Fort Bridger, while Lieutenant Hawkins informed him that he would
leave Oregon City for Fort Hall june 24 with supplies. He carried out his
plan and with fifteen hundred rations and a herd of beef cattle arrived at Fort
Hall after the Mounted Riflemen had left. Joel Palmer served as guide and
took the southern route. *Daily Missouri republican,* december 11, 1849, in Nebraska state historical society *publications,* xx, 217; Bancroft, *History of Oregon,* 1, 567; Loring to Jones, july 22, august 7, 1849.

the command, having been caught by the trappers in the mountains near that place. Although it did not entirely stop desertion it had a tendency to decrease the number. We lost but few at the South pass and Soda springs,[141] where the trails for California leave the Oregon trail.[142] The idea with these men was to attach themselves to emigrating parties as a guard after passing the South pass and Soda springs, simply for their subsistence. But by the time the emigrants arrived there it was as much as they could do to subsist themselves until they reached California without being encumbered by men, who, having violated a sacred oath by deserting the service, could hardly be expected to keep a promise made them. The emigrants, generally, gave no protection to them, but on the contrary were ready to assist us in apprehending them and frequently gave us information which was of great importance.

JULY 11. The first and second divisions left camp at seven o'clock this morning. The third [division], having been required to overtake us, did not arrive until very late last night after a fatiguing day's march of nearly twenty-eight miles – by far too great for the condition of the animals and the country through which they were marching. As several of the wagons did not arrive until after nine o'clock this morning, it was deemed necessary to permit this division to remain here one day to rest their teams and overhaul the train. They

141 Bannock county, Idaho. A group of mineral springs on the east bank of Bear river, about four miles above where it turns abruptly to the west. Sometimes called "Beer springs." Many are found here, but the most famous of them all was named "Steamboat spring," from whose thirty-inch-high cone a jet of warm, gas-impregnated water was thrown several feet into the air to the accompaniment of a sound not unlike the puffing of a steam engine.

142 "Meyers" or "Hudspeth's cut-off" turned off at the great bend of Bear river and struck southwest to unite with the main road, which ran by way of Fort Hall and Raft river, at the City of rocks. The distance from where it left Bear river to the latter place was one hundred fourteen miles. It was first traveled in 1849 and was said to save ninety miles.

had had no rest since crossing the river,[143] and the length of time which they were occupied there [had] thrown them entirely in the rear and out of position.

Provisions being required by the command that left this morning, which were in the train of the third division, I forwarded them in compliance with instructions given. Broken down as the whole train was it would not have been a loss of time to have remained [here] for one day longer. I, however, dispatched them as soon as they were prepared, reported the condition of the teams to the colonel, [and] remain[ed] behind myself to superintend the alterations that were necessary to be made to enable this division to leave in the morning. The day was taken up in overhauling the stores and examining them. I found [them] in a very deranged state, as the loads had been taken out while crossing the river and [were] very much scattered among the train. Having completed the necessary preparations we were again ready to resume the march in the morning.

The night was quite cold, but calm, which was very different from what we had experienced before arriving at Independence rock, for the wind had blown night and day incessantly. We procured as much wood as was necessary for our use from the base of the mountains where it was collected in small quantities. The greater part of our journey having been over a country entirely destitute of wood, I observed that the troops seemed to adapt their wants very much to circumstances and seldom made any talk about the scarcity of fuel.

Since leaving the Platte we had again passed through a dreary, hilly country, in many instances very sandy, meeting with nothing in the least interesting to the traveler. [It was] destitute of vegetation, except the artemisia, which was seen from the highest hill to the

---

143 The Platte river at the Mormon ferry.

lowest valley. [It was] now and then interspersed with alkaline ponds, which were greatly dreaded by the emigrants. This unpleasant sight, as well as the dusty roads, windy weather, bad water, and nothing for our animals to feed on, made us hail the sight of the Sweetwater [river] with pleasure and gratification. This stream, though small, is very beautiful. It rises among the Wind river mountains and after running over one hundred fifty miles empties into the Platte about thirty miles below this place. We were now to travel on its banks for a hundred miles, never leaving it far enough to prevent us from making our encampments on it in the evening until we arrived in the vicinity of the South pass, where the road crosses [it] and leaves it for the last time.

I look on this river as the salvation of the traveler who is fortunate enough to reach it. The water is clear and fine in taste and runs rapid[ly] over a firm, sandy bottom. Its banks are very low and generally well covered with good grass, but this season it had been consumed by the animals of the emigrants who were still ahead of us. The road winds along the river, crossing and recrossing it in many places during the day, and affording us the opportunity to make pleasant encampments on its banks in the evening.

JULY 12. The morning was pleasant, and we got off at half-past six o'clock. Shortly after we left the river, when our road passed over a very heavy, sandy trail throughout the day. It was towards the close of the evening that we came in sight of the high peaks of the Wind river mountains, where they were barely seen to the northwest. Being capped with snow [they] looked like white clouds rising above the distant hills.

We were now getting among the mountains which border the Sweetwater [144] and, although detached from

---

[144] The Granite mountains on the north and Green mountains on the south.

each other, they form a complete range when viewed at a distance. The scenery today was very beautiful, although our road passed over a very sandy and poor country. High cliffs were to be seen with a variety of forms and colors, giving to the eye something pleasing to rest on instead of fields of artemisia, whose unpleasant odor, which is thought by some to resemble that of camphor and turpentine, [continually regaled us]. This scent [is] by no means agreeable at any time, still less when we reflected that we were to have but very little else until we arrived at the Cascade mountains on the Columbia river.

In our march today we saw a large number of cattle which had perished since striking the Sweetwater. I saw one emigrant who had lost four yoke of oxen. [He and] many others [were] going ahead with their packs on their backs, trusting to chance to reach California. They had dreamed of the gold region too long to be discouraged by the loss of a few animals and seemed to be satisfied that they would be able to reach the "diggings" in a very seasonable time. This I very much doubted, for they had then nearly a thousand miles to travel, and no means of carrying their provisions longer than a day or two and were compelled to keep in the vicinity of trains to get a supply. We traveled today eighteen miles, making our encampment again on the banks of the Sweetwater river where the grass was extremely scarce.

JULY 13. It was calm and [there was] every sign of a warm day. We got off at six o'clock and passed along the side of a high cliff, which intercepted every particle of breeze and [gave] us the full benefit of the rays of the july sun. This day's march was through a country which in soil was very much the same as the one of yesterday. We were partly hemmed in today at times by rocks which seemed to be piled one above the other until they reached a height which would justify their being called mountains. These high peaks are of granite formation, and having but little soil are covered with a small quantity of dwarf cedar and a few scattering pine. They are seen on the distant plains and valleys, forming a landscape which is very pleasing to the eye. Here the river winds around the base of these high cliffs, frequently changing its direction at right angles, and leaving scarcely space enough for wagons to pass.

After passing one of these gorges through which the river runs, the road leaves it for a few miles and crosses between two ranges of cliffs whose sides are much broken and made rugged by the effects of time. I came to a place where mountain sheep were seen leaping from rock to rock with as much ease as if they had been on the plain below. Discovering the party which approached them, they soon bounded out of sight, running over the rocks with the greatest of ease. It would be but a few minutes before they would return again, apparently with an additional number, and, after looking over the precipice, would again disappear. [They] seemed amused at the labor of those in pursuit of them, who were struggling among the rocks to reach the top of the cliff.

From the top of these peaks the view of the surrounding country was very beautiful. Many parts appeared rolling, other portions presented plains extending for miles, while in other directions it presented wide valleys and deep ravines. It was from the top of one of these cliffs that the range of the Wind river mountains could be seen in all its beauty. The whole scene was one of grandeur, which is seldom met with on this route, for the scenery is generally not very prepossessing.

Throughout the day it had been very warm and dusty

and the road very sandy in places, causing much fatigue among our mules and horses. We witnessed the same unpleasant sight today in the loss of animals as we had heretofore, and the emigrants were in great danger of being left on the route without means of traveling.

About five o'clock we arrived again on the banks of the Sweetwater and encamped about two miles above where the trail crosses [it] and near a point where the river breaks through a high ridge, forming in its passage a steep bluff which prevents the wagons from passing. The road here leaves the river again and does not strike it for nearly a day's march. The grazing was very indifferent, though better than where we crossed the river.

JULY 14. The mules were getting very much jaded, and every day's march seemed to affect them very much. At the commencement of our journey this morning we traveled along a ridge about three miles, which was extremely sandy, and the artemisia rocked our wagons from side to side until the strength of the wheels was well tested. We struck the road at the head of a low alkaline marsh, which may be looked upon as a natural curiosity. It was at this place that by digging into the ground about twelve inches we came to a bed of excellent ice,[145] which was very acceptable to us.

There is nothing very peculiar in the appearance of this place. The ground is low and boggy, with a number

---

[145] Forty-four miles above Devil's gate. "A number of springs in this little vale furnish water which makes wild grass grow to above ordinary height. In the winter the water freezes by night, but by day the springs renew their flow, thus building up a new coating of ice each night until by summer there are enough layers to allow ice six inches in thickness to be cut. In winter the tall grass withers and bends over—forming a sort of thatched roof for the ensuing summer, which protects the ice to a degree from the burning sun." Hulbert, *Forty-niners,* 147. Reprinted by permission of the publishers, Little Brown and company. This natural wonder was destroyed when the cattle of emigrants devoured the grass covering.

of cold springs oozing from its sides and spreading their waters over the marsh, which soon absorbs it. There is no outlet, except in very heavy rains. I saw on the borders of the marsh a great quantity of this never-ending alkali, and pretty good grass mixed among the large patches of the rush. [The water], being thought to have a deleterious effect on the animals, and [the marsh] being in many places very miry, it was avoided. The ice lies in a bed or strata but a short distance from the surface. It is easily procured and probably one and a half inch in thickness. The bog is in a plain or small sandy valley, very much exposed to the rays of the sun, and one of the warmest places found near the Sweetwater river.

The road two-thirds of the day passed through a low, sandy plain. Not a tree to give us the least shade [was seen], and we found it extremely sultry and warm. Everyone, therefore, who could stop at the ice bed did so and furnished himself with as much [ice] as he could conveniently carry. We arrived at the Sweetwater again about two o'clock and halted for a few hours until the train should come up. I crossed over a high ridge during the morning, which brought me on a very elevated plain. After traveling about five miles I came again to the Sweetwater and followed up its banks until I overtook the division.

To the north the table-land seemed to be very extensive, until the view was intercepted by a high range of bluffs. [This] was broken in many places, giving a view of the valley beyond which extended to the base of the mountains far to the northeast.

It was our intention to have stopped when the trail crossed the river, but there was nothing to be found for our animals to eat. We continued our march over a range of hills about six miles farther, where we struck the river and overtook the other two divisions. The place where we stopped at two o'clock had been made a general resting place for the emigrants. Here were wagons lying in every direction, old clothes – from an old hat to a pair of boots, cooking utensils of every description, and a variety of articles too numerous to mention were scattered about as if there had been a general break-up in camp. It was high time, for many of them had started with an idea that two thousand pounds could be carried without the least difficulty, nor could they be made to believe [anything] to the contrary until it was found [to be] almost too late. I had seen the commencement of it some distance back, but the [road] along here gave full proof of the general feeling among them. In the afternoon I ascended a hill which gave me a much better view of the country than I had witnessed today. We had been fast approaching the high hills to the west for the last few days. From this position it seemed to be the principal range, the rest disappearing into uneven table-land. The view to the north and east was very fine, as the outline of the plains and valleys was very distinct. The Wind river mountains to the north, [which] we were rapidly approaching, presented a very picturesque appearance. The distance traveled today was about twenty-two miles. The weather for the last few days was dry [and] warm in the middle of the day. This morning was beautiful, and although chilly, was very different from that which I had felt in Mexico when approaching mountains covered with snow. There we [had] the mornings very cold and the middle of the day extremely warm.

JULY 15. The two divisions left this morning at seven o'clock, leaving the third to continue its march after resting one day. It was at this encampment I commenced to break up wagons for the first time to repair others, as all our timber had long since been used up. The day was occupied in shoeing horses, mending harness, and making such alterations as might be necessary and proper to facilitate our movement.

Since the rains ceased and we had reached a dusty, uneven country the wheels of our wagons were very much affected by it. In many instances [they were] rendered almost useless by the tires constantly falling off. Having no wood to reset them, I resorted to the plan of calking, and found the wheel to be much better than those which had been reset. I would advise anyone who may be required to travel over a prairie country where wood is scant to provide themselves with the proper materials, and they will never be at a loss to repair their wagon wheels for the road in a few minutes. On this march we have frequently been compelled to stop a wagon in the train and resort to this mode, which was soon accomplished and the wagon off again. Without it we should have been compelled to have abandoned the same.

The country along the river about here had become very hilly and approached the banks of the river so close as to force us among the hills, which was very fatiguing. The country was entirely barren. Not a tree was to be seen of any importance and but very few willows on the banks of the river. It was at this encampment that we found a very cold spring. From the formation of the ground, compared with that where ice had been procured, I have no doubt but what the same could have been obtained here, as the water had the taste of ice water instead of clear spring water.

JULY 16. The division, after passing up the river this morning about two miles turned into a narrow gorge, which, gradually ascending for several miles, brought us to the top of a very high, level country. The river passed through a narrow, deep chasm a short distance above where the road diverged from it and was not touched again until the end of the day's march. About the middle of the day we passed a rapid stream from the Wind river mountains,[146] a tributary of the Sweetwater. Here we found snow on its banks, which had drifted in a large pile in the winter and was at this time at least six feet thick, forming a solid mass of ice.

It was cloudy through the day and drizzled a little, which made it better for traveling, although [it was] somewhat cold and disagreeable. We were now quite near the Wind river mountains [and] we could see the snow falling from the clouds which hung around their peaks. In the afternoon our road lay over a level country, having the mountains to our right and the high table-lands to our left. In the fore part of the day we passed two small valleys which were very sterile, there being but a very scant covering of vegetation [upon] them. We met with many springs in this day's march, which gave us delightful water. They are always acceptable to those who travel and become much fatigued from the effects of the dust and sun. We arrived again this evening on the Sweetwater after a march of twenty-five miles, where I made my encampment on its banks for the last time. As I considered the train in good condition to travel with those in advance, I determined to go forward early in the morning and join the second division again.

JULY 17. Having obtained an escort of four men under Lieutenant Russell [147] we left at three o'clock in

146 Willow creek.

147 Francis Stephen Keyes Russell. New York. Michigan. Second-lieutenant Mounted Riflemen may 27, 1846; brevet-first-lieutenant september 13, 1847, for gallant and meritorious service in the battle of Chapultepec, Mexico; first-lieutenant march 15, 1848; dismissed may 24, 1852; died january 31, 1857. Heitman, *Historical register*, I, 853.

the morning to overtake the second division, which was now one day in advance of us. We were detained some time in crossing the river, as the morning was dark, and [we] did not get over before four o'clock. Here the road diverges from it to touch it no more, and we soon reached the plains which form the South pass. There were none of the party but who seemed to regret leaving the banks of this little stream where we had passed many pleasant nights since the eighth of this month. We soon came to the South pass, which had nothing to mark it except the Pacific spring [148] [which was] near a range of high hills on the left of the road with an alkaline marsh to the right. Here the water collects into a small stream [149] which runs to the west and unites with the Pacific ocean through Green river [and] the Colorado of the west, which falls into the gulf of California. We passed through a barren, sandy waste, slightly rolling in places, [with] extensive plains in other parts of it, until we were compelled to stop on the banks of Dry Sandy [creek][150] in consequence of several of the mules giving out. We had made a march of twenty-two miles and were still some distance from the second division. At this place water and grass were very scarce, and both men and animals fared badly. We found it very warm throughout the day, which made it very disagreeable and fatiguing to us all.

JULY 18. We commenced our journey this morning at five o'clock. It was pleasant [and there was] every indication of a warm day. We had now passed the Snow mountains,[151] which made the temperature very different from that experienced a few days since. There was much less wind and seemed to be moderating very fast.

148 Famous landmark just west of South pass.
149 Pacific creek.
150 Tributary to Pacific creek and noted for being a bad camping place.
151 Another name for the Wind river mountains.

The road passed over precisely the same sandy country that it did yesterday, and we arrived at Little Sandy [creek][152] in the fore part of the day. Here we found many emigrants. Some were lying by, while others were looking for their lost cattle, which had left them during the night and returned on the road many miles. These people could give no correct information of the advance, and it was not until we reached Big Sandy [creek][153] that we learned that the two divisions had taken the Fort Bridger route and that we were on Greenwood or Subblet's [Sublette's] cut-off.[154] As it was impossible now to return and overtake them, and this being a much shorter route, I determined to follow this trail and intercept the command on Bear river. We therefore passed down Big Sandy about three miles and made our encampment, having traveled eighteen miles today.

The grazing at this place, though indifferent, was considerably better than for the last few days, being a little out of the direct route either way and therefore less frequented. Our horses and mules fared finely for both water and grass, compared with the scanty allowance which they got last night. What few sprigs of grass they could collect along the borders of the dry bed of the Big Sandy were pretty well filled with alkali, which lay upon the ground like a white frost on a cold fall morning. The little water which they got at the same place, indifferent as they found it, was drunk for want of better and to allay a burning thirst created by the warm march of that day over a very uninteresting

152 Tributary of the Big Sandy.

153 Tributary of Green river.

154 This route left the main trail west of Dry Sandy, and, after crossing Little and Big Sandy, struck off in a southwesterly direction to the Mormon ferry on Green river. From there it swung a bit further south, then turned to the northwest over Bear river mountains and rejoined the main trail above Cokeville, Wyoming.

country. The contrast was great, and we could not but enjoy our present condition this evening. Even the sound of the waters of Big Sandy, as it ran rapidly over its pebbly bottom, seemed to have a charm in it. It tended to lull us quietly to sleep as we lay close upon its banks brooding over our present and future condition until we should meet the regiment again, which might not be for a week or a fortnight. About nine o'clock at night we were awakened from our sleep by the hailing of a person on the opposite side of the river. [He] proved to be Lieutenant Howland,[155] who had been as far as Green river in pursuit of deserters. [He] gave us the intelligence of the arrival of an express from Fort Vancouver to the colonel.[156] The express-man was left at Green river, his horse having given out. Lieutenant Howland dispatched him to the lower crossing, upon our arrival at Green river, which prevented him from following the command with the letters.

JULY 19. We left this morning at four o'clock and struck across the plains, taking the trail to Green river. There was nothing of importance observed – the whole country from the South pass to Green river being one vast plain. It is bounded by the Wind river mountains to the north, and to the west and southwest by the Green river mountains.

We stopped today at one o'clock to rest our animals. As to grass, there was none to be obtained. The middle of the day being sultry we did not commence our jour-

155 George Washington Howland. Rhode Island. Brevet-second-lieutenant Mounted Riflemen july 1, 1848; second-lieutenant june 30, 1851; first-lieutenant march 3, 1855; captain may 14, 1861; brevet-major february 21, 1862, for gallant and meritorious service at the battle of Valverde, New Mexico; major Second cavalry december 1, 1866; retired april 8, 1869; died december 21, 1886. Heitman, *Historical register,* I, 549.

156 This express carried letters from General Smith, Major Hatheway, and Lieutenant Hawkins. Loring to Freeman, october 15, 1849; to Jones, august 7, 1849.

ney until seven p.m. Then, after traveling all night we came to the ferry [157] on Green river about sunrise in the morning and encamped on the opposite side.

The night's march carried us over a sandy plain and through several deep hollows which gave us some trouble to ascend. Immediately in the vicinity of the river the trail passes down a very steep hill into a deep, sandy gorge which runs to the Mormon ferry. It was very severe for several miles on the mules. The moon shone nearly all night, making it pleasant and much better traveling than in the day.

From the time we left Big Sandy until we arrived on Green river we met with no water, having marched through the day and night a distance of fifty miles without it.[158] This route is generally known as the desert – a very appropriate name, if I may judge from its sterility and dryness, for a more barren region cannot be found between here and the Columbia river. The South pass, being surrounded by mountains and high ranges of hills, may be looked upon as the great plain or dividing ridge which separates the waters of the Atlantic from those of the Pacific, for it is at this place that the waters are seen flowing in opposite directions. The soil is extremely sandy, poor, and barren, and has not one favorable feature to recommend it.

JULY 20. The wagons were ferried across. After mak-

---

[157] Mormon ferry, about twelve miles below Tulsa, Wyoming. A. Delano met Major Simonson and company B here july 3 as they were en route for Fort Hall. This ferry was established june 30, 1847 by Brigham Young. In 1849 he appointed Parley P. Pratt to head a company and take charge of it. On january 14, 1853 it was given to Daniel H. Wells by legislative grant. Delano, *Life on the plains,* entry for july 3; Lund to editor, february 1, 1940.

[158] Estimates as to the distance from Big Sandy to Green river vary, depending, possibly, upon where the latter was struck. Joel Palmer (1845) gives it as forty miles; Edwin Bryant (1846) fifty or fifty-five; Bennett C. Clark and John Evans Brown (1849) fifty-two, and Archer B. Hulbert (1849) forty-four.

ing our encampment the whole of the animals were taken about six miles back of the hills to graze on a small stream [159] which empties into Green river above us, where the grass was pretty good.

There are two ferries here, which are only temporary. The Mormon ferry is about five miles above where we crossed the river, at the foot of a range of high clay bluffs, which we passed to reach this ferry. The country on the right bank of the river is very hilly. On the opposite side there is a range of bluffs, very much washed and broken into gullies. The banks of the river are low and thinly covered with cottonwood, about the same quantity that I found upon the North Platte.

JULY 21. We remained until two p.m., [then] left for Fontanel's [Fontenelle's] fork,[160] about six miles distant. In the fore part of the day we were engaged in getting across the six ox-teams, which, it will be remembered, started from Fort Laramie at the same time with the command. They were directed to continue their march to the same place where we contemplated stopping and there encamp.

A slight shower today made it pleasant, although [it was] hardly sufficient to lay the dust. This was the first shower we had seen since the twenty-fifth of june. As the country through which we had been traveling since leaving Fort Laramie was of a very light clay soil it may naturally be supposed that we had suffered very much with dust for the last four weeks.

After getting under way our road passed down Green river for a few miles, where it turned into the hills and ascended the top of a high range. Here we had a beautiful view of the adjacent scenery. On the opposite side of the river the country was high but level. To the north

159 Muddy creek.
160 Tributary of Green river, emptying into it near Fontenelle, Wyoming.

of us, and in the direction through which our road lay, it was extremely hilly and mountainous. From the top of this ridge we descended into deep ravines, which wound around the hills and crossed other ridges until it arrived on the banks of Fontenelle's fork, where we found good water and better grazing than we had met since leaving Horseshoe creek on the twenty-sixth of june. We made our encampment here for the night – not alone, however, as the banks of the creek were lined with emigrants, who were recruiting their cattle after marching across the desert without grass or water. We now seemed to be getting out of the alkaline country, as there was less on this stream than any I had met before. [There was] certainly much less than on Sweetwater river. The country around us being entirely destitute of wood we were compelled to resort to artemisia, which may answer as a substitute in warm weather, but it [is] a very poor one in winter, as it burns out rapidly without leaving any coals or embers. We were now getting out of the range for game, as buffalo are seldom seen now in great numbers this side of the South pass, although I was told today by an old hunter that he had seen the hills over which we were traveling covered with them a few years since. Since then they had begun to diminish until scarcely any were to be met with this side of South pass. The emigration to Oregon, since 1845, had tended to drive them from this section of the country, as it has done throughout the route. I saw but very few buffalo signs while passing through the plains in the vicinity of South pass. During the three days while traveling across to Green river antelope were seen in large numbers. Deer have been very scarce since leaving the South fork of the Platte. Although we are now in the far west, where we might expect to meet with game in great quantities, I have seen more deer in one day's travel in western Texas than I have met with in the whole of my journey. I have recently met with many antelope, but where they are found in great numbers I have seldom come across many deer.

JULY 22. The emigrants were early in starting this morning, having been here some time. Besides, they were required to travel a long distance today before reaching a good encampment. I did not get to water before twelve o'clock, which I found among the hills in a small gorge, where I saw a grove of hemlock for the first time, also the aspen tree, neither of which were in great quantities. The water was very fine, being near the snow which had drifted on the sides of the hills over which we had to travel. We stopped here until the arrival of our wagons, that were yet some distance behind. Having got in the rear of a long train this morning, they were necessarily detained. While here I passed over the hills and among the valleys, which were quite extensive, for the purpose of looking for game. While returning I came upon a fine elk, but from a want of proper knowledge of hunting them, and not being a very expert huntsman, he soon got wind of me. Frightened at my sudden appearance, he stopped for a moment, then raising himself in all his mountain dignity he bounded off over the hills and was soon out of sight.

Our wagons having arrived, we continued our march over spurs of mountains during the afternoon. So great was the change of the temperature [that] a greatcoat [was] very comfortable. We soon began to descend until we reached the valley, and continued our way until the close of the [afternoon]. It was very unpleasant this evening. The wind blew hard and was accompanied by hail, which lasted but a few minutes. It cleared off as the sun went down and became very cold through the night, making a fire very comfortable. Having provided ourselves with a good supply of wood from the mountains, [we were] enabled to pass the night very pleasantly. This day's march brought us over a very hilly country, particularly in the afternoon. In the fore part of the day it was on a ridge, where the light clay [soil] produced a dust which was almost insupportable. We were fortunate in reaching a place where good water and grass could be procured, as we had traveled twenty miles and our mules had become very much fatigued, so much so as to compel me to leave one on the road. Our encampment was very well selected, being at the base of a range of mountains where we were able to get as much dry cedar and pine as we required.

JULY 23. [We traveled] over a number of spurs of the Green river mountains yesterday [afternoon], which run parallel to each other, forming small valleys. [This gave us] much fatigue. Although feeling it very sensibly, we were ready to renew the journey this morning. We started at five o'clock, keeping a high range [161] on our right until we arrived at Thomas's fork,[162] [when] we passed around it and came into the road which crossed the mountain near our encampment. We passed up the valley for a short distance, [where] we crossed it about twelve o'clock. [Then we] ascended a high hilly country that was very much broken by deep ravines. [In these] and on the sides of the hills [were] small groves of cedar, hemlock, and aspen. Here we had an abundance of wood, water, and grass. [We] made our encampment at five o'clock for the night, after a fatiguing day's journey of eighteen miles.

JULY 24. We started at six o'clock this morning for Bear river. [The road led] over mountains and valleys

---

161 Commissary ridge.

162 Cross is in error here. The stream to which he refers was probably Ham's fork.

and [through what was] probably the most hilly or mountainous part of the route we had traveled. We arrived on its banks [163] at two o'clock in the afternoon, much to our gratification, for we discovered that the troops had not yet passed and in all probability would not for several days. [This] would give us an opportunity to rest, for we stood almost as much in need of it as our animals.

The [march] from the South pass to Bear river was to us a very fatiguing [one], having crossed the desert without grass or water. For the last four days we had been traveling over the most mountainous country which we met with throughout the whole distance. The greater portion of the route between Green river and Bear river is but one series of mountains and valleys where you are constantly rising and descending throughout the day. It is well watered and good grazing is frequently met with. Wood is found along in small quantities, scattered about on the distant mountains, while small groves of aspen and hemlock are seen in the ravines. The whole distance since leaving our encampment this morning has been over mountains [which are] well watered by fine springs running from the hills and ravines. This range continues until you arrive at the valley of the Bear river, and the nearer you approach it the more broken the country becomes. Our encampment was made for the night immediately on the banks of this river, and, fortunately for our horses, the grass was better than any we had seen since leaving the prairies.

---

[163] A few miles above Cokeville, Wyoming.

March from Bear river to Fort Hall

JULY 25 [1849]. We had now fairly arrived in the great valley of Bear river, which had been so much talked of by us. It is a fine valley, in some places three miles wide, and well watered by the Bear river, which empties into the Great Salt lake after having passed through a mountainous region for many miles. We were now to travel along its banks until we arrived at Soda springs, where the Oregon trail turns to the north and the river makes a bend to the south more abruptly than where the trail leaves the North Platte.

The valley of Bear river varies in width from three to five miles. In many places, however, where the river passes through the hills it becomes very narrow. Grass is found in great abundance on the river where the bottoms are wide, but this year it is nearly all destroyed by the emigrants who are scattered along the river as far as the eye can see. We changed our encampment ground today and traveled down the river about eight miles, crossing Smith's fork,[164] a small mountain brook which falls into Bear river probably a mile from where it enters the valley. Here it passes between two high bluffs, about four hundred yards apart, having taken its rise [to] the eastward among the mountains.

We encamped about twelve o'clock and remained through the day, hoping to hear from the command, who were ahead of us one day's march at Big Sandy [creek]. Since then we had stopped two days at Green river and our days' marches between the two rivers

---

[164] Tributary of Bear river, emptying into it near Cokeville, Wyoming.

were of medium length, the country being too hilly to justify long marches.

The mountains in this vicinity are entirely destitute of wood, but small quantities of cottonwood and willow are now and then seen on the river. The willow seldom grows over two or three inches in diameter before it decays. On Smith's fork, as well as other small streams which fall into the river in this vicinity there is also cottonwood and willow, but in no great quantity or size. There is no tree in the forest which grows more luxuriantly in the south than the cottonwood. Every island in the Mississippi and Missouri rivers is covered with it, and it is the same with the ravines and streams in a northern latitude. If cottonwood is not to be found on them you may expect to see no wood of any kind except in the mountains.

JULY 26. The morning was clear and cold. Ice was seen one quarter of an inch thick. Since arriving on Bear river the nights have been very cold, as I have found them since leaving Green river. While crossing to the two rivers ice was formed about our tents every morning. I regret that I was unable to keep the exact temperature through the twenty-four hours, having been so unfortunate as to break my thermometer some distance back and could not procure one from the command.

We commenced our march at eight o'clock for Smith's trading-house,[165] which is about thirteen miles

---

165 Thomas L. (Peg-leg) Smith. To the Spaniards of southern California, from whom he stole horses, he was *El Cojo Smit*. Trapper, trader, desert free-booter, mountainman, horse trader, etc. Born in Kentucky, 1801, he ran away from home to Howard county, Missouri, at the age of sixteen. Hunter among the Osage, Sac, and Fox Indians. Trader to Santa Fe, 1824, with Alexander Le Grand, from which place he went on a trapping expedition to the Gila river. Trapped on the Gila again in 1826 with George C. Yount. Late in the fall of 1827 his leg was shattered by a bullet while in the neighborhood of the sources of the South Platte river. He hacked it off himself with a knife and a key-hole saw and lived with the Ute Indians until the stump was

distant. I crossed Thomas's fork [166] and left the river shortly after, traveling over high hills and through deep ravines very similar to the country which we passed over two days previous to arriving on Bear river. We arrived at the trading-house about two o'clock, after a very warm, dusty, and fatiguing march. I here learned that the difference between the route which I had taken and the one by Fort Bridger was not less than ninety miles, which would make a difference of at least one week. I therefore determined to await their arrival in this vicinity and let our horses and mules take a long rest. They had performed good service and stood greatly in need of it.

It was to be regretted the command did not cross Green river where we did, as it would have given the horses and mules one week's rest on this river, which they had been standing in great need of since arriving at Independence rock. The other route was probably less mountainous, but the grazing was not better and the distance saved by crossing Subblet's [Sublette's] cut-off would have justified their taking it. Being provided with kegs, water could have been carried across the desert. It is frequently the case that you can get it by digging at a place which is about twenty-five miles from Big Sandy and the halfway point between the two rivers. This is easily known from the little valleys that are seen about there and the deep hollows but a short distance beyond.

healed. Thereafter he wore a peg he whittled out himself. He was associated with Ewing Young, Milton Sublette, William Wolfskill, and other famous characters of the early trapping days in the far southwest. Smith's fork of the Gunnison and Bear rivers bears his name. He established a trading-post on Bear river and traded good horses for the broken-down animals of emigrants. Died a pauper in San Francisco, 1866. Bancroft, *History of the northwest coast*, 11, 453-54; Sabin, *Kit Carson days*, 1, 195-96; Hill, "Ewing Young in the fur trade of the far southwest, 1822-1834," in Oregon historical society *quarterly*, XXIV, 1-35.

[166] Tributary of Bear river, emptying into it near Raymond, Idaho.

JULY 27. I remained here during the day. The mules were sent some distance among the hills to graze. Mr. Smith, the trader, visited us and was extremely kind to our party, having a fine beef killed expressly for our use. Since arriving at Green river I observed a great change in the soil among the mountains and ravines. We were now getting to where a fine short grass was to be found on the sides of the hills and ravines. Although not very thick it was considered very nutritious, which I presume must be the case, as our animals would leave the bottoms and climb to the top of the highest hills to hunt for it.

JULY 28. The morning was clear and cold. I left this place at eight o'clock and made my encampment three miles down the river. Our animals were taken to the opposite side and guarded with Smith's horses, being safer with them than by themselves. We were now among the Snake Indians and were visited today by a chief [and] a party [which] accompanied him. They expressed much friendship for us and great pleasure in meeting with white people who had come a long way, not to make war upon them, but to protect them from any aggression from those who were passing in great numbers through their country and of whom they pretended to stand in much fear.

It was, like all Indian speeches, made more for the purpose of exciting sympathy and extracting presents than from the existence of any real fear upon their part. I learned, however, from Smith, who has been a trapper for twenty years in the mountains and much of the time with them, that they have evinced every disposition to be friendly with the emigrants while traveling through their country and will continue to remain so if not molested. They are a quiet race of people who seem to have no desire to make war but [are] ready to redress wrongs when inflicted on them. They were once a powerful nation, but like many others have been broken up and much reduced by still more powerful tribes farther north.

It was here I met with Rocky mountain horses for the first time. They are stout, well-made animals, not so large as our horses, but very muscular and formed to endure great hardship. Nearly all the young men were out hunting, and those who seemed entrusted with the care of the horses could not be persuaded to dispose of one of them at any price. They were in excellent condition, having the full range of the mountains, where they were guarded by small boys who are taught to handle a horse and throw a lasso with as much skill as a Mexican.

The chief appeared to be very much pleased at our arrival and came daily to visit us, accompanied sometimes by all his family. This generally took place about the hour of dining, when they all appeared to have good appetites, judging from the quantity of meat that was consumed. The young boys, who were not over seven years old, brought us great quantities of fish for a few trifling presents. These consisted of the brook and salmon trout which are found very abundantly in this river, as well as [in] all the mountain streams between here and the Columbia river. They were extremely fine and the first I had seen since coming into the mountains. Having but little to do while remaining here we resorted to fishing and were very successful, keeping our mess very abundantly supplied with the finest kind.

Game in this section of the country is scarce, compared with the ranges passed over on the route. We had now gone nearly through the whole buffalo range, as but few are now met with on Bear river. Fifteen years ago they were to be seen in great numbers here but have been diminishing greatly since that time. Antelope are found, though not very numerous. Elk and grizzly bear are more abundant and increase on the range between here and California. Both are found in great numbers in California, where the grizzly bear grows to a very large size. It would seem that the climate is much better adapted to them there than farther north, as they are not very plent[iful] about the Columbia river. I had two pair of elk horns with me, one procured this side of Fort Laramie and the other at Smith's fork. These were considered pretty fair specimens, but not near[ly] so large as some seen in the range of the Salt lake.

JULY 29. The weather continued very pleasant. The mornings were cool and clear; the middle of the days I found very warm but not oppressive. As rain seldom falls here during the summer the evenings are pleasant [until] after sundown, when, like the early part of the mornings, they become cold.

There was nothing worthy of note passed today. The six ox-teams that we left near Green river arrived today with a loss of one wagon. The oxen had been distributed among the other teams, which had aided them considerably in their march. They appeared in tolerably fair condition and I was satisfied they were able to reach Fort Hall before the command, as they now had several days the start. I left at four p.m., and after traveling about eight miles encamped for the evening on a small stream which is formed by several springs coming from the base of the mountains.

JULY 30. We changed our encamping ground this morning by traveling down the river six miles, where we stopped for the day. I dispatched a man to ascertain if any information [concerning] the troops could be obtained and was much gratified to learn that they had

arrived in the vicinity of Brown's trading-house [167] on
Bear river, and would reach me the next day. This was
very agreeable news to all of us. We had been quite long
enough absent and my anxiety had become very great,
for I was aware that the movements of the command
depended entirely on the train, which could only be
kept in order by great care from all connected with it.
I was consoled by knowing that in my absence Lieutenant Frost and the agents would leave nothing unturned
to keep everything in good order which would tend to
facilitate the movements of the command.

The day was passed in wandering over the mountains
in pursuit of game and although scarce we succeeded
in bringing in a fine antelope which came in very apro-
pos. Our stores were nearly exhausted, being entirely
out of sugar and coffee and very nearly out of meat.
The command, therefore, came up in good time to prevent us from proceeding to Fort Hall, as we should
have found it necessary to renew our supply of provisions.

JULY 31. Last night was extremely cold for the time
of the year. Ice and frost were to be seen this morning,
which chilled our horses and mules. This prevented
them from improving as rapidly as they would have
done if the nights had been more mild, as we had now
got to where grazing was very good and clear of alkali.
The whole of this valley is well watered by small
streams from the mountains, which are made by springs
that are found in numbers along their base. The land in
many places along the valley is sufficiently level for irri-
gation and would doubtless produce very well. It is of a

[167] No other reference to a trading-house on Bear river operated at this
time by a man named Brown is known to the editor. Since the distance from
Cross's camp would place the regiment in the neighborhood of Smith's trading-house the question of an error is raised here. Perhaps this latter place
was the one Cross meant.

dark clay soil, lies very light, and could be cultivated without much trouble. The springs are, however, very backward here and [the] winters set in early, when snow generally falls very deep. This may impede the growth of vegetation, and as the summers are very dry, without irrigating the lands they might not produce well. Those who have attempted to cultivate this soil, not being successful, believe it will not produce, but this is by no means a proper test. I am fully convinced that by carefully irrigating the soil it will yield as well as any I have traveled over.

AUGUST 1 [1849]. The mules, being loosed last night, were very hard to catch this morning. This is generally the case with these animals. Where the trains are large and grass scarce it is all-important that they be hobbled. Much time is lost in the morning in preparing the teams for the march when it is sometimes all-important that every moment should be saved. We commenced our march at half-past seven o'clock and soon left the river. [We] passed over some small hills and across a few bad places made by the little streams from the mountains and did not strike it again until one o'clock, when we reached the Soda springs. [These] had been made the theme of conversation among us for many days. The road which we had been traveling had scarcely produced any variety, and we were very desirous of reaching a place which had become so noted among all who have passed here.

Here is the commencement of volcanic signs which the surrounding country so plainly presents. The river for the first time begins to draw within high banks of basaltic rock. The springs are but a few miles from where the river sweeps around a very high peak, which on that side seems to be the terminus of a mountain range.[168] After winding along [toward] the south

168 The Wasatch range terminates here.

among the mountains and hills it finds its way to the
Great Salt lake, about forty miles from here. There
are quite a number of springs here which are certainly
a great curiosity. They occupy altogether a space of
about a mile and a half, are bounded by the river on
the left side and a high range of mountains immediately in the rear of them,[169] which [are] partly covered
with cedar. When you come in sight of the place two
mounds are first seen, which are probably twenty-five
feet high. They are of a whitish cast resembling de-
composed lime mingled with oxide of iron. On top of
one of these mounds and along its side, the water rises
in a small basin and seems to be stationary. Through
[this] gas slowly escapes. The taste of the water is
somewhat metallic and by no means pleasant compared with the springs in the bottom and immediately
in the vicinity of this place. One of them is perfectly
dry, and both have a hollow sound as you walk or ride
over them. There is a beautiful stream of water which
comes from the mountains and passing through a fine,
rich little valley sweeps round the base of one of these
mounds. After running through a cedar grove near
them [it] falls into Bear river about half a mile below.
On the side of this stream several springs are met
with which are not only cool, but so strongly impregnated [with] gas that the taste is very much like that of
soda water. I procured several bottles of it and kept it
some time and found it very refreshing to drink. It was
also used in making bread and was a very good substitute in the place of saleratus.

Previous to arriving at the mounds we passed a
large spring of clear, cold water which bursts from
the ground and forms quite a stream in a very short
distance. It is very pure and not in the least impregnated with gas. Not over a hundred yards from this

---

169 The Aspen range.

spring there is another, the water of which has a metallic taste with gas constantly escaping from the bottom. It differs very much from the spring found in the stream a short distance off.

After leaving the mound and descending the river about half a mile you cross the stream already referred to and come to several springs and small ponds, where the water emits a very disagreeable odor. As you pass on there are several small mounds seen, some of an oval form, while others are conical. [These] are composed of the sediment that doubtless came from the springs when in existence. On the left side of the road and the bank of the river there is another spring where a little stream puts in. [This] is very strongly impregnated and the gas effervesces in [such] great quantities that [it] can easily be heard as you approach it.

Having continued my journey for a short distance to a point where the road passes over a small hill, my attention was drawn toward the river, where many of these small cones are standing. These differ materially in colors. Some are white and others mixed with oxide of iron. I saw some of a beautiful chrome color, of which I procured several specimens.

It was at the side of the river and at this place that I saw the celebrated spring, generally known as "Steamboat spring." The water seems to rise out of the river through a tube of cylindrical form [composed] of carbonate of lime which is about three feet high. Here you hear a rattling noise not unlike the escaping of steam from a steam pipe. It is not loud, but such is the similarity of the sound that it has received the name of the "Steamboat spring." The water here appears to be forced up by the pressure of the gas below, which, escaping at intervals, creates this peculiar sound. The taste of the water is said to be much the same as the other springs in the bottom, but to my taste it was more metallic, warmer, and not so highly impregnated with gas. Many of the mounds that are now dry have been broken to pieces by the emigrants [who were] prompted more by idle curiosity than [by] any desire to obtain information as to the cause which produced them.

Having gathered several specimens which I carried throughout the journey in safety, I continued my march toward camp, which was made about two miles beyond the spring and a short distance from where the river turns to the south. At this place we were near the mountains where we procured as much wood as the command stood in need of for the night. Water from the river was obtained from the only spot where the banks in this vicinity were low enough to admit our horses to water. Here the river sinks between perpendicular banks of basaltic rock which are at least a hundred feet high.

The valley about here is finely watered, not only by the river, but by the little stream which passes the springs that have already been mentioned. Lumber can be easily obtained from the mountains on the opposite side of the river in great quantities, which would answer very well for building purposes should it be required. [It] is the only place on the route where it is found so convenient, except in the neighborhood of Deer creek. Wood for fuel can also be procured without much trouble immediately in the rear of the springs on the mountains. This neighborhood probably produces the best pine and cedar which are met with between the Missouri and the Blue mountains. Grazing about here is generally very fine, particularly in the small valley through which the stream flows, and hay could be procured from it in great quantities for winter purposes.

This place is immediately at the point where the two

trails turn off for California and Oregon and within a very short distance of the Salt lake. It is also but eight days' march to the Sweetwater beyond the South pass, where early in the spring mounted troops would be abundantly supplied with fine grass if it became necessary for them to [make] a summer's campaign. Besides all this, it is no doubt a very healthy place, and I know of no two places better calculated for the establishing of military posts than Deer creek and Soda springs. As two sites have already been located it is hardly possible they will ever be changed. Neither, probably, will be required to be kept up any length of time, as the Indians between here and the Dalles are an inoffensive race who will never be disposed to molest any party as long as troops are on the Columbia river.

I regret that we were prevented from remaining longer at the springs as it would have given us an opportunity of examining them more closely, it being impossible to learn much of them in so short a time. I can say, however, it well deserves the name of "nature's great laboratory" where the earth beneath us is but one great furnace in which many gases are engendered and come forth through the fissures of the earth (that has been rent asunder) to mingle with the pure atmosphere of the surrounding mountains.

AUGUST 2. The morning was cold, and although not cloudy, the atmosphere began to resemble an Indian summer, which always gives the sun a yellowish, sickly hue. We had every indication of a fine traveling day. It was here that we were called upon to part with many of our traveling companions who had accompanied us over the greater portion of the route and with whom we had passed many pleasant hours. They were now about to take the road which leads to California while our trail turned to the north. Doctor [Thomas J.]

White, from St. Louis, who had been employed as surgeon to one of the divisions, and who now holds the distinguished position of speaker of the house of representatives in California,[170] left us with his amiable and accomplished family at this place. Colonel [Edward J. C.] Kewen, the present attorney-general of California,[171] also left us here. It was therefore like commencing a new journey to part with so many pleasant companions. After giving each other a hearty shake of the hand [and] expressing a hope that we might meet under more favorable auspices, we parted. Soon we found ourselves turning north and winding our way up a wide valley which brought us at the close of the evening to the Portneuf [river],[172] a stream which rises in the mountains a short distance from where we encamped. It falls into the Snake river about fifteen miles below Fort Hall. The road today lay along a valley which comes from the north. We met with no impediments except in one or two swampy places which often cause much detention to large trains.

At the commencement of our journey this morning I passed across a valley toward three high hills [which are] situated some distance apart and entirely isolated.[173] They bore evident signs of having once been volcanoes, but [are] now entirely extinct. The inner side of the crater showed the effects of recent heat and the lava, or cinder, lay in great quantities about the valley. Although I had no time to devote to procuring specimens, being constantly required with the train, I gathered some of the cinders and brought them safely with me. [I] intend[ed] them, [together] with the

[170] Elected speaker of the California house of representatives november 13, 1849, but resigned during the first session of 1850.

[171] Elected attorney-general of California november 13, 1849, but resigned during 1850.

[172] Above Portneuf reservoir.

[173] Ten-mile, Broken crater, and China hat buttes.

specimens gathered at Soda springs, the American falls on Snake river, the Hot springs at Malheur river, with other specimens obtained from the inner side of the crater of Popocatapetl near Puebla in the republic of Mexico, for the National institute.[174] The scenery about the bend of the river reminded me of the country near Contreras, in Mexico. In this valley there are many fissures, differing in depth. Some of them are narrow enough to step across, while others are much wider, making the surface so rough and uneven that it was difficult to force my horse through it. In other parts of the valley the earth is extremely spongy and light, and easily beaten into dust when traveled on. This, however, is very much the case with the whole route from Fort Laramie.

The great mass of emigrants ahead of us had now turned off on the road to California, as our trail bore no evidence of having been much traveled this season. It was fortunate for us [that this was] so, for we were soon to enter a country on Snake river that was entirely destitute of grass [as far as] the Cascade mountains,[175] a distance of seven hundred miles.

Several large ponds were passed today which were very similar to those at Soda springs. I observed one or two places which emitted gas and the water tasted very much like the springs heretofore mentioned. In this day's journey we made twenty-three miles, encamping where both grass and water were extremely fine. The hills now began to get scarce of wood, but the small dry willows always found on the banks of these little streams answered as a very good substitute in place of better.

AUGUST 3. The command left this morning at six

174 Smithsonian institution, Washington, D.C.
175 A range of mountains in western United States and Canada.

o'clock. This day's march was entirely among the hills, as our road, after crossing a very miry swamp, passed along the side of a hill some distance and entered a gorge. After winding around the base of the hills for some time [it] began to ascend and [continued to do so] until the animals were completely broken down, as well as ourselves. The day being warm, it was felt still more so among the surrounding hills, which seemed only to admit a slight breeze to create a dust that became almost insupportable, [it] being often so thick as to hide teams and wagons. The drivers at times scarcely knew in what direction they were traveling and left it more to the instinct of the animals than to their own judgment. Our encampment was made about six o'clock this [afternoon] in a small ravine among the mountains and on a small brook [176] coming from a fine spring near by which gave us delightful water that was extremely refreshing after so dusty a ride. The hills were covered with small groves of aspen, and the tops of the mountains were in many places interspersed with cedar and sugar-loaf pine.

The second division overtook us, having traveled yesterday about thirty miles and twenty-five today. This had the effect of breaking down many of the mules, which must always be the case when persons not connected with the department have the entire control of regulating the days' marches. On a long journey like this, where we travel over a country unknown to any excepting the guides, it is often the case that too much latitude to regulate the distance to be traveled is given them. If they feel a desire to travel twenty-five miles to reach a place where grass and water can be had, the command is generally required to travel it, when by a little trouble on their part it might be pro-

[176] Ross's fork of the Portneuf.

cured by shorter marches. On the route to the South pass I would have wanted no better guide than the Mormon guide book,[177] which I found to be very exact throughout that distance. It has noted down every hill, valley, and stream you meet with, stating with great precision the several points where good encampments could be reached and the distance between each place. We had but few along and it is hoped, for the benefit of emigrants, they may become more freely circulated.

AUGUST 4. We commenced our journey today for Fort Hall, which was not more than an ordinary day's march, but the fatigue of the teams of yesterday and the heavy, sandy road that we were to pass over between this and Fort Hall made it very doubtful if we accomplished the distance today, [it] being twenty-two miles. The first division left the encampment at six a.m. The morning was cold and as clear as you generally find in this country. Being calm, it indicated heat in the middle of the day. We descended a long hill which brought us into a sandy plain. This extends to Fort Hall and [to] the banks of the Portneuf [river]. After taking a circuitous route through the hills [it] strikes the road again at the base of the hills which we had just descended, making [the distance] eighteen miles from our encampment of the second. We continued along its banks for some distance, [then] it diverg[es] from the road and passing through the plain reach[es] the Snake river valley where it falls into that river about fifteen miles below Fort Hall.

Throughout the day the sand was very heavy, and the middle of the day [was] extremely warm. During

---

[177] *The latter-day saint's emigrants' guide: being a table of distances, showing all springs, creeks, rivers, hills, mountains, camping places, and all other notable places from Council Bluffs to the valley of the Great Salt lake, etc.* (St. Louis 1848). Reprint by A. William Lund, assistant historian of the Church of Jesus Christ of Latter-day Saints, n.d.

the day the train became, in many instances, completely exhausted. At sundown we were just entering the valley of the Snake river, Lewis's fork of the Columbia river.[178] [We were] compelled from necessity to leave some of the wagons on the plain until the next morning, the mules having become too much exhausted to get them along.

As you cross the valley to approach the river there are many small streams to pass over, where the banks are miry and dangerous. [This condition was] rendered still [worse] in proportion to the number of wagons that had passed over them. It was therefore very late in the evening before the regimental train got into camp. The supply train [was so late that I was compelled] to park it until the next morning on the banks of a very miry pool. To have attempted to pass it in the night would have endangered the wagons. This was in sight of the command, which had nothing to do but to ride forward in the morning and rest quietly until the arrival of the two trains in the [afternoon]. It was a very severe day's march, and though not a long distance, [it] was felt by the whole command, even by those who had but little to do and were therefore very little exposed.

AUGUST 5. The morning was pleasant and presented, as usual, a smoky atmosphere. I gave orders to commence crossing at daylight so as to reach camp as early as possible. Several wagons were still on the road, but [they] were brought in during the morning. We had now arrived at Fort Hall, our last resting place. The condition of the trains, which were destined to carry us a distance of seven hundred miles farther before

[178] Named "Lewis's river," 1805, by Captain William Clark, in honor of Captain Meriwether Lewis. The "Hobak" and "Mad river" of the Wilson Price Hunt expedition, 1811, and now known as the Snake river.

any aid could be obtained after leaving here [was not encouraging]. These were the same teams which, from their condition at Fort Kearny, induced me to call for a board of survey, being fully satisfied that their condition did not justify the hope of our arriving with them at our place of destination without great trouble and loss of property. It was now important to reorganize the whole train by leaving such animals as were unfit for present use and [the] unserviceable wagons at Fort Hall, which was to be occupied by two companies of the rifle regiment that had recently arrived.[179]

The regimental train was the most injured by the march. The drivers, being enlisted men, were entirely ignorant of such duty. [They] took no interest in learning [nor in] improving the condition of their teams. Having found among the train that had recently come up a number of very fine mules [I was] enabled, together with what I had, to refit the whole train once more and place them in a condition to commence the long journey which we still had before us. The best drivers were taken from Fort Hall and substituted in place of the soldiers [from] the regimental train. The most indifferent teamsters of the supply train were paid off, and others left at Fort Hall to be discharged as soon as they received their pay. We were therefore kept busily engaged through the day in making preparations to renew the march.

AUGUST 6. The morning was calm and pleasant and, although cloudless, [it] was smoky as usual. We had now entered a country entirely different from that we

---

179 Companies G and B under Major Simonson. They arrived at Fort Hall about two weeks ahead of the regiment, therefore their animals were rested. Loring to Jones, august 7, 1849. Major Simonson was relieved of the command of this post, arrested for some military dereliction, and Brevet-lieutenant-colonel Porter placed in command. Loring to Freeman, october 15, 1849; Steele, With the rifle regiment, 2.

had recently traveled. We were approaching the Blue mountains [180] and the Cascade range which are constantly on fire during the summer and fall, as well as other mountains that are thickly wooded. The sky in this vicinity presents a hazy appearance, caused entirely by the smoke from the burning mountains, which increases to such an extent as to hide the neighboring hills as we advance. This gives to the sun a yellow hue and [to] the day the appearance of an Indian summer. The weather was fast changing and felt more like autumn in latitude 37° than that which should have been experienced in latitude 45°.

We were busily engaged today in making such alterations and improvements as remained unfinished yesterday, and succeeded in preparing the first division [181] to leave on the seventh. We entirely overhauled the public stores and made a report of their condition, leaving such as were unnecessary for the march at this post. This day was a very busy one and my clerks, as well as myself, were extremely fatigued when we retired to rest at eleven o'clock at night. All resting days for the troops are generally the reverse for the staff officers. There was none of us but what was always glad to commence the march again. It has often presented itself to my mind very forcibly how little is known of the fatigue which is felt by the members of that portion of the command who are always looked to for the success of the daily marches or the accomplishment of a journey. It is to be regretted that the labors of the day, as well as the responsibilities, could not be more equally divided and felt by all. While laboring

---

180 A range of mountains in northeastern Oregon through which the regiment would pass.

181 At Fort Hall the command was divided into two divisions. Brevet-major Stephen S. Tucker commanded the first, and Lieutenant-colonel Jacob B. Backenstos the second. Loring to Freeman, october 15, 1849.

during the day in superintending the movements of
large trains, particularly through mountainous passes
and broken countries, I have come into camp completely overcome by heat, covered with dust, and exhausted by mental as well as bodily labor. I have heard
those around me, whose duty was but little more than
to go forward and luxuriate on the banks of some
pleasant brook until the arrival of the train, speak of
their fatigue as if they had in reality been called on to
perform some laborious task. Who is it on a march
like this experiences trouble but the one who is always
looked to for the preservation of the means which is
to insure success, who must always be diligent and
watchful over all around, be the trouble what it may,
trusting but little to anyone and [relying] on his own
untiring zeal and industry for the safety of all?

AUGUST 7. All necessary arrangements being made
for the first division, the march was renewed at twelve
o'clock. The day was passed in completing all unfinished business and preparing the second division to
follow in the morning. Reports were made to the chief
of the department,[182] as well as to Colonel Mackay [183]
at St. Louis, suggesting the propriety of furnishing
the acting assistant quartermaster [184] at this post with

182 General Thomas S. Jesup.

183 Colonel Aeneas Mackay. New York. Assistant deputy commissary of
ordnance march 12, 1813; retained as first-lieutenant of ordnance february 8,
1815, to rank as of march 12, 1813; honorably discharged june 15, 1815; reinstated as second-lieutenant of ordnance december 2, 1815, with brevet of first-
lieutenant from march 12, 1813; transferred to corps artillery may 17, 1816;
first-lieutenant december 1, 1816; transferred to Third artillery june 1, 1821;
captain december 31, 1822; captain assistant quartermaster july 15, 1824;
brevet-major december 31, 1832 for ten years faithful service in one grade;
major quartermaster july 7, 1838; lieutenant-colonel deputy quartermaster
general april 21, 1846; colonel may 30, 1848, for meritorious conduct particularly in performance of his duties in prosecuting the war with Mexico; died
may 23, 1850. Heitman, *Historical register*, I, 670.

184 Lieutenant F. S. K. Russell.

such instructions as might be deemed necessary for his future guidance. When I left St. Louis I received no orders relative to the several posts that were to be located, neither were any instructions given to me while on the march. What orders the colonel had previous to starting I know not, and I therefore could not give any definite instructions which might be proper to regulate the officer in charge of the department while building quarters for the companies left, either here or at Fort Laramie. I however gave such instructions as I thought most proper, presuming that on the receipt of my report at St. Louis, Colonel Mackay would give such orders as he might deem advisable. We retired this evening to rest at half-past eleven o'clock, after riding, walking, and writing throughout the day and much of the night, having again completed a new train which was to last us to the end of our journey, there being now but two divisions instead of three. One of the companies was left but another was taken from here, which still made the number of companies the same. The decrease of provisions and stores had greatly diminished the supply train and it was thought advisable to concentrate the troops [for] the remainder of the journey.

March from Fort Hall to Fort Boise

AUGUST 8 [1849]. The morning was pleasant. The second division commenced their march at ten a.m., and encamped on the Portneuf [river] about eight miles from here. I left at two o'clock and passed Fort Hall, a trading establishment of the Hudson's Bay company. This place is about three miles below where two companies of the rifle regiment have chosen for the site of their new post.[185] It is built of clay and much in the form of Fort Laramie, having a large sallyport

185 The two companies under Brevet-lieutenant-colonel Porter immediately set to work erecting quarters for the new post, which was called "Cantonment Loring." Captain Howard Stansbury, who said this place was five miles above Fort Hall, arrived there september 22, found the troops living in tents and busily engaged in erecting permanent quarters. When he left for Salt Lake City Porter accompanied him for the purpose of examining Cache valley to determine its possibilities as a wintering place for stock. Both officers agreed it was an ideal place. Consequently Porter sent all his mules and part of his oxen thither in care of twenty-four teamsters and a number of herdsmen, while Stansbury sent only a part of his. The winter proved unusually severe, snow fell to an unprecedented depth, and more than half the entire herd was lost. Stansbury, *Exploration and survey,* 94, 95; Porter to Hatch, february 24, 1850. From the very first there seems to have been doubt that a post could be maintained here. On october 30, 1849, Colonel Loring sent back orders and instructions to Porter to the effect that in the event the train of supplies from Fort Leavenworth did not arrive the post was to be abandoned and the troops marched to the Dalles. This train arrived, however, and on december 31 Porter reported supplies on hand sufficient to last his command until the latter part of september 1850. An error in computing the daily consumption was made, for on february 24, 1850, Porter reported that the supplies would last only to june 20. This being the case, and pursuant to Colonel Loring's instructions of october 30, 1849, he abandoned the post about may 1, 1850, and arrived at Fort Vancouver the twenty-eighth of the same month. Stansbury, *Exploration and survey,* 93; Porter to Hatch, february 24, 1850; Hawkins to Porter, february 24, 1850; Hatch to Porter, april 28, 1850; Loring to Freeman, april 28, 1850; to Jones, june 30, 1850; *Daily Missouri republican,* june 16, 1850, in Nebraska state historical society *publications,* XX, 222-23.

which fronts the Portneuf, with its walls extending back toward the banks of Snake river. There is a blockhouse at one of the angles. The buildings inside are built against the side of the wall and of the same materials. The main building is occupied by the proprietor, while the others are intended for storerooms and places for the hands who are employed in the service of the company. The rooms are all small and by no means comfortable. Being generally intended for one person they are contracted and dark, having but a small window and one door.

This place is occupied by Captain Grant,[186] who has been here fourteen years. He informed me that he had endeavored to cultivate the soil, but to no success. As they seldom have rain during the summer the ground becomes very hard and baked, transpiration water from the river not being sufficient to keep it moist. The ground presented to me a fine, dark alluvial soil, [which] by proper cultivation [should] produce well. I have seldom met with any of the traders, however, either on the upper Mississippi [river] or this route, who have turned their attention to agriculture enough to speak with any experience or certainty on the subject.

There are along the river small quantities of cottonwood, particularly in the vicinity of where the two companies are located. With the exception of this advantage I do not admire their location for the post. I presume the troops, however, will not be required to occupy this post very long, as it seems to be out of position, not being able to draw properly the necessary supplies for it from either Fort Leavenworth or

186 Captain Richard Grant. He was at Saskatchewan in 1834 and at York factory 1837-1841. In this latter year he was transferred to the Columbia district and assigned to Fort Hall in 1842. Cross was therefore in error when he said Grant had been here fourteen years.

[Fort] Vancouver. While the former is fourteen hundred miles, land transportation, the latter is upwards of seven hundred miles, having the Cascade and Blue mountains to pass over, which are very formidable barriers. The whole country is a dreary and barren waste [and] there is little or no vegetation. There is very good grazing on the prairie or bottom land about here and around in the vicinity of where the post is to be established, which is four miles above Fort [Hall] and [at] the same point where our command struck the river. Here the troops are able to procure as much hay as may be required by them. In this country it is expected that horses will be hardy enough to endure the winters by running at large and grazing on the bottom lands.

The two drawings of the outer and inner side of Fort Hall, or the trading-post of the Hudson's Bay company, will give you a correct idea of their rude construction, and I find but little difference in any of them on the route to the Columbia river.

Having left Fort Hall, I joined the second division about five o'clock, divided the train into sections, and assigned the several wagonmasters to their respective places. I was again prepared to commence the journey for Oregon City, or the Dalles on the Columbia river.

AUGUST 9. The morning was quite cold. The command left at half-past six o'clock and crossing the Portneuf soon ascended a steep bluff which borders on a plain that is five miles wide. Here the road runs along the bluff, giving us a fine view of Snake river valley below. It is wide and much cut up with small streams which either [rise] from the springs on the side of the bluffs or from springs which are found boiling up in the valley. [These send] forth water in such quantities as soon to form large streams. As the

OUTSIDE VIEW OF FORT HALL, 1849

INSIDE VIEW OF FORT HALL, 1849

road wound along the top of the bluff the valley presented a beautiful view as compared with the surrounding country.

We had now fairly commenced the remainder of our journey to Oregon City, with the best outfit we could procure from the materials obtained at Fort Hall. Now we were to pass through a more dreary and barren country than heretofore, a small specimen of which had been before us during the day. From the bluffs to the range of hills which runs parallel to the left bank of the river, about five miles off, the land is a poor, light, barren soil, covered with artemisia. Neither the hills nor the plains produce one stick of wood.

On the opposite side of the river the country is a vast plain. With the exception of the Three buttes,[187] which are high peaks standing alone on the plains and giving a little variety to the scenery, there is nothing to be seen in the distant view but artemisia, which is always present to the sight, let the eye turn in any direction it may. The picture, on the whole, was anything but a pleasing one. When we reflected that we were to travel several hundred miles through a country presenting nothing more pleasing than barren hills and sterile plains, having artemisia to burn, as well as food probably for the animals, it was certainly discouraging.

A journey of seven hundred miles at any time, where everything is plent[iful], is no small undertaking. Still greater must it seem to be to us when we had traveled constantly for three months and had only accomplished fourteen hundred miles, two-thirds of the journey, over probably the most uninteresting route which can be found on the northern continent. But

187 Pillar butte, Big butte, and Old crater.

stout hearts and willing dispositions to brave difficulties were able to accomplish many hardships and
to make impossibilities possible. When I reflected on
the fatigue which had been endured, and likely to be
renewed again, I began to think that if we reached our
destination safely nothing in the way of traveling hereafter can be looked upon as impossible.

We continued the march during the day through
dust half-leg deep, for we had now struck a soil that
was so light and spongy as to make it dangerous sometimes when riding over it. The mornings and evenings
are exceedingly keen, while the middle of the day is
very warm. We suffered severely from the heat today,
and find that we experience two extremes of heat and
cold during twenty-four hours. We made our encampment at the close of the evening in the valley of the
Snake river, having entered it for the first time, and, I
may say in truth, for the last time where grass was to
be found on its banks in any great quantity.

AUGUST 10. The morning being pleasant, the march
was resumed at the usual hour. Our encampment last
evening seemed to be the terminus of Snake river valley, as the appearance of the river entirely changed
after a march of about five miles, which brought us to
the American falls.[188] The sound of [these] was heard
some time before reaching them, as the wind came
from the southwest, directly from them. The scene
was truly magnificent. Here was an entire change in
the face of the country as well as [in] the river. But a
few miles back we had looked on it running quietly
through a wide, fertile valley and winding around
islands studded with trees. Now [it] became contracted to a space of not more than four hundred yards
and in a short distance was precipitated over huge

188 In Power county, Idaho.

rocks to resume its course through a deep canyon, the perpendicular walls of which were formed of basaltic rock.

In the center of the falls there is a ledge of rocks dividing the river into two parts, which has a few scattering dwarf cedars on it that seem to spring from the crevices of the rocks and are nourished by what little earth is found upon them. Between the right bank and this ledge, the column of water, after being whirled among the rocks, has a perpendicular fall of about eight feet. That on the left is much less, and [the water] finds its way below by passing round and over large masses of rock that lie in its way, until it reaches nearly the base, where is a small fall of a few feet high. While the right bank commences to rise quite high and perpendicular, the left bank is somewhat broken with shelving rocks projecting over the water.

[There are] many places which appear as if they had been intended as caldrons or reservoirs for molten lava, which by some convulsion of nature had been thrown out and scattered about the falls in small fragments. [These] could be seen everywhere. The inner sides of these basins are entirely glazed, as if submitted to the action of very strong heat, while others resemble very much the appearance of a surface polished by the water. Many small pieces of stone were lying in different directions, which were evidently volcanic productions. I obtained several specimens of the rock and some large pieces of obsidian. The latter seemed to be scattered in small fragments for miles around on the plain, as it could be picked up wherever you went.

The road passed along the bluff, bending to the right, which soon caused us to lose sight of the falls. In this day's march we crossed many gorges or deep ravines that were much broken and very difficult to travel over. They were the outlets to streams from the hills, are often very miry, and the hills which we ascended very sandy and difficult to get over.

The river today has been much broken up by the rapids. Since leaving the falls they are frequently met with. One of these I observed is very beautiful. Here there is an island in the middle of the river about a quarter of a mile long, which seemed to be one mass of rock.[189] Its top was covered thickly with scrub oak and small stunted cedar. The rapids commenced about half a mile above it and forming a series of small falls, passing on both sides of the island with much rapidity and force of current, continued in this way for about half a mile below it. The growth on the island (which in this vicinity is a very rare sight), the beauty of the rapids, the deep canyon through which the river passes, and the surrounding scenery, so different from any passed before, made the whole landscape here one of beauty and interest. Toward the close of the evening we passed many ledges of rocks [190] which formed a complete valley, having an outlet so narrow that but one wagon could pass at a time. These seemed to be the effect of some volcanic action. The right bank of the river along here rises to the height of at least fifteen hundred feet, [is composed] entirely of basaltic rock and resembles very much the palisades on the Hudson river a short distance above New York. On the left bank, the ground, although much broken, is not so rough and there are some places where you are able to drive your train or take your horses to water.

It had been very fatiguing through the day. As there is no way of heading the ravines they were obliged to be crossed, and we did but little during the day except

189 Cedar island.
190 Massacre rocks.

cross one ravine to come soon to another, so that [the afternoon] had passed away before we reached our encampment. After sundown we came to what is called Fall creek,[191] a rapid little stream having in the vicinity of the road many cascades where the water rushes from one to the other with great force, forming a very pleasing little picture. The side of the hill around which we had to pass before crossing the stream was very broken and sandy. On the opposite side of this little brook the hill was so steep as sometimes to require sixteen mules to a wagon and as many men as could well get hold of a rope to get it to the top. This will give you some faint idea of the very great detention often met with on this route and how long the delay would be in crossing one hundred sixty-six wagons. It was, however, accomplished, and we reached camp after nine o'clock at night, where we had neither wood to make fires nor grazing for our animals.

AUGUST 11. The morning was cold and the mules, for want of something to eat, had wandered over the hills and among the ravines to pick up what they could find, as it was impossible to keep them confined to any particular spot. This prevented us from starting early and we did not commence our march until about half-past seven [o'clock], passing through a rough gorge and afterwards over level plains through the day. We crossed Ogden's river [192] at twelve o'clock. The road turns off to the south for California,[193] which was

191 So named on account of the succession of cascades, which were sometimes called "petrified beaver dams."

192 It was given this name as early as 1826 by Peter Skene Ogden. Jason Lee (1834) said it received the name "Raft" river from the fact that some traders crossed it on a raft in time of high water.

193 At the site of present Yale, Idaho, the road to California left the Oregon trail and ascended Raft river, passed the City of rocks, and fell upon the headwaters of the Humboldt river in northeastern Nevada.

taken by the Californians who were still along. After passing over a plain about five miles wide we ascended a steep hill by the assistance of soldiers, which was the only obstacle met with during the day. Our road, take it altogether, was a good one, and our march was not so severe as yesterday. But for the dust, we should have traveled very well.

The scenery today was not very interesting, as the road led a short distance from the river. [This] intercepted the view we otherwise would have had of its singularly formed banks, which sometimes vary from two to five hundred feet high. The mountains to the left [194] began to show the unevenness of the country to the south and west. A range of mountains to the north,[195] a long distance off, seeming like distant clouds rising above the horizon, began to indicate that we might realize some change for the better in the scenery before many days. This range was probably seventy miles off. A little after sundown, after having had the teams in harness for fourteen hours and accomplishing a march of twenty-five miles, we arrived at a reed swamp, where the mules and horses fared well compared with that of last night.

AUGUST 12. The morning was calm and the day pleasant. The command got off at the usual hour. After passing around the swamp some distance and over a plain for about ten miles, we came to Snake river again and made our encampment for the day. The grazing was very indifferent, but the march would have been too great to have continued it to a better place. The distance which we would have been compelled to travel for water [was] twenty-three miles, and no intermediate point between where we could have fared better than here.

194 Raft river and Goose creek mountains.
195 Saw-tooth mountains.

From Bear river to this place every stream abounds in fish of the finest kind. The speckled as well as the salmon-trout can be caught in great quantities. Everyone who could find time resorted to his hook and line, and we fared sumptuously when we were fortunate enough to procure fuel to cook them.

AUGUST 13. It was at this encampment that I met with a family in great distress, consisting of a man, his wife, and two little children, who had by great labor reached this far on their route to Oregon. Their oxen had entirely given out and they were now left alone to starve. They might have returned to Fort Hall, [it] being only five days' journey back. Their condition was one that could not but excite sympathy, and I accordingly made arrangements to take them along. It was about six o'clock in the morning when we got under way. The Dutchman and his family were called for, who from their movements seemed to think that time was of little value, as they were much longer in getting themselves ready than we were willing to lose. They were ordered to abandon wagon, oxen, and baggage, taking only such articles, with their clothing, as were indispensably necessary. The woman seemed to be disposed to hang on to her wagon as her only wealth, and when brought from it by her husband her lamentations of grief, with those of her children, were really distressing. The Dutchman took it more philosophically, although at first he was somewhat loath to leave his all. [He] smoked his pipe with as much composure as if he were still wandering in dreams to that golden region where his imagination had so often led him, [there] to rear fortunes which were soon to vanish again.

We marched about twelve miles and encamped for the day, having learned from the first division ahead of us that the distance would be too great to reach grass and good water. [We] therefore remained on the banks of Snake river again for another night, although it was desolate to look around and see what the horses were to get for their subsistence. The scenery for the last two days was much the same, the picture being made up of distant hills, barren wastes [and] wild sage, with not a tree to intercept the view.

AUGUST 14. As the first division was not far in advance of us, I left the second at five o'clock in the morning to go forward. The road lay along the bank of Snake river nearly all day, which still continued to pass through a deep canyon of perpendicular rock. [This] appeared to have been made by some convulsion of nature, apparently simply to give room for the waters of Snake river, for the country on the opposite side was as dry and sterile as on the side we were traveling.

We passed several islands during the morning similar to those already described, which, with the rapids about them, presented quite a picturesque appearance. We here stopped for a short time, when Major Crittenden,[196] being expert with the hook and line, caught from among the rocks which formed small eddies a fine mess of fish, principally speckled salmon. Our march was then continued until about four o'clock in the afternoon, when we arrived at Rock creek [197] and continued down its banks to a bend where the road diverges, making our encampment for the evening on its banks.

---

[196] George Bibb Crittenden. Kentucky. Brevet-second-lieutenant Fourth infantry july 1, 1832; resigned april 30, 1833; captain Mounted Riflemen may 27, 1846; brevet-major august 20, 1847, for gallant and meritorious service in the battles of Contreras and Churubusco, Mexico; major march 15, 1848; cashiered august 19, 1848; reinstated march 15, 1849; lieutenant-colonel december 30, 1856; resigned june 10, 1861; major-general Confederate army 1861-1865; died november 27, 1880. Heitman, *Historical register*, 1, 337-38.

[197] In Jerome county, Idaho. Not to be confused with Rock creek in Blaine county, same state.

Our march today brought us about twenty-three miles over a dreary, sandy plain, crossing the dry bed of a creek, where the water lay in holes. The bottom of this creek, as well as its banks, was of volcanic formation and a solid mass of basalt. Rock creek is a small stream which comes from the neighboring hills and falls into Snake river, having for an outlet a very deep canyon, from where we made our encampment to the river. The stream itself is not more than fifteen feet wide. The canyon through which it passes is in many places from fifty to one hundred feet high and varying in width from one hundred to two hundred yards. In some parts of the canyon we met with a little willow growing immediately on the borders of the stream. In other places it becomes so narrow as to exclude everything in the way of vegetation. In the vicinity of our encampment the banks are low, forming a handsome bottom studded here and there with willows and with better grass than any we had met with since leaving Fort Hall.

The evening was pleasant, although the day had been very warm and dusty. Toward the close of the [afternoon] the fishermen sallied forth with their hooks and lines and soon returned laden with as fine Rocky mountain trout as I had met with. After having our supper of them, which we had served up in fine style by a very excellent cook, we all turned in for rest to be better prepared for an early start in the morning. As I had once got[ten] in the rear a day and found it very difficult to overtake the command, I determined not to get in[to] the same unpleasant predicament again.

AUGUST 15. We commenced preparing for a start this morning at three o'clock, but did not get off until some time after four o'clock, as the morning was dark and smoky. We traveled rapidly for about eight miles

until we arrived at the creek again.[198] At this place
we waited for our wagons, which soon came up. Having assisted them out of the canyon, which was no easy
work, we continued on until the middle of the day
when we came again to the banks of the river which
were at least two or three hundred feet in height. I
attempted to descend into the valley through which
the river ran for the purpose of procuring water, but
it was so fatiguing, both for myself and horse, that I
returned without being able to accomplish it.

It was at this place we could easily hear the sound
of a waterfall, which from the noise we at first supposed might have been the Little falls of Snake
river,[199] but as we were still twenty miles from that
point we were soon satisfied that it did not proceed
from there or [from] the small cascade on the opposite
bank which is mentioned by Colonel Fremont as the
Subterranean river. We were much surprised to learn
the next day that within ten miles of this place there
is a cascade which in height is not surpassed by the
Niagara falls. The guide who was with the command,
having traveled this route very often, was shown the
place by an Indian. He took Mr. George Gibbs and
Lieutenant Lindsay to the place, who pronounced it
one of nature's great wonders. The river here becomes
a little contracted and passes through a chasm of solid
rock. It commences to fall about a quarter of a mile
above the last pitch and after forcing itself among the
loose rocks which lie in its way takes a perpendicular
pitch of at least one hundred sixty feet. It is even
thought to be a greater height. They descended to the
foot of the falls after much difficulty and some length
of time, where they were better able to judge more

198 Near Twin Falls, Idaho.
199 Otherwise known as Twin falls.

accurately of its great height. There seems to be but
one opinion, that it equalled in grandeur [and] in
proportion to column of water the Niagara falls. Having been the first who had ever taken the trouble to
examine them carefully and wishing to change the
name said to have been given them by a priest many
years since, they decided on that of the Great Sho-
shonie [Shoshone] falls, instead of Canadian, as being
the most appropriate.

The road does not pass there and probably its nearest point is not less than eight or ten miles, which is
probably the reason why it is so little known, for I
have never seen it mentioned by those who have
trapped in this country for years. Their time is generally occupied and they take no interest in riding, much
less walking, twenty miles out of their way to see a
river tumble over rocks of any height. Besides, they
are generally ignorant Canadians who have but very
little curiosity to notice such things.

We continued our journey until sundown when we
came to the foot of the Little falls of the Snake river,
commonly called Little Salmon falls and encamped
for the night immediately on the banks of the river.

Our teams came in quite late and very much exhausted, not having had any water since leaving Rock
creek and [having] traveled twenty miles since leaving
that stream. This place gave the mules but very little to
subsist on, [what there was] being principally long,
coarse, sour grass, which has but little nourishment in
it at any time and much less toward the close of the
summer. The river here presented a very beautiful
view. Our encampment was on its banks and immediately at the foot of the falls, which could be seen from
the bend above and until it again changed its direction
below. The fall passes over several ledges of rock

which extend across the river and somewhat parallel to each other, giving it in its fall, when viewed at a distance, the appearance of heavy waves.

The scenery is very different from what we have witnessed since leaving the American falls. The banks on both sides at this place become entirely changed. On the opposite side they take the form of small hills which gradually rise one above the other, bringing you again to a vast plain beyond them. The right bank presents broken bluffs, which form quite a valley between them and the river. Two small brooks pass out of the ravine, one at our encampment and the other three miles below. [The latter], called Little Salmon creek, runs with much rapidity, falling over rocks and forming cascades in its way.

This was one of the severest day's marches I have ever experienced. It was excessively warm [and] without the least air. The hills on each side seemed, as it were, to reflect the rays of the sun so as to strike us with double force until it became almost insupportable. Previous to reaching the bank of the river about the middle of the day, we resorted to making a shade with our blankets by hanging them over the artemisia shrubs, which afforded us considerable relief for a time. The dust appeared to be greater today than I had experienced since leaving Fort Hall. The road was so pulverized that by every revolution of the wheels it would fall off in perfect clouds.

AUGUST 16. The morning was pleasant for traveling, but the atmosphere was filled with smoke, which continued to increase as we gradually approached the Blue mountains. We commenced our journey at an early hour, and after traveling a few miles came to where the first division had encamped the previous evening. They [had] got[ten] under way previous to

our arrival there, leaving a few men to collect together and take charge of the straggling horses and
mules which had strayed off among the hills. Those
broken down, which were so reduced in flesh that they
were constantly giving out and increasing the *cavayard* daily, [were] anything but a pleasing sight to
look on, for by the additional increase we were rendered less able to facilitate our journey.

The bank on the opposite side of the river had again
resumed its rocky appearance and looked in many
places as if it were a solid mass of masonry. We had
not proceeded far before we came to where the water
burst forth from the rocks in many places, while a
pretty little stream of several feet in width tumbled
forth from the top of the rocks and formed a very
beautiful cascade in its descent to the river, making
the whole scene one of beauty seldom to be met with.
For several miles water in large columns was constantly bursting from the banks of the river.[200] [These]
must have proceeded from the volcanic formation of
the ground on the opposite side [where there were]
fissures which received the waters collected from the
neighboring hills and valleys. [Due to the] porous formation [of the ground, the water] finds its way in this
manner through the earth until it reaches the river. I
regret that we were prevented [by] the want of time
and the little grazing which could be had about here
for our horses from remaining a few days, so that we
might have carefully examined the country on the
opposite side in order to have become better informed
of the causes which produced this singular freak of
nature.

The formation of the banks of the river below this,
and almost throughout the whole distance which it

200 Thousand springs, a few miles above Hagerman, Idaho.

passes from the time it leaves the American falls until
it unites with the Columbia river, [is much the same],
seldom becoming in any place low enough to allow the
wagons to pass. Whenever [this] did occur the distance was not longer than from five to ten miles and
often much less. The river here is seen running through
a deep canyon or opening in the earth. Its banks in
many places are of solid rock. When it does not take
that appearance, it generally proceed[s] from the
mouldering of the rocks from the sides. The earth
from the plains being deposited on its banks and covering up the detached rocks gives it the appearance of
an embankment. I have often come on the banks of
this dreary, barren, sterile river in my daily marches
and invariably found it the same uniform canal, a spot
which could not have been more uniformly defined if
it had been cut by the hand of man.

We soon came to the Big Salmon falls,[201] having
traveled about eight miles this morning. These falls are
somewhat similar to those already described, except
that large rocks are seen projecting above the surface of
the water, against which it dashes in parts of the falls
with great violence and forms in one place a perpendicular fall of six or eight feet. It was at these falls that
we met a few Indians for the first time since leaving
Fort Hall. [They] had assembled here to lay in their
supply of salmon for the winter, as well as to subsist on
them during the fall. There were twelve lodges, if they
may be so termed, some oval in form, and others of a
semicircular shape, [all] opening toward or from the
sun as might be required. These lodges were made of
green willow brush, their tops bent over and fastened
together. When fresh they look not unlike a willow
grove, but when the leaves become withered they re-

201 Near the mouth of the Salmon river.

semble, at a distance, bunches of dry weeds and might
have been easily passed without being noticed. The men
were good-looking, well formed, and appear stouter
than the generality of Indians farther north. They are
thick-set and well built, and there is nothing sullen
about them, a quality you meet with among the northern tribes on the Mississippi [river]. On the contrary,
[they] appear pleasant and fond of talking, and from
what little I saw of them [they] are a harmless and inoffensive race of people. The women whom I found at
the lodges were in appearance inferior to the men. I
saw none who possessed the least beauty. All [who]
were there are principally the Root Diggers, who live
in abject poverty compared with the balance of their
nation. They are in fact nothing more than the degener-
ate portion of the Snake nation, Bonarks [Bannocks]
and Nez Percés, who prefer living among the neighboring hills and subsist by digging roots (from whence
they take their name) [to] following a more noble oc-
cupation of catching beaver and hunting big game. It
was amusing to see them watching for fish, [for] they
throw a spear with as much precision as an arrow.
[They] no sooner caught [one] than they would plunge
into the rapids and make for our side to dispose of it.
They appeared to have but little idea of the value of
money, as they sold for an old tin cup, partly without a
bottom, ten times its value. I purchased as much for two
cartridges as they had asked me for a blanket. Their
way of estimating the value of [an] article is, not what
its real worth would be to them in the way of war, but
simply [how it might] gratify their fancy. I presume
the tin cup would have made them many trinkets compared with a piece of money ten times its value, which
shows they go a good deal for quantity and at the same
time still more to gratify their taste. These people were

almost in a state of nudity, the men having a covering about their hips made of rabbit skins, while the women had for petticoats dressed skins and for robes either undressed rabbit or squirrel skins, which were a substitute for blankets.

In Captain Bonneville's adventures Washington Irving says, "Some of these people, more provident and industrious than the rest, lay up a stock of dried salmon and other fish for the winter. With these they were ready to traffic with the travelers for any object of utility in Indian life, giving a large quantity in exchange for an awl, a knife, or a fish-hook.

"Others were in the most abject state of want and starvation, and would even gather up the fish bones the travelers threw away after a repast, warm them over again at the fire and pick them with the greatest avidity.

"The farther Captain Bonneville advanced into the country of these Root Diggers, the more evidence he perceived of their rude and forlorn condition. 'They were destitute,' says he, 'of the necessary covering to protect them from the weather and seemed to be in the most unsophisticated ignorance of any other propriety or advantage in the use of clothing. One old dame had absolutely nothing on her person but a thread around her neck from which was pendant a solitary bead.'

"What stage of human destitution, however, is too destitute for vanity! Though these naked and forlorn-looking beings had neither toilet to arrange nor beauty to contemplate, their greatest passion was for a mirror. It was a 'great medicine' in their eyes. The sight of one was sufficient, at any time, to throw them into a paroxysm of eagerness and delight. They were ready to give anything they had for the smallest fragment in which they might behold their squalid features."

The road leaves the river at the falls and ascends a

long hill for about three miles, where, after four hours'
labor, the whole train succeeded in reaching the top.
Here the country to the left presents a series of plains,
rising one above the other, causing the ground between
them to be somewhat uneven and broken. To the north
you have a fine view of the mountains which we had
been approaching for several days. These were the
Salmon river mountains.[202] We arrived at the close of
the afternoon on the top of the bluff, which was, as usual
so high, steep, and rocky as almost to deprive us of
getting our mules into the canyon. The rear of the train
arrived about eight o'clock. The night being dark, we
were prevented from getting the remainder of them
down to water. They were therefore turned out to
graze among the sand-hills and artemisia, there being
scarcely a particle of grass either on the bluff or in the
canyon. The whole day's march, after passing the falls
in the morning, was over dry, barren plains entirely
destitute of water and in places extremely heavy [with]
dust half-leg deep. The mosquitoes at our encampments
were very annoying to ourselves as well as to our animals, and we had been troubled by them since striking
the Snake river. The teams came in very much broken
down, and it was as much as we could do to make daily
alterations among them, so as to prevent them from
impeding the movements of the command and entirely
giving out.

AUGUST 17. Every day's journey brought us into a
worse country, if not for ourselves, certainly for our
teams. Many of our mules had been carried into the
canyon last night and the balance were driven down
early this morning, after much trouble, to get water. As
we had to travel sixteen miles today before either grass
or water could be obtained, over an uneven country, or

202 A range of mountains in Custer and Lemhi counties, Idaho.

encamp where we would have to fare worse than last night, our march was commenced as early as the state of things would permit. The whole train did not get off until ten o'clock, as we had much trouble in collecting the mules this morning, and still greater to get them out of the canyon. Many of them being unable to ascend the bluff [were] therefore abandoned.

The morning was calm and clear. The road lay over a very broken country, having to ascend high hills and then cross deep ravines all day, although to look at it at a distance it did not seem to present any of these obstacles. These ravines were frequently difficult to pass through, being the outlet for the water from the hills and plains and for the water made by the melting of the snows. [The country] was sometimes very much broken. Our road necessarily carrying us along near the river, it was often very difficult to cross the gullies which were frequently met with in this day's march, for this light spongy earth is easily washed into a very uneven surface along this river.

After sundown the train arrived at a very steep hill or bluff, where the road descends to the river. [The hill] was too much to attempt to descend at that time of the afternoon. I therefore remained on the plain all night, as the greater portion of the train did not arrive until nine o'clock. The march had been throughout the day over a country entirely destitute of water. Although the river was not far off the steepness of its banks would have prevented us from getting at it, and besides the bluffs about here were very much broken. The command had succeeded in reaching the river at the termination of the day's march, and the train sufficiently near it to drive the mules into the bottom where they could remain in safety until the morning. They were between the river and the high bluffs, which were very good barriers to their getting off.

AUGUST 18. It continued pleasant last night until midnight, [then] the wind, shifting to the north, gave us a norther in all its fury. Those on the top of the hill got the full benefit of it. Wagon covers were torn to pieces and our tents blown down over us. In the morning we were completely buried alive in sand which had drifted on the tents as they lay over us. The morning continued very windy, raising clouds of dust so thick that the wagons, in descending the hills, were completely enveloped. The bluffs about here have very much the appearance of chalk banks and are equally as light. It was very difficult to descend the hills, and in spite of all efforts to the contrary the wagons would get such headway as to render it dangerous to hold on to ropes attached to them. I here witnessed the capsizing of several, throwing boxes and barrels in all directions. One of them turned over entirely, injuring nothing except a few wagon-bows.

Having arrived at camp this morning, the train was too much broken down to continue our march today. In consequence of it we remained here, arranged the loads, broke up such wagons and teams as impeded the movements of the train, and turned out the mules and horses to roam over the hills and in the bottoms to get what could be found.

AUGUST 19. It was thought advisable to undertake to cross the river here,[203] as grass was getting scarcer. I examined the river opposite two small willow islands and thought it practicable, as the water in depth would not come up to the wagon-beds. The river banks were immediately cut down from one island to the other. On going with the party to the right bank, the current was discovered to be so strong as to force one of the men imperceptibly down into deep water before getting across. He was soon carried beyond his depth by the

203 At Glenn's Ferry, Idaho.

force of the current and drowned before any aid could be given him.[204] This created a panic among some of the others, and I did not get them back to the island without considerable difficulty and great apprehension for their safety.

Having completed cutting down the banks one of the wagons was then tried, which, after much labor against the current, succeeded in reaching the right bank in safety. Fearing that more property would be lost than the necessity of the case would justify, the idea was abandoned and we remained on the left bank, trusting to our luck while traveling over what might truly be called a desert, and about as bad as generally falls to the lot of anyone to be found on.

The second division had arrived in a worse condition than the first. [It] was directed to encamp here for a couple of days to rest the animals and let them get what little grass might be obtained in the ravines and gorges among the hills in this vicinity.

The banks of the river now began to change their appearance and the steep, rocky cliffs so long met with were in places rapidly disappearing. This part of the river was the first we had met with since our departure from Fort Hall where the banks would enable us to pass if the stage of water had permitted, although we had traveled a distance of one hundred eighty miles.

AUGUST 20. We continued our march at eight o'clock this morning along the river, where the bank is somewhat sloping, until we arrived on a small stream which ran from among the hills. [Here] we found better grazing than could possibly have been expected. The road was level and not very heavy today, although somewhat rocky. As the distance was not as far as we usually traveled the trains came in but little jaded. [With] what

---

[204] Private John C. Scott. Monthly returns, Mounted Riflemen.

ARTEMISIA PLAINS ON SNAKE RIVER

CAMP GROUND OF AUGUST 23, 1849
At bluffs on Snake river

little grass they [were] able to pick up from among the willows [the teams were] better prepared to renew the journey in the morning than recently.

AUGUST 21. The road continued along the slope of the hills for some hours, where the rocks lay so thick that we were greatly impeded in our march. The balance of the road was not very difficult to travel over, meeting only in some few places with heavy sand. We got in today much better than I anticipated, for such was generally the state of the teams when we left in the morning that there was no great certainty of our reaching camp at night. We arrived about five o'clock in camp after traveling twelve miles, and to the agreeable surprise of all we had plenty of long, coarse sour grass which resembles very much broom-sedge in appearance. This induced the commanding officer to lay by one day. The day was extremely warm. Being sometimes among the hills we were deprived of the breeze and got the full benefit of the sun. It was very pleasant in the morning and bid fair to be so throughout the day.

AUGUST 22. Having remained here during the day, the horses and mules were taken to an island where very good grass for this country was found, but not such as we would expect to travel horses on hundreds of miles. Such arrangements were made today to facilitate our movements in the morning as are generally required after a few days' travel. The second division came up and remained one day after our departure. The day was extremely warm, although the evenings and mornings continued to be pleasant.

AUGUST 23. Our march was commenced this morning at the usual hour. Leaving the banks of the river about three miles from our encampment we passed into a deep, narrow gorge, which brought us upon a plain that gave a beautiful view of the surrounding country. To the north there seemed to be a series of plains rising gradually above each other, where a range of mountains might be seen at a very long distance. The country to the southwest was much the same as that which we had recently passed over, being a light, sandy soil. In the whole of this view not a tree could be seen, but the artemisia was everywhere presented to the eye. In our march today we passed a small stream of good water. After crossing it we soon entered a deep canyon and continued down it until we arrived once more at the river, after which our road diverged from it and brought us into camp toward sundown. Our animals were taken to the opposite side of the river to graze for the night. The day, with the exception of the dust, was very pleasant, by no means severe upon the teams, and we marched today twenty-one miles without any serious difficulty.

The view which is here attached is [of] the bluffs immediately in the rear of the encampment, and they are frequently met with throughout this part of the country. As I have heretofore stated, the country sometimes for miles is very level. Then again you come to places which, from the nature of the soil, become wasted, as you see in the drawing. It is nothing but clay and easily yields to the weather.

AUGUST 24. The morning was cloudy and extremely smoky. It became warm and sultry in the night and began to rain at three o'clock in the morning, but not enough to lay the dust. This was a very novel sight to us, as a shower of rain of any importance had not been seen since the twenty-fifth of june. Our guide, having been in the country many years and being well acquainted with every stream and watering-place along this route, informed us that the distance today must exceed twelve or fifteen miles. Our march the next day would have to be increased to twenty to reach a place where grass and water could be obtained [even] in small quantities. Our third day's march would be nearly twenty-eight miles, as the country was entirely destitute of both grass and water. After that we should soon reach Fort Boise [205] and there would be but little difficulty afterward until we arrived at the Blue mountains. This was cheering news, for we greatly required a change for our teams, which were fast on the decline, and the horses of the command were no better.

We commenced the march at half-past six o'clock this morning, passing along the borders of Snake river for some distance before leaving it, and arrived at Bruno [Bruneau][206] creek early in the afternoon, where we encamped for the night. The distance being short today and the road not uneven, [we were] enabled to pass over it without any trouble. The character of the scenery in this short march was such as had been met with for several days. The bluffs along the river were much broken, and rising one above another appeared, at a distance, like high hills or mountains. In reality they are only the termination of a series of plains when you approach them.

AUGUST 25. Last evening the wind shifted to the northwest and brought over a dark cloud, accompanied by a heavy wind, as well as a little rain and hail. It lasted but a few minutes and made the balance of the evening very pleasant. As it continued to blow, it was

205 The original site of Fort Boise was on the Boise river, about five miles above its mouth. Built by the Hudson's Bay company, 1834, to compete with Nathaniel Wyeth's Fort Hall, in 1837 it was moved to the east side of Snake river, about a mile below the mouth of Boise river. After 1846 the profits of both Fort Boise and Fort Hall fell off sharply. In 1853 the post was partially destroyed by the Snake river, and owing to an Indian massacre in the vicinity the place was abandoned in 1855. Though Cross spelled this "Boissé," the editor has changed it throughout to "Boise" to conform with modern usage.

206 A tributary of the Snake river in eastern Ada county, Idaho.

cold in the night, and not less so this morning. With the wind, which threatened our tents, and the stumbling of the mules over our tent-cords all night, sleep was out of the question. There were but very few who commenced their journey this morning any better prepared for it than they were yesterday. It was two months today since we left Fort Laramie. When we reflected on the condition of the teams at that time, the many changes which the trains had undergone, and the distance we had traveled over, as well as the great variety of country through which we had come, it all seemed to be a dream and could hardly be realized. The journey was not yet accomplished by several hundred miles, and that portion of the route through which the road passed was considered by mountaineers equally as bad in many places as the route from Fort Hall to this place. Of all countries for barrenness I have ever seen it certainly exceeds any, and I doubt if it can be equaled in any part of the continent.

We had now to march twenty-eight miles before meeting with water of any importance. As to grass, there was none to be seen, [and we would be compelled to] pass over some very fatiguing places for the teams. We commenced the march as early as the arranging of the trains would permit. Our road soon brought us to a steep ascent and then into a valley where we met with the only water for the day. Having crossed this little stream we passed into a deep gorge which brought us to a very long, steep descent that gave us great difficulty. It required nine yoke of oxen to take up the first wagon. The others required ten mules and as many soldiers as could well get hold of a rope to bring them to the top of the hill, which they succeeded in doing after about three hours' work. I mention these facts to show the many obstacles that were daily met with about this time, when it was impossible to make any calculation for more than from one day to another how long the teams, or even the horses of the command, would last unless we succeeded in reaching a place where we would be able to make shorter marches and procure food for them. Nothing up to this time had saved us since leaving Fort Hall but the decreasing of the loads, which took place every three or four days, the breaking up of wagons, [and] turning the most indifferent mules into the drove and taking the best [to] replace them. It may be said that the condition of our mules did not justify such long marches, but we were driven to it from compulsion, as neither water nor grass were to be had at any intermediate point. When we were compelled to stop at night the grazing was poor enough to create starvation among them. We were perfectly aware that the marches were too long, but we [had] to travel them or be in much worse condition. There was not an evening ever passed but what the agents were made to give in a detailed account of the state of the teams and what changes might be made in order to move to any advantage the next day.

If the mules had been in good condition when the march first commenced, and [the] loads light, there would not have been any trouble on the whole route, but this was not the case. Their condition did not justify their even starting for Fort Hall, and by the time they arrived there, with all the care taken of them, they were in no condition to continue a journey of over seven hundred miles through a desert waste like that found on the banks of Snake river.

The road from here continued in many places to rise gradually, making the hauling so severe on the animals that at sunset they were completely broken down. This compelled me to stop them on a barren waste, where neither water nor a sprig of grass [were] to be obtained. Here they were kept several hours, when they were again put in motion and reached camp at one o'clock in the morning. The regimental train was compelled always to reach camp as soon as possible. Although possessing by far the best mules, it did not arrive tonight until very late and some of the [wagons] not until the next day. In this day's journey there was nothing of the least interest. The hills to our left were gradually increasing and those to the north partly intercepted our view of the range of mountains in that direction. The country through the [afternoon] was somewhat rolling, but for several hours before arriving in camp it commenced gradually descending.

I have in many places spoken of the formation of the bluffs along the borders of the river and those among the ravines through which we have passed as being broken and rugged. The one bordering on Snake river where we encamped, and around which we traveled last night through a small valley made by a plain until near one o'clock this morning, [is typical]. This was [the] termination [of the plain, which was bordered by] the river and the high hills to our left. The soil is extremely light, being composed principally of clay and sand which is easily washed by the melting snows in the spring and heavy rains early in the season. It not infrequently takes a variety of forms, which, if the imagination is allowed free scope, would bring forth buildings in every shape. Old towers, fallen castles, and old fortresses with broken and tumbling walls seem to have the appearance of having long since been undermined by time and only wanted the ivy to complete the touch.[207] This bluff has stood many a blast and pelting storm until it show[s] the effects of it by the many rude, sharp

207 Castle buttes, about seven miles below Grand View, Idaho.

peaks, and rugged breaks which are easily perceptible. Toward the top [it] had been so changed that its formation was not unlike a human figure, which from its peculiar position attracted the attention of us all. On approaching these bluffs one would suppose that it would be impossible ever to get over them. On the contrary we find that there are ravines and gorges which bring us to the top where the bluffs disappear, and we find ourselves traveling over apparently level country. Thus it has been ever since leaving Fort Hall, but much more so along here than [at] the commencement of our journey from that post.

AUGUST 26. The camp wore a gloomy aspect this morning. There was not one among us but felt that many more days like that of yesterday would bring us all on foot and probably be the destruction of the trains. The colonel therefore determined to change only the encamping ground today and stop at the first convenient place. We left at ten o'clock and found a fair encamping ground about six miles below on a small creek, where water was found in holes and the grazing tolerably fair. This gave us the opportunity of collecting the wagons which did not reach camp last night.

AUGUST 27. We commenced the journey at the usual hour, traveling down the river. Through the day we passed several lodges of Indians who were fishing. As soon as they saw us they were ready for trading and appeared not to be very particular as to what they got in exchange. They are, like all Indians, fond of trinkets and care but very little as to quality. The india-rubber boat [in] which Lieutenant Jones [208] had descended the

---

[208] William Edmonson Jones. Virginia. Brevet-second-lieutenant Mounted Riflemen july 1, 1848; second-lieutenant november 30, 1850; first-lieutenant october 31, 1854; resigned january 26, 1857; brigadier-general Confederate army 1861-1864; killed in action at Mount Crawford, Virginia, june 5, 1864. Heitman, *Historical register*, I, 583.

river for several days greatly excited their curiosity, being the first they had ever seen. They appeared much puzzled how it could be so easily made.

In the march today I visited two hot springs a short distance on the left of the road, which have not been mentioned by anyone before.[209] They are about halfway between the river and the hills. The water was extremely hot – too much so to immerse the fingers. The taste was a little metallic, but it gave no unpleasant smell. From the appearance of both I presume they come from the same fountainhead, as the one below seemed in its direction to diverge from the same point. The ground around the springs was extremely dry and light, [and] in many places my horse would sink half-leg deep. There was no vegetation except a few rushes that grew on the banks of the little brooks which make from them. [These springs] were, in appearance and temperature, very much like those on the Malheur river. Our camp this evening was made on the Snake river again and [was] about as good as those we generally met with. The distance traveled was fourteen miles and [was] performed much better than could possibly have been expected.

AUGUST 28. Having made necessary arrangements last night for our march [in the] morning, I retired for the night, much worn down in mind as well as body. The wind began to blow and the sky was overcast with thick clouds, which indicated a violent storm. About three o'clock the bugle gave us the signal to commence preparing for a start. The animals were pretty well scattered, and it being a windy morning, we had much difficulty to collect and catch them. As the sun came over the rugged cliffs the clouds dispersed and the day was fine, except the heavy wind which continued to

209 Givens Hot Springs, Owyhee county, Idaho.

blow directly into our faces, much to the annoyance of the whole command, but still more to the teamsters. So great were the clouds of dust that the trains were entirely enveloped. It was utterly impossible for [the drivers] to see which way they were driving. [They] could therefore only allow their teams to follow those in the advance, for it was too severe to expose the eyes to it for any length of time. The road today was quite sandy and heavy, which made it, as such roads generally did, hard to get over. After a fashion we got into camp towards the close of the [afternoon], all much gratified that a short march tomorrow would bring us to Fort Boise, where better prospects for our future march might be reasonably expected.

AUGUST 29. The command commenced moving at seven o'clock, which was generally as early as we could at present make arrangements to move. The wind continued to blow all day, giving us the full benefit of the dust. Soon after leaving camp the river turned to the northeast, making a large bend. The road diverged to the left through a dry, sandy country. Throughout the day several mules as well as horses died, and some became so exhausted as to compel us to leave them behind. This was certainly not to be wondered at, when we bear in mind the state of the country through which a command as large as this had been traveling. [It was] entirely destitute, I may say, of the least subsistence for our mules and horses. As to what grazing they got since leaving the bottoms at Fort Hall or since they passed the American falls, where the entire face of the country commences to change, it was of but little importance and barely kept them alive. Sometimes [it did] them much more injury than good. It is true that on our march each encampment would present some little difference, but in not more than one or two instances did

we ever arrive at an encampment where we supposed
they could be the least benefited, and I have merely
spoken of the advantages of each encampment by comparison with others since leaving Fort Hall.

We arrived at Fort Boise about five p.m. and encamped on a small creek called the Owyhee, about
three-quarters of a mile from the trading-post of Fort
Boise, which is on the opposite side of Snake river and
immediately on its banks. This is another trading-post
established by the Hudson's Bay company for the same
purpose as that of Fort Hall. The walls and blockhouses
are placed at the corners so as to protect the several
sides, and the sallyport or main entrance opens on Snake
river. Inside the walls the buildings are arranged
around the four sides, one story high, and similar in
formation in every respect. The material of which they
are formed is of clay. In dry climates this makes very
excellent building [material] and is found to be very
durable. Some of these buildings are used as storehouses, together with the blockhouses, to keep their
peltry. They are contracted, and by no means intended
for anyone to occupy who is used to the comforts of life.
The *engagés,* however, never being accustomed to better, are perfectly reconciled, and so long as they get their
daily food are perfectly happy to breathe out their
lives in this manner among the Indians, who to them are
somewhat like what the peons are to the Mexicans.

We had been three days traveling on the banks of
Snake river. The bottoms had become somewhat extensive, changing entirely their appearance as the hills
began to slope gradually, until Snake river was found
once more passing through low ground, unincumbered
with basaltic rock.

A gentleman by the name of Craige [210] is the super-

210 Craige (Craigie, Craig) succeeded Payette at Fort Boise in 1844 and
probably left about 1852, as Archibald McIntyre was in charge there in 1853.

Outside view of Fort Boise, 1849

Inside View of Fort Boise, 1849

intendent of this trading-post. [He] has been here for a period of thirteen years [and] informed me that he had cultivated the soil a little, though not very successfully. He thought that corn might be raised by planting it early in april, as the rainy season generally sets in about that time on this river. His cultivation had been principally confined to raising vegetables, and [he] had succeeded tolerably well, except in light seeds which required moist ground.

The view which we had today of the Salmon river mountains, as well as towards the Blue mountains, was very beautiful. The scenery in this neighborhood is bold and picturesque, although destitute of trees to give it that finish which is so indispensably necessary.

March from Fort Boise to the Grande Ronde

AUGUST 30 [1849]. Preparations were made last night to send to Fort Vancouver on the Columbia river for transportation to meet us at the Dalles, as it would be impossible to get the stores and troops over the Cascade mountains with the present means of transportation. One of the guides was therefore sent by me in compliance with the orders of the commanding officer, with instructions to return without delay after he should receive an answer from the officer in charge of the quartermaster's department at that place.[211]

The command started for Malheur river,[212] about fifteen miles from here, where we were to enter a hilly country and get better grazing than we had had heretofore, which was so necessary to prevent our animals from starving. The move was made about eight a.m., after which I visited the fort for a short time, where I saw about two hundred Indians who had kept up a great noise all night. Some were dancing, while others were playing a game on which they would sometimes stake all they possessed, even to their leggins and blankets.

The road led up through the hills by a narrow gorge for about four or five miles, [which] brought us to the top of them and into a similar gorge. This looked as if

[211] Captain Rufus Ingalls.

[212] So named in 1826 by Peter Skene Ogden on account of the loss of furs and goods stolen by Indians from a cache. In his journal he sometimes speaks of it as "Malheur" and again as "Unfortunate" river.

it had really been intended for a public highway (for it could not have been more regular in its descent) and it brought us down to Malheur river [213] without the least fatigue to our animals early in the day. Here we made our encampment,[214] intending to make every preparation before renewing our march to the Dalles.

AUGUST 31. The morning was pleasant after sunrise, but cold before day broke, and ice remained in our buckets of water quite thick until half-past seven o'clock. The day was calm and warm at noon.

An order was issued to leave the principal portion of the train behind, with all the broken down horses and mules, to be escorted by one company [which was] left for that purpose.[215] These preparations being required, it [was] necessary to overhaul all the stores and distribute them, so that they could be carried without impeding the movements of the first division or incumbering that portion which was to follow on after us. All necessary instructions were given by me to prepare the stores for distribution, so soon as a proper examination and alterations were made with the wagons to receive them.

The Malheur is about twenty yards wide and comes from a lake [216] that is found among the hills of the Blue mountains, about forty miles from here. The range of hills through which it passes is not very high and forms

213 Two roads ran from this place to Malheur river. One led north down the Snake river about three miles, then turned northwest up Locket gulch and to present Vale, Oregon. The other took a northwesterly course to the same place. The former route was the one followed by the regiment.

214 At Vale, Oregon.

215 ". . . the command was here dismounted and the horses driven the remainder of the march. Five companies, with their baggage and provisions, were placed in advance, the remainder of the train, the weakest horses, and one company followed by easy marches under command of Brevet-lieutenant-colonel Backenstos." Loring to Freeman, october 15, 1849.

216 Malheur lake, in Harney county, Oregon.

a small valley, which is abundantly supplied with very good grass, particularly near Snake river. Our horses, by ranging among the hills and valleys, were able to get very good grazing, which they so greatly stood in need of, as they were now on the verge of starvation. The river not only abounds in fish of every kind, which were caught in the greatest quantity, but ducks and geese were constantly flying from the river to the lake, [and] the bottoms were filled with them.

A very serious accident occurred in camp this evening, [in which] a corporal [was wounded by] the accidental discharge of a carbine by one of the wagonmasters. It had been carelessly thrown into one of the wagons to be transported, although [this was] against orders. With men who seemed to have but very little forethought, as was the case with many of them, we might congratulate ourselves on having no more accidents than really did occur.

SEPTEMBER 1 [1849]. The morning was calm and pleasant. Having commenced the unfinished business of yesterday, the stores were weighed and arranged in the two trains by placing about seven hundred to one thousand pounds in each wagon, in proportion to the strength of the teams.[217] The commissary stores were daily decreasing, which would greatly relieve the teams

---

217 "The number of teams in the first division are as follows: ten wagons with commissary stores, one with ordnance, and one with quartermaster's stores. One ambulance, one forge, and a mess wagon for the wagonmasters and assistants. The number of men in all will be twenty-nine. The second division will have nine wagons with supplies, six with ordnance, and seven with hospital stores, also four with quartermaster's stores. One with public property, one for the mechanics, one mess wagon and six empty wagons, in all thirty-seven. One of the empty wagons will have to carry the sick of the second division. . . In the movement of the second division train I hope that it will be required to move by SMALL MARCHES and that the movement of the escort shall not govern it, for I feel assured that if the teams ARE PUSHED many of the animals as well as public property WILL HAVE TO BE ABANDONED." Cross to Hatch, september 1, 1849.

[which] were weak and [showed] the probability of being more so before arriving at the Dalles.

At sundown every change had been made that the trains could undergo. The regimental train was in charge of Lieutenant Frost, and I left it with him to make such changes as might suit the commanding officer, and such alterations as I thought indispensably necessary.

The companies in leaving Fort Leavenworth had been provided with good teams, but many of them were allowed to be too much overloaded for so great a distance. As [this] had been done under the inspection of officers of the department, as well as those immediately interested in the success of the journey, I could make but very little change after overtaking them on the prairies. The consequence was they had become very much broken down by being overladen. Having completed the alterations necessary to facilitate our onward movement I made my report at eight p.m., finishing two of the most laborious days' work that had been done on the journey. As nearly all the horses of the six companies had partly given out and many of them [were] completely broken down, they were left to be brought on with the second division train. The men who were on foot were placed under the command of Lieutenant Lindsay, who commenced the march quite early this morning in advance of the train and those who were mounted.

SEPTEMBER 2. The morning was very smoky, which prevented us from catching our mules and leaving before eight o'clock. The second division was directed to change its encamping ground, remain one day before it renewed its march, and Lieutenant Frost was left in charge of the public property to conduct it to the Dalles. The road here crossed the Malheur river and ran along a valley for some distance.[218] From thence it gradually passed over small hills and finally descended by a gorge to Birch creek, where we made our encampment at sundown. This day's march brought us twenty miles. [It] was performed in shorter time and with much less difficulty than any day's journey since we left Fort Hall. The road was good, as the rise and descent among the hills was very gradual throughout the day. Besides, the number of wagons broken up had given us an additional number of good mules, and the most indifferent had been turned out to be driven. This gave us an opportunity to travel rapidly, as we were no longer encumbered by them.

Doctor Moses and myself visited the hot springs at Malheur river this morning and [found the temperature of] the water was 196°. This spring is on the right bank of the river, about two hundred yards from where the road crosses, and at the end of a range of hills that runs parallel to Snake river from Fort Boise. The ground about this spring was extremely warm [and] the heat could plainly be felt through the boot by standing on it for a short time. I could detect no peculiarity in the taste of the water, although muriate of soda was incrusted on the pebbles about the spring. There was nothing very peculiar in the formation of the several springs, which were at a short distance from each other at this place. The water was very shallow and came from the bank with but very little force, showing that the fountainhead of the spring was very little higher than where it came from the earth. The soil in the bottom, through which we traveled in the morning, is dark and resembles that on Bear river. Wood is not to be obtained on the hills or in the ravines in this vicinity, and is as scarce here as at Fort Boise. A little willow is

---

218 Willow creek valley.

found on Malheur river, which never fails to be seen on all the streams in Oregon.

I was not aware that the water of this spring had ever been analyzed. Being somewhat anxious to know its qualities, I procured a small quantity and carried it with me through the whole journey. [I] have since ascertained that it was examined by Colonel Fremont while on his exploring expedition through this country in 1843 and 1844. If I had taken the same trouble with the water at the hot springs I visited before arriving at Fort Boise it might have been to some purpose, as I am inclined to believe it has never been analyzed. I presume the two springs are much the same, as they are nearly of the same temperature and resemble [each other] very much in other respects.

SEPTEMBER 3. We made an early start this morning and a few miles brought us again alongside of Snake river, where we were now to leave it for the last time.[219] No river has been passed on this march with more heartfelt joy. It here turned to the north, forming a large bend, passing through a range of high hills, [and] making a deep canyon on its way through them. We soon passed out of sight [of it], as the road gradually crossed a ridge and descended to Burntwood creek.[220] [This stream], turning to the northeast, breaks through the same range of hills, leaves a deep canyon in its passage, and falls into Snake river not far from where we left it. These openings in the mountain hills are very striking and worthy [of] the notice of those who travel this way. Our road ran along the stream throughout the day, leaving it but once until we made our encampment at four o'clock, when we stopped again on its

219 Farewell bend, above Blake's Junction, Oregon.

220 Tributary of the Snake river in northeastern Oregon. French-Canadian trappers called this stream "Rivière Brule."

banks. [We were] completely hemmed in by the mountain hills that form a ravine through which this little stream passes.

Since leaving Fort Boise the country began to change rapidly from plains and broken clay banks to that which is more hilly. Although the hills are not very high [they] were gradually increasing and continued to rise rapidly until we arrived at the foot of Blue mountains. These hills were well covered with bunch grass, which was very strengthening and much sought after by the mules, and we were fortunate in getting it for them through to the Grande Ronde.

SEPTEMBER 4. We commenced the march at half-past six o'clock this morning up the ravine, which became so narrow that the road passed along the bed of the river for some distance. [Then] it again turned to the right and winding around the base of the hills through a very narrow gorge brought us once more on level ground, where the face of the country was entirely changed. Mountains were to be seen all around and it appeared a mystery how we had extricated ourselves from those left behind us with so little difficulty or how we were to pass those ahead of us. This brought us again to Burntwood creek, where we encamped for the night.

In this day's march the road lay much of the time on the creek, seldom leaving it except when it became too much encumbered by rocks to allow us to pass. There is much cotton[wood], birch, and willow wood on this creek, [which] in many places is quite large. We also met with wild cherry and hawthorne here. Although filled with fruit, the trees grow to a very limited size.

The ravine through which the Burntwood passes is too narrow to be cultivated, but the soil is rich and ought to yield very well. The evening was spent in reaching the tops of some of the highest mountain hills, where the view of the adjacent country well rewarded us for our trouble. A few scattering hemlocks were seen in the ravine where we made our encampment, and the distant hills and ravines were interspersed with several groves of cedar and pine. Our encampment lay in a fork formed by Burntwood creek and a little brook which falls into it. [We] crossed the creek thirteen times and traveled about fifteen miles. Although the road was altogether quite rough, we accomplished the day's march without any trouble.

SEPTEMBER 5. Our location last night was a very good one, as we had wood, water, and grass in abundance. The night was quite cold but clearer than usual. Such is the density of the smoke that sometimes as we approach the Blue mountains it frequently intercepts the view of the adjacent country. We commenced our march at seven a.m., turning immediately up the side of the little creek which ran by our encampment. After passing around the base of these hills, which are entirely detached, [we] again reached a part somewhat more level. We had not traveled long before we began to descend gradually through a valley. Towards the close of the [afternoon] we came to a small mountain brook where birch and cottonwood were found on its banks and scattering pine on the sides of the hills.

We traveled about sixteen miles today, the greater portion of the road leading through much more open ground. Although we were still surrounded by ranges of mountain hills [we were] not so much confined to narrow gorges as [on] our march of the third and fourth. There was nothing, however, striking in this day's march. The gorges and ravines are very similar, and [there is] very little difference in the ranges of mountains which completely surrounded us. We were, however, daily approaching the Blue mountains, where pine and hemlock would take the place of [the] artemisia, which was gradually decreasing.

SEPTEMBER 6. After passing this morning through the valley in which we encamped last evening the road brought us to the top of a high ridge, giving us a beautiful view of the mountains running east and west and parallel to the ridge over which we were passing. The sight was very fine, as these mountains were the first we had seen covered with pine since leaving Soda springs. This range is high and rugged, with its base well wooded. Those to the left were equally so, while the Blue mountains to the northwest reared their peaks in dark blue masses high above the rest. [They were] covered with as beautiful timber as can be found between here and the Pacific ocean. The valley between these two ranges is probably six miles wide. The soil appeared light, spongy, and of a quality very similar to that on Snake river.

About five o'clock in the afternoon we came to the valley of the Powder river. [Here we] encamped for the night on what was once the bed of the river, which now runs near the base of the mountains and about two miles distant. This valley has many advantages over those I have passed on the march besides having a fine stream running through it. The mountains in the vicinity are covered with pine and hemlock, which is easy to procure. The soil is light and sufficiently level to be irrigated and will no doubt yield well when properly cultivated.

SEPTEMBER 7. Last night was very pleasant compared with many we had [seen] since coming among the mountains. In the early part of the morning the view of the mountains on the east was destroyed by a dense smoke and fog, which we have frequently met since leaving Fort Hall. It soon began to disperse, which

CAMP GROUND, SEPTEMBER 5, 1849

Two miles from camp, September 6, 1849

gave us a fine view before the middle of the day. The morning was pleasant and the day warm. We continued down the valley for eight miles, where we crossed the river and made our encampment on its bank but a short distance from where it turns to the right. Running through a range of mountain hills, over which we passed this morning, it flows into Snake river.

We remained here tonight, having fine water, plenty of wood for ourselves, and good grazing for our mules and horses. This stream is about thirty feet wide, is clear, and runs quietly over a gravelly bottom.[221] Here brook trout and salmon are found in great numbers. Being late in the season, the salmon become very poor in these streams and many of them die. It is said by mountaineers that they get weak and sickly and never return to the Columbia river from this stream. Be that as it may, there is certainly a great difference in the taste of the salmon fish caught near the Pacific and in this stream, and there is very little doubt but what numbers of them perish here. We saw much sign of it about the banks of the creek. Those that were caught had a whitish appearance, very different from the healthy salmon found in the Columbia river, and were not fit to eat. From all the information I can obtain, gold can be found on the headwaters of Powder river,[222] but the Indians are unwilling to risk themselves in that vicinity, as they would come in contact with hostile Indians who reside in the mountains and immediately in that neighborhood. I have no further knowledge of this fact myself than what I obtained from the guide and others who have resided among them.

[221] Durkee creek.

[222] Rises in the Blue mountains, western Baker county, Oregon. Cross struck it a few miles below Baker, Oregon. In 1861 E. D. Pierce, with twenty companions explored Malheur, Burnt, Powder, and Grande Ronde rivers in search of gold. By october of that year forty men had arrived and taken claims in the Grande Ronde valley.

SEPTEMBER 8. The morning was so smoky as to prevent us from seeing much of the country through which we were to travel today. The road after leaving Powder river valley turned again among the hills, which were interspersed [with] small groves of hemlock. The view which we had of the Blue mountains was very beautiful. We were soon to reach them and again have the pleasure of entering a thick, dense forest, the beauty of which we had so long been deprived.

We traveled until about two p.m. over an uneven country, then descended a mountain for a mile and a half, which brought us to the Grande Ronde.[223] [This is] a beautiful valley, or more properly a basin, for it is entirely surrounded by the Blue mountains on the north and northwest and spurs of the mountains to the east, one of which we had traveled over during the day. At the base of the mountain we crossed a small brook which came from the deep gorge to our left. After running along at the base of the one we had just ascended it passes through the Grande Ronde valley and falls into the Grande Ronde river, which is a delightful, cold stream that comes immediately from among the mountains. We continued our march through the valley until we reached a small stream near the head of the valley where the road ascends. Here we stopped for the day, intending to remain a day or two, before attempting to cross the Blue mountains.

This valley is a fine, dark soil, very level. Water issues from the base of the mountains which completely surround it [and] it may be easily irrigated. [It] is, for a settlement, the prettiest place I have passed on the route. The range among the hills and in the valley is very fine for grazing, while it is well protected by the

223 A valley in northeastern Oregon formed by the Blue and Wallowa mountains and drained by the Grande Ronde river.

mountains against the northern winds in winter. The
thick wood would give shelter to cattle and all other
stock, while the valley and mountains would supply
them abundantly with grass to subsist on during the
winter. The only objection, therefore, which can be
made to this section of the country is the great difficulty
in getting produce to the Columbia river. This could
be easily remedied, and the day is not far distant, no
doubt, when a railroad will overcome these objec-
tions.[224] The distance between here and the Dalles is
about two hundred five miles, as the road now runs,
passing through the Umatilla valley,[225] which would
avoid the high hills and present not the least obstruction. There is timber enough to be found here and at
the Dalles to build a railroad to the Atlantic ocean.

SEPTEMBER 9. The morning was much clearer than
when we entered the valley. It gave us a fine view of
the range of mountains to the north and west, as well
as the extent of this beautiful valley, which surpassed
any we had seen on the march.

A number of Indians came to our camp last evening
and this morning, bringing some of their most INFERIOR
HORSES with them to exchange for blankets, tobacco,
and trinkets.[226] These animals were very wild and
equally vicious, [and] they could scarcely be approached without our running the risk of being bitten
or kicked by them. They are generally ridden with a
lariat fastened simply round the lower jaw, while a
small pad with wooden stirrups constitutes the saddle.

[224] The Union Pacific railroad reached Huntington, Oregon, november 25,
1884, where it joined the Oregon Railway and Navigation company's line
from the west.

[225] Although Cross consistently spelled this "Eumatilla" the editor has
changed it to conform with modern usage.

[226] Colonel Loring formed a favorable opinion of these horses. Loring to
Freeman, october 15, 1849.

The Indians never mount their horses on the left side. The bridle is of but little use to them in guiding, as it is principally done by pressing the legs close to the side of the animal. The least touch of the bridle is sufficient to guide in any direction.

Having been directed to proceed to the Dalles to make necessary arrangements for transporting the troops by water to Fort Vancouver on their arrival, I hired a guide and also several horses, which would enable me to travel the distance without any delay, and made every arrangement for an early start in the morning.

March from the Grande Ronde
to the Dalles

SEPTEMBER 10 [1849]. Having made all necessary preparations [227] last evening, I started this morning at half-past six o'clock in company with Lieutenant Lindsay and two soldiers as an escort. The road lay up the valley for three miles, [then] we commenced to ascend a very long, steep mountain. After considerable work we got to the top of the ridge and five miles farther descended to its base, which was as difficult as the ascent. This brought us to a beautiful mountain stream called the "Grande Ronde" river, that passes between the ridge which we had just come over and those on the other side, which we were about to travel over. This stream runs into the Grande Ronde valley and being met by other small brooks gives an abundance of water to it.

Our route lay along the side of the mountain. After riding about two hours [it] brought us to the top of what seemed to be a wide ridge. The whole distance traveled until we crossed the mountains was over slightly rolling ground, except for ascents, which were made by small valleys or ravines in the mountains.

Our horses were put into a canter, in the true California style of riding, and kept so until the close of the afternoon, when we again came to clear ground on the opposite side of the mountain. After traveling along on the ridge and winding for some time down its side,

227 Cross committed the responsibility of representing him and bringing the trains safely through to James B. Leech. Cross to Leech, september 9, 1849.

which is entirely destitute of timber, we reached the Umatilla river. [It] has its rise in the Blue mountains and flows into the Columbia river ninety miles from the Dalles.

The soil of the mountains is of dark vegetable mould and thickly covered with timber, consisting of hemlock and fir which is hardly surpassed by any in the United States. The timber is not generally as large as that on the banks of the Willamette, but equally as tall and abundant. While on the mountains we came to water several times during the afternoon's ride. Although we had to encamp twice [while] crossing [them we] found enough to answer our purpose.

The distance traveled today was nearly fifty miles, and we were all tired enough to make our encampment for the night, which was easily done since we had nothing but our blankets. We all lay down by a fire under a wide-spreading cottonwood tree on the bank of the river for the night, after each man had cooked his own dinner and supper in true mountain style. It is merely necessary to remark here that for better than four months our dinner and supper were generally served up at the same hour. It depended generally upon the time of encamping and the means of cooking it whether we were fortunate not to go without either. [Upon] entering the Umatilla valley I was struck with the fine range for stock which presented itself to my view, as the country though high and rolling is not broken. It is covered from the base to the top of every hill with fine bunch grass, which is so much sought after by stock in this valley.

SEPTEMBER 11. Last night was very cold and the morning calm and very smoky. Our horses had strayed off, which prevented us from starting before seven o'clock. We [then] passed along the Umatilla valley

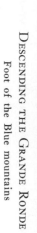

DESCENDING THE GRANDE RONDE
Foot of the Blue mountains

DESCENT AFTER LEAVING THE BLUE MOUNTAINS

until near the close of the day, crossing and recrossing
it several times in our ride. At nine o'clock in the morning we came to where the Cayuse Indians were located.
Their town, which is temporary, consisted of a number
of lodges made of mats and bushes, much larger than
those made of buffalo skins. As they expected us they
were all on the *qui vive*. Some were out to meet us,
while others gratified their curiosity by gazing at us.
Old women and children were to be seen in numbers,
but the smaller boys were out attending to the droves of
horses which belong to the band.

I have seldom seen a more beautiful sight than I
witnessed in examining these large droves of horses that
could be seen throughout the valley and among the
hills. They are stout, well built, and very muscular, but
not tall, and look to me as [if] formed for great durabil-
ity and strength. Having remained with the Indians
a short time, I again continued my journey until twelve
o'clock, when we came to a burial-ground near the road
and not far from the banks of the Umatilla.[228] Here the
dead were deposited of those who had been killed by
the Oregonians in the campaign against them after the
death of Doctor Whitman. The ground was nicely
staked in and at the head of the graves a long pole was
planted, probably to designate the person who was interred. There were several places of the same kind, I
observed, all of which were very handsomely fenced in
so as to protect them from the wolves and keep the remains of their friends secure from being harmed or
molested. I saw for the first time since leaving Fort
Leavenworth signs of agriculture. These people had
been taught by the first missionaries established among

---

[228] A battle between the Oregon troops under Cornelius Gilliam and about
three hundred Cayuse Indians was fought in this neighborhood february 24,
1848, in which eight of the latter, including chief Gray Eagle and a medicine
man were killed. This was probably their burial place.

them the use of implements for husbandry, and had begun to cultivate the soil.[229] The remains of the old fences
enclosing fields that had been cultivated bore ample
proof of their progress toward civilization. The death
of Doctor Whitman and the chastisement received from
the whites for it put an end to tilling the soil and they
have done but little [of it] since. We stopped about
noon for a short time, having come near[ly] forty
miles, and then continued our journey, leaving the
Umatilla and striking the Columbia river as the sun
was setting. The last fifteen miles of our road was over
a barren, sandy plain, giving a view of the country for
miles beyond the Columbia, both up and down the
river. [It is] even more barren than that of Snake river.
There the wild sage could be seen in a flourishing condition. Here the ground seemed too sandy to produce it,
although it was still to be seen.

There is some good land on the Umatilla river but
generally it is too sandy. The river is narrow, and at this
time the water lay in holes where we crossed it for the
last time but a short distance from where it empties into
the Columbia river. Its bed and banks give ample sign
of volcanic action. Some time before arriving at the
Columbia river I saw at a distance a deep canyon
through which it passed, but could not well distinguish
it until I nearly reached its banks. I was at first somewhat disappointed in its appearance, expecting to see
something more magnificent. The river is about six
hundred yards wide where we struck it, and the banks

229 In 1836 Marcus Whitman established a mission among the Cayuse Indians at Waiilatpu, twenty-five miles east of Fort Walla Walla. He and his
helpers not only preached to them but also taught them agriculture and animal husbandry. At the outbreak of the Cayuse war, following the murder of
Whitman and members of his household november 29, 1847, Taitu and Five
Crows, with their bands of followers, were living on the south bank of the
Umatilla where they had been located for a number of years. Here they had
made some crude and partially successful attempts at farming.

are not more than six feet high, with a gentle, sandy slope to the water's edge. [It] quietly rolled along with but very little current. The whole country presented a scene of barrenness seldom met with, for not a tree was to be seen far or near. It was a delightful evening, quite calm and warm, though a little smoky. [This] prevented us from viewing still further the sterility of a country where so much has been said in its praise and against it. Our horses were hobbled and turned out to graze on what little grass could be found among the willows, which were growing in detached places where we encamped for the night. We had traveled today at least sixty miles. As the day was warm and we were not accustomed to such violent exercise, [we] were very much fatigued.

The day's ride had brought me to the banks of the Columbia river, four months and eleven days after leaving Washington city. We had gone through much fatigue and many perplexities, had escaped the cholera and surmounted many difficulties, and when we reflected that we had at last reached the Columbia river, though not at the end of our journey, it filled each one's breast with feelings which cannot be easily described. We now began to think that by a little more perseverance our journey would soon be brought to an end. The fatigue endured would only render the trip more interesting when we look back on it hereafter, [and] it would be a source of pleasure to reflect on the hardships endured and what we had encountered during a period of five months.

SEPTEMBER 12. We set out early this morning, as it bid fair to be a pleasant day. The air was sharp and keen, [and] the slight breeze made us feel it the more sensibly. Our trail lay along the banks of the river, and we had not traveled far before we passed on the right bank some thirty lodges of the Walla Walla tribe who had come down to fish. Their lodges in small numbers could be seen during the day. We continued along the bank until twelve o'clock, when we stopped on Rivière de Canal [230] to graze and rest our horses, having come twenty-five miles. Here the road leaves the river and strikes it twelve miles below. From thence we continued along the bank of the river until near sundown, when we again encamped on its banks, or rather between perpendicular cliffs and the water's edge. The plate here annexed is a scene on the Columbia river where we descended to [it] after traveling twelve miles. [This] fully explains the formation of the columnar basalt which you meet with from this point along the banks of the river to its mouth. [Sometimes] it is higher [than this]. They are frequently found standing alone, and some of the pieces of rock, of an octagonal form, are from eight to ten feet long, piled one on the other for hundreds of feet high. It forms the [bank] of the river in places from five hundred to one thousand feet high. In other places [it is] much like that on Snake river. Having [planned to] remain here for the night, our horses were again let loose to graze on what could be found. The scarcity of grass justifies me in saying that none but a Rocky mountain horse could have stood such rides on so little food.

SEPTEMBER 13. The day was calm, and the whole country seemed to be shut out from view. Last evening and this morning you could not see across the river at some of the bends. The rapids at our encampment looked very beautiful,[231] and the water ran in other parts of the river with a very rapid current. From here to the

---

[230] This stream was in the neighborhood of Willow creek, but has not been identified.

[231] Possibly Rock creek rapids.

Dalles, about twenty miles, we passed rapids constantly. Our ride this morning soon brought us to John Day's river,[232] a small stream about thirty yards wide where we crossed it at its junction with the Columbia river. The road passed over the plain and among the hills about this river. [These hills] are extremely rugged and high, giving [one] great trouble to get over them. Our path still remained on the banks of the river. [It] was only an Indian trail, [but it] was nearer and still more convenient for water. At twelve o'clock we arrived at Shute's [Deschutes] river,[233] or more properly Fall river. It contracts here and forms a very pretty fall before it reaches the Columbia, which is not more than two hundred yards from it. This stream is probably one hundred yards wide and is very difficult to cross when the water is high. When this is the case the animals have to be swum across to an island below the falls and the loads and wagons taken over in canoes, which [are] entirely managed by Indians. The country between here and the Dalles becomes very hilly and not very unlike that crossed on Burntwood creek [Burnt river]. [It is not unlike] the gorges which take you to the river at the foot of the Dalles, or Old Mission, established several years since by the Methodist missionaries.[234] We remained a short time at this place and renewed our journey to the Dalles. The road from here leads up a long hill, and after passing along the bluffs at least two miles turns to the left. Then passing over

---

232 Called "LePage" by Lewis and Clark in honor of a member of their party. Renamed for John Day of the Wilson Price Hunt party, 1811-1812.

233 Called "Towahnahiooks" by Meriwether Lewis, "Kimmooenim" by Gass, and "la Rivière des Chutes" by French voyageurs.

234 About the middle of march, 1838, Daniel Lee and H. W. K. Perkins left the parent mission on the Willamette, traveled by canoe to the Dalles, where they chose the site for a new mission. It was known both as the Dalles and Wascopam mission.

the ridge it strikes a small stream at its base. This unites with another called the Walla Walla fork,[235] which empties into the Columbia river at the Dalles. This stream waters a very fine valley about halfway to the Old Mission. All the ravines you meet with have good water and plenty of bunch grass.

While passing down the ridge we had a fine view of the commencement of the falls before reaching the Dalles. When near them we again left the river and passed over the ridge, which brought us to where we had a fine view of what is called the Dalles of the Columbia, a series of falls that present a very imposing sight. When it is first seen it is but little more than a rapid. Here the whole river passes over a ledge of rock that extends across [it]. [This] causes an interruption in the current and makes a very small fall. After this the water is seen passing rapidly between flat table-rocks whose surfaces have been worn smooth by the friction of the water in higher stages of the river. The next seen is where the water falls into a contracted part of the river, the middle of which is interrupted by large masses of basaltic rock which are perfectly level and smooth on their surfaces. Finally, the river becomes still more contracted, and passes through a deep canyon of the same formation with a rapid current, which forms in its way large eddies and renders it, at this stage of the river, extremely difficult to get a boat above them.

From the top of this hill we had a fine view of the valley which is made by the hills receding a little and curving with the river. [It] is probably ten miles long, though in no part is it more than half a mile wide. We continued our journey to the Old Mission, where I met

---

235 Probably Fifteen-mile creek. So named because the road crossed it fifteen miles from the site of the present town of The Dalles. Eight-mile and Five-mile creeks join it before it reaches the Columbia river about four miles above the town.

Lieutenant Fry,[236] who had at that moment arrived with the boats for our transportation to the Great falls of the Columbia river,[237] forty miles below. It was about two o'clock when we arrived, and we were all greatly pleased, not only in reaching a point which really seemed to be the termination of the journey, although there was still much to do, but we had the pleasure of meeting with those who could give us some intelligence in the way of late news from the states, of which we had so long been deprived.

SEPTEMBER 14. This morning was very pleasant, but we were prevented from seeing any distance [by] the constant clouds of smoke which [so] filled the atmosphere that it was impossible to see. Yesterday evening our view did not extend a mile from the mission. The wind had been prevailing from the southwest so long that the sky was entirely overcast.

Lieutenant Fry left this morning, accompanied by Lieutenant Lindsay, for Fort Vancouver. I wrote the quartermaster [238] to send more boats if they could be obtained. [I] also wrote to Colonel Loring, giving him my views relative to the disposition to be made of the whole command.[239]

236 James Barnet Fry. Brevet-second-lieutenant Third artillery july 1, 1847; second-lieutenant First artillery august 20, 1847; first-lieutenant february 22, 1851; brevet-captain assistant adjutant general march 16, 1861; captain assistant adjutant general august 1, 1861; major assistant adjutant general april 22, 1862; lieutenant-colonel december 31, 1862; colonel provost marshal march 17, 1863; brigadier-general provost marshal april 21, 1864; colonel march 13, 1865, for gallant and meritorious service in the battles of Shiloh, Tennessee and Perryville, Kentucky; major-general march 13, 1865, for faithful and meritorious and distinguished service in the provost marshal general's department during the war; died july 11, 1894. Heitman, *Historical register,* I, 439. He left Oregon for the United States september 5, 1850. Talbot, *Journals,* 103.

237 The Cascades. Called the "Great Chute" by Lewis and Clark. Forty miles below the Dalles.

238 Captain Rufus Ingalls.

239 "My plan is this, cross such animals (as can travel to the ferry opposite

The Old Mission has gone greatly to ruin. It is composed of a dwelling-house, which we now occupied, and three more buildings, one of which, opposite the one fronting the river, had been used as a schoolhouse. These buildings would all have made good quarters for a detachment of troops (which was suggested in my letter to the colonel), who could have remained here and taken charge of the stores and public property this fall. The buildings rest on the side of the picket-work, which is made of heavy pine logs brought from the neighboring mountains, where wood for fuel and timber can be procured in great abundance. The out-buildings have all been destroyed and the whole is going to decay since the war with the Cayuse nation, at which time it was abandoned. There is a fine spring but a short distance from the house, and the whole valley, which lies between the mission and the river, is finely watered. The soil is very sandy, [and] as the valley shows signs of volcanic action I presume the soil would produce fine grain, particularly oats. It is not unlike the soil which you meet with at the base of volcanic mountains in Mexico, which yields admirably well.

The hills on the other side of the river are entirely destitute of wood. [This] begins to show itself at the bend of the river below the Old Mission. Those immediately in the rear have a little scrub oak and pine, but neither is found in great quantities as much of it

Fort Vancouver) about twelve miles below here, send wagons to transport the stores at the portage, send such portion of the command by land as can't be transported in the vessel, place on her merely the stores actually necessary for the troops at their place of destination, and while that is transported and the vessel returns, the three boats can carry down such stores as may be required this fall, leaving the balance of the stores, wagons, broken down mules, etc. under the charge of an acting assistant quartermaster until it may be deemed necessary for them to be forwarded to such place as may hereafter be designated." Cross to Hatch, september 14, 1849; also found in U.S. Senate. *Executive documents*, 30 cong., 2 sess., no. 1, pt. 2, 234.

METHODIST MISSION AT THE DALLES

From a contemporary painting by William Henry Tappan

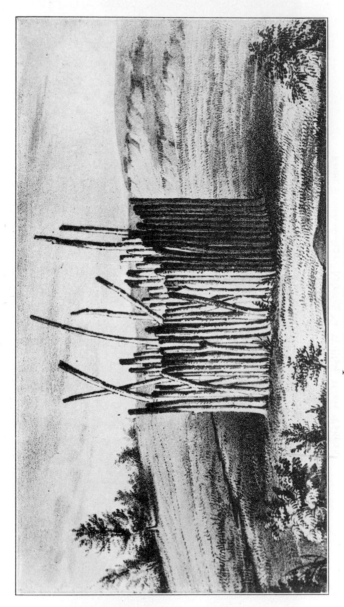

Indian Burial Ground

has been destroyed. The mountains immediately in the vicinity, however, are abundantly supplied with pine, which is accessible and can at any time be obtained for building purposes in greatest abundance. The country between here and the base of the Cascade range affords mountain bunch grass in great quantities. On the Walla Walla fork and over the whole range of country between here and Deschutes river there is fine grazing. The small valleys on the streams afford an abundance of grass for a large number of horses, cattle, or sheep. From my own personal observation I know of no place that possesses more advantages for a post than this. Troops are able to move from here at all times, in any direction, either up the river towards the headwaters of Deschutes river or even towards Puget sound, as there is fine grazing and no very great obstruction direct from Fort Walla Walla[240] by Mount St. Helens. As regards the trouble of getting supplies, this would not be attended with half the difficulty in the spring, when boats can come over the falls. The great trouble would be for mounted troops to move from [Fort] Vancouver in this direction.

SEPTEMBER 15. There was very little wind today, which made it warm in the middle of the day and very smoky. This prevented us from seeing the beauties of the surrounding scenery. When the weather is clear the view of Mount Hood[241] to the west about thirty miles, and Mount St. Helens,[242] to the north, is very

---

[240] Built by Donald McKenzie of the Northwest Fur company on the east bank of the Columbia river about half a mile above the mouth of the Walla Walla river. First called Fort Nez Percé, its name was later changed to Fort Walla Walla. With the merger of this company with Hudson's Bay company, 1821, it became the property of the latter.

[241] A peak of the Cascade range in Hood river county, Oregon. Elevation 11,225 feet. Highest point in Oregon.

[242] In Skamania county, Washington. Elevation 9671 feet. It was an active volcano in 1842 and 1854.

beautiful. The former appears quite near, compared with the latter, as you have merely a sight of the top of St. Helens, which about this time is generally covered with snow. As our journey had given us much fatigue, having [ridden] in [a] little more than three days two hundred five miles and been on the road better than five months, we made this a resting day and began to feel as if we had nearly completed our journey. At any rate, we could now take our time, as we were in striking distance of our place of destination where aid could be obtained at any moment if required.

SEPTEMBER 16. Being desirous of examining the country before the arrival of the troops to see where our horses and mules could be kept, I left this morning in company with Mr. Switzler,[243] who had come in charge of the Indians, and traveled down the river fifteen miles.[244] Here the river takes a bend and forms a valley entirely surrounded by high mountains, where there was but one place through which you could pass, giving room merely for a wagon. At this place grazing is very fine, and any number of animals could be kept there entirely secure. It was also the place where the emigrants had crossed their horses and cattle in 1845. I returned to the Old Mission about four p.m., after a fatiguing day's ride, not so much [because of] distance as from a bad horse and the effects of the three days' ride from the Grande Ronde, from which I had not recovered.

SEPTEMBER 17. The day set in cloudy, with a warm wind from the southwest. I was prevented from going to the Big falls [245] this morning because of sickness pre-

---

243 John Switzler. He went to Oregon in 1845 and settled on the south side of the Columbia river opposite Fort Vancouver, where he began the operation of a ferry the next year. The troops which marched from the Dalles on the north side of the river were ferried across the Columbia river on his boat.

244 Neighborhood of Mosier, Washington.

245 The Cascades.

vailing among the Indians who had come up with the transportation. They were afflicted with fevers [induced] by constant exposure and severe labor in ascending the river over the falls. As the mackinaw boats [246] had become leaky by the rough usage received among the rocks in ascending the river, I had them pulled out and repitched. The Indians were getting very impatient, [for] they are a restless set of people and cannot be confined long in one place.

SEPTEMBER 18. The boats were this morning again placed in the water ready for use. The weather still continued smoky, the wind from the southwest being stronger today than [at] any [time] since our arrival. It brought over thick clouds of smoke, which still kept hidden from us the beauties of the adjacent mountains. As evening came on, however, it was calm and pleasant, and the troubled waters seemed to become more quiet and glided along with their usual tranquility.

SEPTEMBER 19. This morning an Indian came from the first division, bringing a letter from the headquarters of the regiment, which was answered by the same express. The morning [was] cloudy and cool enough for a fire. Several persons arrived from Deschutes river to make necessary preparations for descending the Columbia river, if it were found more advantageous to do so than to attempt to cross the Cascade mountains.[247] Having learned from these men that the stage of the water would cause a detention of the command at the

---

246 The mackinaw was a flat-bottomed boat much used by traders on northern and northwestern waters.

247 Until the opening of the Barlow road across the Cascade range near the southern flank of Mount Hood, 1846, the Dalles marked the end of the journey for wagons. Despite the extreme difficulties incurred upon this route it became the regular road to the Willamette valley. Many emigrants, however, chose to abandon their wagons at the Dalles. Some resorted to pack trains, while others descended the Columbia river upon rafts or in boats. This latter method of travel was not without difficulties and dangers, for rapids had to be run and three laborious portages made.

river, I determined to undertake to carry one of our boats to that place, if it were possible to get it through the Dalles. With this assistance the stores could be easily ferried, but to bring across the whole command in canoes would be an endless job. Necessary instructions were given to make the attempt in the morning with one boat, and as the start was to be an early one we turned in early, to be better able to commence our journey at the proper hour.

SEPTEMBER 20. The morning was quite calm, after a very windy day yesterday. The mackinaw boat went off early this morning, much to the delight of the Indians. They were very anxious to visit the Indians above, who had assembled in large numbers to fish for salmon and to see the soldiers, who had attracted much curiosity among them. I was very anxious for the command to arrive, for we were here without one comfort or the means of securing any. I had now been from the first division nearly two weeks [and] without a tent or the means of cooking. The only thing we could really boast of was a coffee-pot and a bowie knife. As to a plate of any kind, all had been left behind and a common pine board was used as a substitute. This mode of living will do sometimes and can be endured for a time, but it was a mode of living I began to grow weary of the nearer I approached civilization. Each man had his blanket and overcoat for a bed, which on a plank floor was not the most agreeable way of lying and a poor substitute for a good soft bed made of grass. The boat was well manned, having a fine boat's crew of twelve Indians who made it glide through the water like a "thing of life."

The interpreter was taken sick with chills and fevers, and there was but little change among the Indians. [The sick] had increased to five patients, and [we had] no medicine to give them. I began to feel that my pleas-

ure [at] seeing the command would only be equaled by
the sight of our resting place of a few days since. An
emigrating party came in this morning from Deschutes
river. [They] were compelled to take their wagons
apart, but thought that in a few days the river would be
low enough to drive across. I therefore determined to
go up in the morning, where I hoped to find my boat
safely landed, which was sent yesterday to their assistance.

SEPTEMBFR 21. I left at seven o'clock this morning
for Deschutes river with the expectation of meeting
with the troops, but was informed by some emigrants
whom I met on the road that they left them yesterday,
and [that] it would take them until late this evening to
arrive [at] that place. These people were in advance of
their party, going to the Dalles, which seemed to be the
general rendezvous for such as feared to undertake at
this time the crossing of the Great Cascade range, particularly [those] with weak teams.

I learned on reaching the crossing that the troops
would not be there until the next day. I regretted that
my boat had not arrived, nor could it be got over the last
fall. The Indians labored all day to succeed, but becoming disheartened had finally abandoned all further
attempts, and were enjoying the hospitality of their
friends when I assembled them together to return to the
Old Mission through the same deep cuts among the
rocks [which] they had yesterday toiled almost in vain
to overcome.

This ride gave me a fine opportunity of again carefully examining the falls, as well as the Dalles. The
whole distance, since we struck the river on the eleventh, has been through a deep canyon of dark columns
of basaltic rock, in many places five hundred feet high.
A column of water, which in places was six hundred

yards wide, now contracted to fifty yards and passed through a small canal. From the top of the cliff, where we could pass, the rocks [seemed to] lie side by side, apparently so near [each other] that it would be but little trouble to pass entirely across the stream [on them] as if they were stepping-stones. Having carefully examined them and the great expertness of the Indians in catching salmon, I again passed over the road, which lay among the little ravines and gorges, and arrived at the Dalles just as the sun went down. [I was] soon followed by the boat, which the Indians were successful enough to bring in safety through the Dalles. My horse was not the best I had seen and went [only] as long as I applied the whip to him. After a ride of thirty miles, in which I labored much more than the animal, I reached the mission much more worsted than the horse. [I] was very glad to return him to his owner, who never troubled himself about the fleetness of his pony so long as he could reach his point of destination without much bodily labor or trouble to himself.

SEPTEMBER 22. The day was extremely pleasant, the morning was clear, and we were gratified with a view of Mount Hood, which lay in a westerly direction. It appeared quite near, although thirty miles from us. The weather had not been cold enough to cover it with snow and [had] only left but a little trace of it. Although this mountain is seen partly from the Old Mission, the prettiest view is from a ledge of rocks on the side of the valley which is between the mission and near the point where the troops embarked. The several views that are here placed in order from Deschutes river will give the river through to the bend below the Dalles. [This stretch] is probably from fifteen to twenty-five miles in length. That of the Old Mission, the valley, and the point where the troops embarked, will give a far better

The Columbia river, near the Dalles

The Columbia river, below the Dalles

idea of that country than any description I can write of it. I will here take occasion to say it is the case with all the drawings annexed, and my principal object in having the sketches taken was that the whole country should be delineated more perfectly in the description by them.

Lieutenant Lindsay arrived today, bringing one whale-boat and a ship's boat, which made an addition to our little fleet. He also brought along a fine party of Indians, all good oarsmen, who were greatly required. These Indians had been so much under the good discipline of the Hudson's Bay company that they had only to be commanded to obey promptly. The crew who had been left here were nearly all sick and but little use to us at this time. The command arrived late this evening and encamped about three miles from us. All preparations were now made for a speedy departure.[248] As I was well aware that we had much more freight than could be taken down for some time, I prepared a raft by taking a portion of the pickets from the Old Mission, which [was] sanctioned by the colonel, and having given orders to commence [building it] early in the morning it was soon completed.

SEPTEMBER 23. The morning was clear and pleasant, but indicated wind. Mount Hood was again seen today, as the atmosphere was very clear, which sometimes it is not for a week. You are better able to judge of the clearness of the atmosphere by the distinct outlines of that mountain than [by] the hills immediately around here.

[248] See Loring's account, page 340. Cross gave instructions to Lieutenant Frost concerning the transportation of supplies over the mountains. "I desire that the teams which you take with you may carry the quartermaster's stores for which I am accountable, as well as those under your own charge, placing in each wagon not more than three hundred and fifty pounds. . . I wish no INTERFERENCE IN ANY MANNER DIRECTLY OR INDIRECTLY BY ANY OFFICER WHO MAY ACCOMPANY THE TRAIN. Messrs. Leech and Kitchen will accompany you as well as William Frost." Cross to Frost, september 27, 1849.

An order was issued regulating the departure of the troops in the following manner; Brevet-major Ruff [249] was to accompany the boats with as many persons as could conveniently go, as they had become barefooted and unable to walk. The remainder were to march down by land twenty miles below, on the left bank of the river, with such horses as could well go this route, and there to cross. Then they would proceed to Fort Vancouver by land. I dispatched a wagon with one of the boats and a team with two teamsters to transport the stores at the half-mile portage.[250] The boats were to be taken over the falls by the Indians, and from the foot of what is called the Upper falls. The open boats were then to proceed to the foot of the Lower rapids, a distance of three miles, and there embark on a schooner [251] employed to transport them to Oregon City.[252] Major Ruff was to send back the boats to transport the remainder, and in the meantime improve the portage so as to admit a wagon to pass.

This evening we commenced to load, but the company stores came so slow that very little was done and it was postponed until morning. I was taken with a violent cold which partly deprived me of my voice, but it did

[249] Charles Frederick Ruff. Pennsylvania. Second-lieutenant dragoons july 1, 1838; resigned december 31, 1842; lieutenant-colonel First regiment Missouri volunteers june 18, 1846; resigned from volunteers september 17, 1846; captain Mounted Riflemen july 7, 1846; brevet-major august 1, 1847, for gallant and meritorious service in the affair at San Juan de los Llanos, Mexico; major december 30, 1856; lieutenant-colonel june 10, 1861; Third cavalry august 3, 1861; retired march 30, 1864; brigadier-general march 13, 1865 for faithful and meritorious service in the recruitment of the armies of the United States; died october 1, 1885. Heitman, *Historical Register*, I, 850.

[250] This portage was on the north side of the river. Bonneville dam now levels this portion of the stream.

[251] This vessel was the property of the Hudson's Bay company.

[252] Located at the falls of the Willamette river, Clackamas county, Oregon. Although the original destination of the regiment was Fort Vancouver, the lack of quarters there and the possibility of obtaining them in Oregon City brought about a change of plan.

not prevent me from continuing the labor of getting off the troops and loading the boats under my own special superintendence, as all were very anxious to reach the place of destination.

SEPTEMBER 24. Mount St. Helens was very plainly seen for the first time this morning to the north, though much hidden by mountains in that direction. Since my arrival the smoke has been so dense as to exclude the scenery in the immediate vicinity, but the top of this mountain, rising over the neighboring mountains, could now be plainly seen capped with snow. This view, with that of Mount Hood to the west, the mountains covered with pine around us, and the hills to the east destitute of wood, gave us a new picture, [which was] much more agreeable than the monotonous scenes so constantly presented to our view on our march. The whole landscape reminded me very often of the scenery in Mexico, [though it] was not nearly so picturesque. There is a boldness about the rugged cliffs in that country which these do not possess.

The boats were all loaded and off at half-past nine o'clock. Major Ruff and family and fifty men – also a large quantity of company and private baggage – were transported in three mackinaw boats, one yawl, four canoes, and one whale-boat. The party on foot, [the] mounted men, and eleven pack mules left at eleven o'clock to cross the river about twenty miles below at an Indian village where the guide was directed to hire Indians to cross them to the right bank of the river.[253] This made our camp look very deserted. The second division had not yet arrived, and if the march was made properly could not arrive for several days, as the broken-down condition of the animals would not possibly justify long marches.

---

[253] Near present Hood River, Oregon. The guide was W. W. Raymond.

SEPTEMBER 25. The day was calm and warm, and [there was] nothing to prevent the boats from reaching the Cascades early today. Having learned that the second division was at Deschutes river, much to my surprise, and in a very bad condition, I dispatched fifteen teams to assist them to this place. The raft was completed, and from all appearances it was thought at least four or five tons could easily be carried. The Indians were coming down constantly with their canoes to hire, but the greater portion were small and but very little calculated to carry freight, although there are canoes among them which are large enough to carry twenty persons.

SEPTEMBER 26. The day was extremely pleasant, and everything [was] favorable for the party who had embarked, as well as for those who were still left behind. Lieutenant Frost and Doctor Moses arrived today at eleven o'clock and the division late this afternoon. I learned today from Lieutenant Frost the manner in which the march of the second division had been conducted, which convinced me that the state of the train left by me at Malheur river must be deplorable. I do not hesitate to say if a different course had been taken this train could not possibly have become so disordered as it was represented. It arrived and showed that my predictions were not far from what had actually occurred. It was fortunate that preparations had been made to go from here by water. I found the whole train on its arrival [so] completely broken down [that it] could not possibly have gone any farther. I beg leave to call your attention to Lieutenant Frost's report in the appendix.[254] Mr. Raymond,[255] the guide, returned to-

254 Concerning the condition of this train Lieutenant Frost said, "although you left the train in MY charge as A A Q M, yet the commanding officer of the escort (Brevet-lieutenant-colonel J. B. Backenstos) having in the first place assumed command of THE ENTIRE TRAIN AND ALL CONNECTED WITH IT, in writ-

day, having crossed the party of men and horses without any trouble by the Indians, who are generally a very hard-working race of people when they are made acquainted with the work required to be performed.

SEPTEMBER 27. I now commenced to prepare the train to cross the Cascade mountains with such stores as could be conveniently carried. All the wagons were examined and thirty left here, together with one hundred ninety mules, which from weakness were unable to leave here before they were rested. Good grazing was to be found, and I therefore placed them in charge of our guide, who intended to remain here. With the Indians to guard them they would become sufficiently recruited to drive down by land to Fort Vancouver this fall. The wagons could be of no use below and were as well here as to have had them shipped to Fort Vancouver. Besides, this could not be done as the stage of the water did not admit of it, and even if carried to Oregon City they could not be used. The boats having all arrived, the Indians returned without the headman – a Canadian, who had entire control of them – he having been detained at the falls to act as interpreter to Major Ruff. This embarrassed me very much, and I therefore was compelled to hire one to assist me while here.

SEPTEMBER 28. Captain Van Buren's [256] company left

ten orders proceeded to give orders to the quartermaster's agents without my KNOWLEDGE OR CONSENT and enforce obedience, and in the exercise of this assumed authority ABANDONED WAGONS and property without consulting me, and without my consent, and against my remonstrance, so that I was deprived of all POWER to protect the PUBLIC PROPERTY left by you in my charge as well as that in my OWN POSSESSION." Frost to Cross, october 26, 1849.

[255] This was no doubt W. W. Raymond, who, with his wife, went to Oregon on the "Lausanne" in 1840, and occupied the Methodist mission farm on Clatsop plain.

[256] Michael E. Van Buren. Maryland. First-lieutenant Mounted Riflemen may 27, 1847; brevet-captain august 20, 1847, for gallant and meritorious service in the battles of Contreras and Churubusco, Mexico; captain october 9, 1847; died july 20, 1854, of wounds received july 11, 1854, in action against

last evening for Oregon City. Lieutenant M'Lane [257] took his departure with the broken-down horses of the command this morning which in my opinion should have been left here. Having no control over them they were driven across to Oregon City, losing nearly two-thirds while crossing the Cascade mountains.[258] The

Comanche Indians near San Diego, Texas. Heitman, *Historical register*, I, 980.

[257] George McLane. Delaware. Second-lieutenant Mounted Riflemen may 27, 1846; brevet-first-lieutenant august 20, 1847 for gallant and meritorious service in the battles of Contreras and Churubusco, Mexico; first-lieutenant october 9, 1847; captain september 13, 1847, for gallant and meritorious service in the battle of Chapultepec; captain december 30, 1856; killed october 13, 1860, in action against Navajo Indians at the southern base of Black Rock, New Mexico. Heitman, *Historical register*, I, 674. Upon arriving in Oregon he was given charge of the commissary department at Fort Vancouver. Talbot, *Journals*, 97.

[258] The destructive effects of this long march upon the animals of the regiment are disclosed in the following report. ". . . from the commencement of the march until our arrival near Fort Hall in Oregon we found ourselves enveloped in a crowd of California emigrants whose myriads of animals caused the grass to be very scarce over this portion of the route, where we had expected to find it in abundance. For the want of sufficient forage therefore our animals were very much reduced in flesh, just at the time when, departing from Fort Hall, we entered upon a barren desert country covered alone with 'artemisia,' a wild sage, and extending with little interruption for six hundred miles to the foot of the Cascade mountains.

"Notwithstanding orders dismounting the command and requiring the soldiers to lead their horses, and although every effort was made by officers and soldiers to save our animals, still they literally starved to death as we proceeded, until on arriving in Oregon City, we had the mere skeletons of only about one hundred left. These, for the want of sufficient forage, were turned out to graze during the winter, according to the general custom of the country. An unusually heavy snowstorm falling soon after upon their weak and debilitated frames and burying the grass beyond their reach, nearly completed the destruction of the few that survived the starvation and hardship of the march.

"In addition to the foregoing I have the honor to state that eight companies with about six hundred horses of the regiment of Mounted Rifles constituted the marching force as far as Fort Hall, where two companies with about one hundred fifty horses remained as a garrison and the remaining six continued on with about four hundred fifty horses. This number of animals dwindled away from day to day until upon reaching the Cascade mountains it was reduced to between two and three hundred. The road through these mountains [is] about one hundred thirty miles in length through a dense fir forest, teams having been all properly examined, the march was commenced by them this evening.

SEPTEMBER 29. Nothing of any importance was done today. The weather continued pleasant, but [there was] every appearance of heavy winds. Lieutenant Denman [259] and family were still here, also a guard of nine men and a large quantity of company and private baggage to go to the Cascades. I therefore wrote to the commanding officer to return the boats, which would enable me, with the assistance of the raft, to finish the duties at this place. This was done, and they arrived in due time.

SEPTEMBER 30. The raft was loaded today with old harness and heavy private boxes that were too large to be placed in a mackinaw boat, and all necessary arrangements made for its departure in the morning. Eight trusty men were placed on board, sufficient to manage it and relieve each other from here to the falls.

OCTOBER 1. The party designated to go with the raft left at six o'clock this morning. The day was calm, it moved off quite manageable, and I heard early next morning that it was progressing finely.

---

where not a single blade of grass could be found for four days. The consequences of this entire destitution upon the enfeebled animals can easily be imagined. The road was strewn with the dead and dying. Officers and men were obliged, and actually did, support the poor animals up the steep ascents by putting a rail behind them and pushing them forward. Notwithstanding all this zeal, however, they were only able to get about one hundred through the mountains." Frost to Jesup, november 16, 1851.

[259] Charles Lewis Denman. New York. Second-lieutenant Mounted Riflemen may 27, 1846; first-lieutenant may 15, 1847; resigned november 30, 1850. Heitman, *Historical register*, I, 367.

To Fort Vancouver by water

OCTOBER 2 [1849]. The balance of the stores were all placed in the boats [and], with the assistance of an increased number of canoes, we left the Old Mission with delight in the hope of soon arriving at the end of our journey. The day remained calm and warm until the afternoon, when a light breeze sprang up, which continued to increase as the sun went down.

The bold mountain scenery soon commenced on both sides of the river, rising gradually in some places from the water's edge. [It was] covered with pine and capped with scrub oak, [which was] only fit for fuel. Other parts of the mountains presented steep, rugged cliffs, sometimes rising perpendicularly from the water and in many places broken into rugged and steep cliffs. About thirteen miles below the Old Mission we passed several rocks standing in the river, which had once been a burying ground for the Indians. Their object, doubtless, was more to secure their dead from the prowling beasts of prey than [to] any romantic feeling on their part. There were many places for the deposit of the dead, which reminded me very much of old tombs in a dilapidated state, but on a closer examination [they] were found to be made of bark and supported by sticks and boards driven in the ground.

The main channel of the river here passes between these rocks and the projecting rocks from the shore, through which a large arch that can be seen in low water presents a singular appearance. The ravines or deep gorges run far back in the mountains and are covered with pine and oak. The scenery, altogether thus far, was very picturesque.

Seven miles from here we came to an Indian village on the right bank of the river in a small valley, where the troops under Major Tucker crossed.[260] Passing back over the mountains they followed a trail which leads to the falls and thence to Fort Vancouver. It is a small bridle-path and entirely impracticable for a wagon road. The river takes a bend here, showing high mountains on the right bank. Those on the left form something of a valley, with but little timber compared with the opposite side. I may remark here that since starting from the Dalles the timber on both sides of the river has appeared very small, with but few exceptions.

The evening was fast drawing to a close when we met Mr. Prew [261] returning with one boat for me. He had been all day making twenty-two miles. As we had a fine breeze from the northeast, which was increasing, I left the canoe and took the barge, leaving it to follow and was soon out of sight. The river began to approach the high mountain range and in many places [it] reminded me, as the moon shone upon the scenery, of the highlands of the Hudson river. I continued down the river with increased rapidity as the wind began to blow a gale from the northeast.

Proulx had given me the very unpleasant tidings that since the evening of the first nothing had been heard or seen of the raft, [when] it passed down with sail hoisted and going rapidly. [It] was then only fifteen miles from the head of the falls, [and] there appeared no disposition on their part to stop. As he would

260 Near the mouth of the Klickitat river.

261 Prou, or perhaps more properly Proulx. Two men by this latter name were in Oregon in 1849. They were Charles and François, the former being recorded as a Hudson's Bay company employee. He was probably the man to whom Cross refers.

have seen them while ascending the river I was satisfied they had violated my orders and perished on the falls. This sad information, the dim, hazy appearance of the heavens, and the roar of the Great falls as we approached them, made it anything but agreeable. In addition to this it was near ten o'clock at night, and the wind began to blow very hard as we approached the falls, which made it very dangerous.

We were now near the rapids, [where] we were struck by a squall. Before the Indians could lower the sail we found ourselves on the flat rocks. We soon became righted, and taking to our oars once more passed down the right bank of the river as if we were on the wings of the gale and rounded to between the shore and the island. Here one of the clerks and [an] agent had landed and were out on the rocks with a signal light for those coming down the river. From this point up the river the scenery is very beautiful, and the drawing of it is a fair representation of the country along the banks to its mouth.

[We] made [our] bed among the willows, each contributing his all in the way of blankets. By the assistance of the thickets and a fire which our Indians kept up, the night was passed much more comfortably than could have been anticipated. It was after ten p.m. and the night [was] much colder than any we had experienced since coming on the Columbia river. We had made forty miles today since eight o'clock and were within a quarter of a mile of the head of the portage.

OCTOBER 3. The morning began to moderate, but still the wind continued to blow from the northeast. It came down the river and had the same effect in the change of temperature as the northers have in Texas and Mexico. As the head of the portage was but a short distance from our encampment of last night, I reached it at an

DEPARTURE OF THE TROOPS FROM THE DALLES

Landing place near the Cascades

early hour this morning. The boats, which had become a little scattered in the gale of last evening, soon followed. We were all ready at an early hour this morning for a final debarkation. Each one had his story to tell in what manner he was saved from going over the falls in the fury of the gale and [some] were worse for a hat. Silk handkerchiefs were called readily into requisition by those who had been so unfortunate as to lose their hats in the bustle and confusion of the blow.

To those who knew nothing as to where the portage was to be made at that hour of the night and in the midst of the blow, which was strong enough to silence the sound of the angry waters as they whirled and boiled among the rocks with deafening sound, it was not an easy task to make themselves safe. I was glad to see them all arrive without any greater accident. About a mile from the head of the falls the river changes its direction and makes a sweep to the right, forming a bend. At the head of [this] there are three rocky islands with a few scattering fir trees, where the channel passes between them and the right bank. Here is the commencement of the strong current. The other two are opposite the first small fall. The boats all pass between the shore and island. Descending rapidly, they cross a small chute or fall, and by the dexterity of the helmsman swing into an eddy where the landing is made. [This] is the head of the portage and halfway to the foot of the falls. From this point the portage is made either in a wagon or by hand for about half a mile over a very rugged road that brings you to the foot of the Great falls and the head of what is called the Lower rapids. From thence to the foot of the Lower rapids it is about three miles, which [distance] is passed in boats with some difficulty, but in safety when [they are] managed by skillful helmsmen who know where the different points are to guide their boats.

The Cascades or Great falls of the Columbia river are not more than three-quarters of a mile in length, and there is no part where the water has a perpendicular fall. At the commencement of the rapid the rocks project from the left bank and form a reef partly under water until it nearly crosses to the upper island. This is the first ripple where the water receives an increased velocity. [It] glides swiftly down for about a quarter of a mile, when it passes a high rock and in a short distance meets with some half dozen more, where it commences to boil and foam with all its fury. The river between the island and left bank contracts considerably, and the whole column of water of the Columbia river passes down over masses of rock, forming in its way whirlpools through the whole distance which cause the water to roll up as if there were some immense pressure below. It makes a magnificent scene. The sublimity of it can hardly be described or surpassed. A continuation to the foot of the rapids will make a distance of four miles. There are several pitches, which are made by the several ledges of rock extending across the river. [These] make it dangerous, particularly when the river is low, as was the case at this time. In high water not only the lower rapids are passed in ascending, but the big falls also, and in fact all the obstructions which are not only met with here and [at] the Dalles, but [at] other places of less importance.

On arriving at the portage this morning I learned that parts of harness and pieces of boxes had been found in the eddies below the falls, which fully confirmed my fears concerning the raft. The sun had scarcely risen above the mountains when I discovered two men on the opposite side among the rocks. From their destitute condition I was satisfied they were some of the men I had sent with the raft. [When] a canoe was dispatched and returned with them I learned that those in charge of the raft had continued to descend the river during the night of the second instead of lying by, as I had directed. [This] brought them to the falls about two o'clock in the morning and much sooner than they had anticipated. Finding themselves in danger they tried to cross to the right bank, but being unsuccessful [they] were carried on to the first rapid. So great was their surprise that they were not conscious of their real danger until in the heaviest of the water, when in an instant all went down. Six men were buried within the whirlpools.[262] These two men who were saved, having but little clothing on, were better prepared to extricate themselves than the others, who had made no preparation to meet this awful catastrophe. Not coming in contact with the massive rocks [they] were carried by the heavy columns of water to the eddies below. Here they were thrown by the counter currents into shoal water among the rocks without being injured, except a little bruised.

While passing over the rapids they were kept under the water. Sometimes [they were] thrown to the top by the pressure beneath, which enabled them to breathe for a moment. [Then] they were soon drawn under again. They were much exhausted and remained until daylight among the rocks. One of them passed down the river and did not meet the other till near the close of the day, not being aware that any person but himself was saved. Thus ended the lives of six valuable men. The destruction of the raft and the stores on it were of no importance compared with the loss of the men.

---

262 The men who were drowned were James Sharkey, William McLaughlin, Bailey Vaughn, James McStaffie, Joseph Kinlock, and John Walker. Kansas City (Missouri) *journal-post,* november 28, 1915. Other deaths in the regiment since july 4 were Private John C. Scott, july 19; Private Frank Lewis, august 13; Private Herman Williams, august 19; and Private Andrew Munch, september 1. Monthly returns, Mounted Riflemen.

The boats were immediately unloaded, but Mr. Proulx, the Canadian who had charge of the Indians, deemed it too dangerous at this stage of the water to attempt to pass the boats over the falls. [He] assembled the Indians, and with about forty of them transported three mackinaw boats, one yawl, and a whale-boat half a mile over one of the most rugged roads I have ever traveled. [It] was filled with rocks and [passed] through a thick pine forest. The stores were carried in a wagon and every preparation [was] made to leave by sundown. This was performing the work [in less time] than that [usually consumed] when boats were [taken] down by water. It may never be equaled again, much less surpassed. Having no further use for the canoes, which had been employed at the Dalles to assist in transporting the stores to the falls, they were all discharged and a large mackinaw boat substituted. This was too large to bring over the falls when the first were brought to the Dalles.

The banks of the river about here are extremely rocky, [while] the mountains are high and steep and thickly covered from their base to the top with pine, fir, and hemlock. The timber on the right bank of the river is much better than that on the left, as the mountains are not so high and the land more rolling. Much of the timber has been destroyed by fire along this part of the river, as it [has been] through [to] the Pacific.

OCTOBER 4. At sunrise the loading was renewed and finished by half-past eight p.m. Then the boats were taken by Mr. Proulx to the foot of the rapids. The detachment under Captain Claiborne [263] was marched

---

263 Thomas Claiborne. Tennessee. Second-lieutenant Mounted Riflemen may 27, 1846; first-lieutenant february 16, 1847; brevet-captain october 9, 1847 for gallant and meritorious service in the battle of Huamantla, Mexico; captain august 30, 1853; resigned may 14, 1861; colonel in Confederate army 1861-1865. Heitman, *Historical register*, I, 302.

down, while Lieutenant Denman and his family walked
to the foot of the rapids as they were at that time considered too dangerous to venture a boat. It was thought
better to let the stores go [in boats] and the men could
walk.

I had heard much of the petrified forest [264] and went
in search of it, but found nothing of any importance.
The small pieces of petrified wood which I found were
of an inferior quality, but the specimen which I procured and brought with me is probably six inches in diameter. I was, however, much gratified and well paid
by the walk, as I was enabled to examine a burial
ground of the Dalles Indians which was on the high
banks of the Columbia river in sight of the rapids and
[in] one of the most secluded and romantic spots nature
could have formed. It was in a large, dense grove of
hemlock and fir trees whose limbs spread a shade over
the whole spot. [These] almost excluded the light of
heaven which seemed, in defiance of the foliage, to shed
its rays now and then upon the tombs of the dead.

There were several repositories, rudely made of
boards placed upright and covered with others and the
bark of trees. Many had crumbled away by the effects
of dampness and the hand of time. [Owing to] their dilapidated state heaps of bones of all sizes and ages were
lying about, and I may add with all propriety, all
shapes as far as the head was considered.[265] These people have a singular fancy, peculiar to themselves, of
flattening the forehead to correspond with a line to the
crown of the head. The back of the head is made per-

---

264 A short distance below Bonneville, Oregon. First seen by Lewis and
Clark october 30, 1805. They attributed the phenomena of trees standing in
the water to a slide, which they thought had occurred some twenty years previously. While grading for a railroad along here in the middle 1880's innu-
merable buried logs in various stages of petrification were found.

265 These were the skulls of Salish or Flathead Indians.

fectly flat. Many of these skulls had been removed and scattered through the woods by persons, whose curiosity being satisfied, had dropped them where the wagon wheels had pounded them into dust. Towards the lower part of the rapids there is quite a clearing at what was once an Indian encampment. Here the timber is very fine and easy of access.

Having all arrived, we soon got under way, each boat unfurling what little sail the Indians could raise. They are never backward in spreading their blankets whenever a fair wind offers, which sometimes does not occur for weeks. The wind was fair and as we strung out we produced quite a fleet, the whole number of [craft] being five mackinaw boats, one barge, and one whale-boat.

The scenery continued to present a bold appearance until we descended about halfway to [Fort] Vancouver, at a point called Cape Horn.[266] From this part of the river the mountains begin to fall off gradually until a flat country is seen on the left bank. The banks and islands were studded with sycamore, while the hills on the right were covered with pine. Ten miles below Cape Horn the islands are large, and being filled with sycamore [they] resemble very much [those of] the Mississippi valley. About six miles above Fort Vancouver we passed a saw- and flour-mill [267] which is the property of the Hudson's Bay company.

From here the mountains recede until the country on the left bank becomes quite low. [Here is] a beautiful country for agricultural purposes, [lying] between [Fort] Vancouver and Oregon City, which is twenty miles from the fort. The whole of the boats arrived at Fort Vancouver at five o'clock in the [afternoon], hav-

266 A palisade of basalt on the north bank of the river in Skamania county, Oregon. It was about two hundred feet high.

267 Near the site of Camas, Washington.

ing run forty-five miles [today]. They accomplished the distance from the Dalles in three days, [it] being ninety miles, and were detained one day at the falls. Here we met that portion of the command which had left several days before us.[268] Some of the parties had only arrived one day before, having been detained by heavy head-winds.

OCTOBER 5. The fogs and smoke had become so thick that it was with great difficulty that we could cross the river. The schooner was necessarily detained here. The troops, as soon as they could get over, took up the line of march to Oregon City, where they were glad to reach so as to say they had arrived at the long-looked-for place of rest.[269] Oregon [City] is not a very prepossessing place in its appearance, for like all new places in the western country the stumps and half-burnt trees lie about in every direction. It is immediately at the Willamette falls, hemmed in by the river in front and a ledge of rocks immediately in the rear. To get from Fort Vancouver to Oregon City, which is the capital of the territory, one [must] be a good woodsman, as there is nothing but a crooked bridle-path through as dense a forest as can be found in any country. In going to and coming from Oregon City Captain Ingalls [270] and my-

---

[268] This was Major Tucker's command which arrived at Fort Vancouver september 30.

[269] The regiment arrived at Oregon City october 9 and took up quarters in six rented houses. These provided quarters for officers and men, offices, a hospital, and storehouses. In addition stables and mule lots were secured. The total amount paid for these accommodations was $611.66 2/3 per month. Complaints were immediately made that the buildings were not satisfactory, either as to quantity or quality. Cross, who was responsible for locating the troops, advised the breaking down of partitions where possible, the assignment of two officers to a room, and the securing of additional quarters if necessary. Cross to Hatch, october 11, 1849; U.S. Senate, *Executive documents*, 31 cong., 2 sess., pt. 2, 287.

[270] Rufus Ingalls. Maine. Brevet-second-lieutenant july 1, 1843; second-lieutenant First dragoons march 17, 1845; brevet-first-lieutenant february 4, 1847, for gallant and meritorious service in the conflicts of Embudo and Taos,

self [got] lost repeatedly, and that too within a mile of
the city.

Fort Vancouver, which is the headquarters of the
Hudson's Bay company, is on the right bank of the
river. It is situated on a beautiful plain about five miles
long and probably three-quarters of a mile wide. The
country gradually rises and runs back for ten or fifteen
miles, passing through several plains, some of which are
cultivated. On one of these plains there is an excellent
seminary where the children from the fort and neighborhood are educated.[271] Immediately in the rear of the
fort and on the rising ground, the company of artillery
under Brevet-major Hatheway [272] have put up tempo-

New Mexico; first-lieutenant february 16, 1847; captain october 22, 1854,
which he vacated the same date; captain assistant quartermaster january 12,
1848; major quartermaster january 12, 1862; lieutenant-colonel assistant
aide-de-camp september 28, 1863; brigadier-general volunteers may 23, 1863;
honorably mustered out of volunteer service september 1, 1866; major-general march 13, 1865; lieutenant-colonel deputy quartermaster general july 28,
1866; colonel assistant quartermaster general july 29, 1866; brigadier-general
quartermaster general february 23, 1882; retired july 1, 1883; died january
15, 1893. Heitman, *Historical register,* I, 562.

271 This school, which was a short distance north of the fort, was conducted
by Mrs. Richard Covington, who arrived in Oregon from London a short
time before 1849.

272 John Samuel Hatheway. New York. Brevet-second-lieutenant of artillery july 1, 1832; second-lieutenant august 31, 1836; first-lieutenant july 7,
1838; captain march 3, 1847; brevet-major may 20, 1847, for gallant conduct
in the battles of Contreras and Churubusco, Mexico; died march 31, 1853.
Heitman, *Historical register,* I, 511. On may 25, 1849, Captain Rufus Ingalls
arrived at Fort Vancouver and found Major Hatheway's command living
in tents. On june 12, he commenced the erection of buildings for them. Soldiers
on extra duty with extra pay, were set to work cutting logs and rafting them
down the Columbia river to the Hudson's Bay company's saw-mill. This work
was not very successful, due to dissatisfaction and desertions among the men.
On october 17, Captain Ingalls reported that he had erected one building
90 by 25 feet, containing twelve rooms, for the use of officers and men; another 24 by 12 feet, for officers' kitchen and servant's room; two, 40 by 20
feet each containing two rooms, to be occupied as company messroom and
kitchen, hospital and bakehouse, and two large, two-story buildings 50 by 40
feet each, to be used as quarters for the troops. About sixty thousand feet
of lumber, costing thirty-six hundred dollars were consumed in this work.
In addition, about ten other buildings for the use of quartermaster's and

rary quarters and have made themselves very comfortable. This place would be a fine location for troops. Indeed it is the only spot between here and the mouth of the river where the mountains will admit of it. As to Astoria, its location is on the side of a mountain and about seventeen miles from Cape Disappointment. [It] has eleven houses, or huts, but there are not more than two or three that are fit to live in. There is no regularity in the place, no streets, and the hemlock and fir grow within three steps of their doors. The site of Fort Vancouver and that of the Dalles are the only two points where a proper location might be made for a post.

There is not one feature in the country east of the Blue mountains to recommend it. The plains which we passed over for days and weeks through dust and heat, and sometimes thirst, are enough to appall the stoutest hearts. With the exception of the country about the Grande Ronde and Blue mountains, which is covered with verdure, tall fir, and spruce pine of the finest description, the eye never sees a tree and seldom a mountain, except in the distance. The Blue mountains have their charms, for they dispel the unvaried sight so long looked upon and present to view something that gives new life and vigor to all who pass them. I cannot say that of the country which you pass after crossing that range of mountains to the Columbia river. The soil is of a light clay, in many places very sandy, particularly on the Columbia river. For eighty miles down it and up to Fort Walla Walla, [it] is entirely barren and sterile, as much so as is found on the borders of Snake river. From the point where you strike the Columbia river to the Dalles, and particularly about John Day's river, it is extremely broken and uneven. The sufferings of the

commissary's departments and stables were rented at the cost of $218 per month. U.S. Senate. *Executive documents*, 31 cong., 2 sess., no. 1, pt. 2, 184-89.

animals along here were greater and many more were lost than on any other portion of the route.

The route is destitute of timber. This side of Fort Laramie pine in small quantities is found in the distant mountains. In the vicinity of Deer creek, and up to the Mormon ferry, cedar and pine can be obtained from the mountains in great abundance. At Soda springs we find it equally as plentiful, but from there to the Blue mountains it is not to be met with. These mountains are thickly covered with as fine fir and spruce pine as you will meet with from the Dalles to the Pacific ocean. At these points, however, timber could be procured, but at considerable expense, to erect a railroad from the Missouri to the mouth of the Columbia river whenever it may become practicable. I look upon it as the best natural highway on the North American continent. The worst place to encounter is the Cascade mountains, not from their height, but because travelers arrive late in the season when their animals are exhausted. At any other time they could pass without difficulty.

From the North Platte to the Dalles the trail passes over a sterile waste, which can scarcely ever be inhabited unless there are more facilities for getting to and along the route than exist at present, or will [exist] probably for many years. Bear river valley is the best, except that portion in the vicinity of Fort Hall, which is extremely limited. The climate is severe, snow generally falls very deep, and ice is found in the summer. I made inquiries relative to the cultivation of the soil at Forts Hall and Boise and learned that it would be attended with much difficulty, great uncertainty, and no profit.

The country on the Columbia river has, I think, been much exaggerated, and that portion of it from the Dalles to the Pacific ocean does not come up to my expectations. The mountains approach the river so near

that it leaves neither valleys nor plains of any importance, except in the vicinity of Fort Vancouver. The
country between this point and Oregon City is of a
light, rich soil, rolling enough to make it fine for cultivation, and is covered with timber of the largest kind
which extends from the Columbia to the Willamette.
The land from the base of the Cascade mountains to the
junction of the two rivers will bear comparison with
any in the states. Grain is raised in this country in great
abundance, consisting of oats, barley, and wheat. Corn
cannot be raised. The wheat on the Klamath river near
the seacoast is, I think, of an inferior quality, as the
sample I procured will show. Vegetables of the finest
kind grow without the least trouble on the Columbia,
although the season during the summer is extremely
dry. From the nature of the soil there is much transpiration water which keeps the ground moist [so that it]
only dries as the river gradually falls.

On arriving at Fort Vancouver and finding the senior
quartermaster of the Pacific station [273] there, I gave no
instructions nor made any changes in the territory relative to the department, except so far as related to the
want of the command to which I belonged. During this
march I have studied the interests of the department,
but separated as the command was, in three divisions,
you can readily see under what disadvantages I was
compelled to labor. Besides, the condition of the train
when it left Fort Leavenworth was not such as should
have been furnished a command destined to cross the
Rocky mountains. Your attention is particularly called
to the report of Lieutenant Frost in the appendix.

My duties had now nearly come to a close, and from
this time to the eleventh of november I was employed in
paying off the teamsters and collecting money. This I

[273] Major D. H. Vinton. Headquarters for the quartermaster's department
of the Pacific division were at Benicia, California. Oregon comprised the
Eleventh military district, with temporary headquarters at Fort Vancouver.

was enabled to do through the kindness of Mr. P. S. Ogden,[274] chief factor of the Hudson's Bay company, who advanced money enough at par to finish my duties, besides turning over to Captain Ingalls a few thousand dollars for the use of the department. The kindness of Mr. Ogden, in many instances, in accommodating the officers of the department places it under many obligations to him.[275]

I do not know that I can make any better suggestions relative to the establishment of posts than have already been made by those more competent than myself.[276] The route has already been occupied by troops at Fort Laramie and Fort Hall. The latter, I have already remarked, is entirely too far to be properly supplied from Fort Leavenworth or Fort Vancouver and probably one at the Dalles will answer every purpose. It has also been thought that one at the head of the Willamette valley would be proper, as the Indians in that direction are very hostile and troublesome to travelers going to and from California.[277] As to Puget sound, I have no great information, but from the number of Indians in that vicinity I should think it the proper place for the principal depot and for a large garrison. Besides, navigation from the Pacific through the sound, which is about one

[274] Chief factor of the Hudson's Bay company at Fort Vancouver. He was a son of Chief-justice Ogden of Quebec. In 1811 he joined the Northwest Fur company and upon Dr. John McLoughlin's resignation, 1846, succeeded him. He died at Oregon City in 1854.

[275] "Through his aid and counsel Indian labor has, in a measure been made available for many of our purposes. Horses, sailboats, batteaus, etc., have been freely placed at our disposal at a moderate compensation, when, not infrequently, it has inconvenienced the company to do so." Report of Major D. H. Vinton, in U.S. Senate. *Executive documents,* 31 cong., 2 sess., no. 1, pt. 2, 262.

[276] Posts were established near Fort Vancouver, at the Dalles, Astoria, and at Nisqually on Puget sound. Loring to Jones, january 8, 1850. The latter post was called Fort Steilacoom.

[277] Fort Lane was established in the Rogue river valley, 1853, by Major G. W. Warren for this purpose.

hundred fifty miles [long], is entirely free and uninterrupted. I see no reason why a route cannot be established between Nisqually [278] and Fort Walla Walla. Troops could move during the year through this part of the country and even as far as Fort Boise, which would supercede the necessity of keeping up Fort Hall, unless it can be supplied from the Mormon settlement. It is scarcely necessary for me to say that mounted troops are indispensably necessary for these remote posts, for this has long since been known to the department.

My duty having ended, I left Fort Vancouver on the eleventh of november, and owing to the great fogs which prevail during the fall and winter on the river did not arrive at its mouth until the close of the month, which prevented me from reaching San Francisco in time for the steamer of the first of december. I left that place on the first of january, passing Monterey, San Diego, Santa Barbara, Mazatlan, Acapulco, and Chagres, by way of Panama and the isthmus, touching Kingston, and arrived at New York on the eighth of february, having traveled over two thousand miles by land and five thousand by water between the tenth day of may 1849 and the eighth day of february 1850.

I have been much in the field with the troops for the last six years. The labor, as well as the anxiety of mind which I have experienced while on this march have been enough to wear down the stoutest frame. The information which I have obtained is herewith laid before the department.

It affords me pleasure to speak of the assistance given to me by Lieutenant Frost, whom I found indefatigable in the performance of his duty as acting assistant quar-

---

[278] Fort Nisqually was founded at the southern extremity of Puget sound in 1833 by Archibald McDonald as a fur-trading post for the Hudson's Bay company.

termaster. He had charge of the regimental train and conducted it across the Cascade mountains. The loss which was sustained on the march was wholly unavoidable and can only be attributed to the weakness of the animals for the want of grass. The several wagons which we left on the Cascade mountains will be brought on during the fall, [or else] next spring. I also received great assistance from Messrs. Leech, Bishop, and William Frost.[279] The latter was attached to the regimental train. These agents used every exertion for the preservation of public property throughout the march.

In making out this report I have endeavored to condense it as much as possible – so much so that I have not given that description of the country which may probably be expected, but I hope that while the drawings will partly make up the deficiency, the few remarks I have made without any comment will give the department some idea of what we passed over and met with on the march to Oregon City. And if it will give the least satisfaction to you, as chief of the quartermaster's department, I shall feel myself rewarded for the no little trouble I have taken to arrange this journal for your inspection.

All of which is respectfully submitted for your consideration.

Respectfully, sir, your obedient servant,

OSBORNE CROSS

Major and quartermaster.

To Major-general Thomas S. Jesup
Quartermaster general U.S. army
Washington City, D.C.

---

279 William Frost was wagonmaster for the regimental train. Z. C. Bishop was general superintendent of divisions and trains. James B. Leech was agent and wagonmaster for the first division, G. M. DeL. Porter for the second, and George W. Earhart for the third. Other wagonmasters were James Krutchfield and Edward Gaines. Under them were twelve assistant wagonmasters. Bennett to editor, january 27, 1939.

The Diary of George Gibbs

March from Fort Leavenworth to Fort Kearny

We reached Fort Leavenworth the eighth of may 1849 and found that the regiment had encamped in a position about five miles off, called Camp Sumner. Riding out we were most kindly received by Colonel [William Wing] Loring and the officers, and passed our first night in camp. The next day was spent in the purchase of mules and saddle horses and in stowing the wagons. Orders had been given for the march of the regiment on the tenth, and we had little enough time for preparation.

The regiment is thus disposed; the main body consisting of five companies, which are to be hereafter joined by a sixth, all under command of Brevet-colonel Loring, is to march to Oregon, there to be posted in garrison at such points as may be deemed most advisable, Fort Hall being, it is understood, one of them. The companies are A, [Captain Michael E.] Van Buren; D, [Captain Llewellyn] Jones;[280] F, [Brevet-lieutenant-colonel Andrew] Porter; H, Brevet-lieutenant-colonel [Jacob B.] Backenstos;[281] K, [Brevet-major Stephen S.] Tucker. Company I, [Brevet-major Charles F.] Ruff, is to join the regiment at Fort Kearny. Brevet-major [John S.] Simonson [282] with company B, [Cap-

---

[280] Llewellyn Jones. New York. First-lieutenant Mounted Riflemen may 27, 1846; captain december 31, 1847; major september 28, 1861; colonel march 13, 1865 for meritorious service; died july 17, 1873. Heitman, *Historical register*, I, 581.

[281] Jacob Benjamin Backenstos. Pennsylvania. Illinois. Captain Mounted Riflemen may 27, 1846; brevet-major august 20, 1847, for gallant and meritorious service in the battle of Chapultepec, Mexico; resigned june 30, 1851; died september 25, 1857. Heitman, *Historical register*, I, 179.

[282] John Smith Simonson. Pennsylvania. Indiana. Sergeant, Captain Knapp's

tain Noah] Newton,[283] to which on reaching Fort
Kearny his own company G is to be added, is to proceed
to Bear river, where he is to be stationed. Brevet-lieutenant-colonel [Winslow F.] Sanderson [284] with company E, [Captain Thomas] Duncan,[285] and company C,
[Brevet-lieutenant-colonel Benjamin S.] Roberts,[286] is
ordered to Fort Laramie.

Field and staff officers are Major [George B.] Crittenden, Captain [J. P.] Hatch,[287] adjutant, and Lieu-

company (Dobbin's regiment) New York volunteers may 1 to november 8,
1814; captain Mounted Riflemen may 27, 1846; brevet-major september 13,
1847, for gallant and meritorious conduct in the battle of Chapultepec,
Mexico; major september 16, 1847; colonel may 13, 1861; retired september
28, 1861; brigadier-general march 13, 1865, for long and meritorious service
in the army; died december 5, 1881. *Ibid.*, I, 888.

283 Noah Newton. Connecticut. Ohio. First-lieutenant Mounted Riflemen
may 27, 1846; captain january 8, 1848; died august 30, 1853. *Ibid.*, I, 746.

284 Winslow F. Sanderson. New York. Ohio. Captain Mounted Riflemen
may 27, 1846; brevet-major august 20, 1847, for gallant and meritorious
conduct in the battles of Contreras and Churubusco, Mexico; major january
8, 1848; died september 16, 1853. *Ibid.*, I, 859.

285 Thomas Duncan. Illinois. First-lieutenant Mounted Riflemen may 27,
1846; captain march 15, 1848; major june 10, 1861; brevet-lieutenant-colonel
april 8, 1862, for gallant and meritorious service in action near Albuquerque,
New Mexico; colonel and brigadier-general march 13, 1865 for meritorious
service during the war; lieutenant-colonel Fifth cavalry july 28, 1866; retired
january 15, 1873; died january 7, 1887. *Ibid.*, I, 388.

286 Benjamin Stone Roberts. Vermont. Brevet-second-lieutenant First dragoons july 1, 1835; second-lieutenant may 31, 1836; first-lieutenant july 31,
1837; resigned january 28, 1839; first-lieutenant Mounted Riflemen may 27,
1846; captain february 16, 1847; brevet-major september 13, 1847, for gallant
and meritorious conduct in the battle of Chapultepec, Mexico; lieutenant-
colonel november 24, 1847, for gallant and meritorious conduct in the action
with the enemy at Matamoros and Pass Galaxara, Mexico; major may 31,
1861; colonel Fifth New Mexico cavalry december 9, 1861; colonel february
21, 1862, for gallant and meritorious service at the battle of Valverde, New
Mexico; brigadier-general of volunteers june 16, 1862; brigadier-general
march 13, 1865, for gallant and meritorious service in the battle of Cedar
Mountain, Virginia; major-general of volunteers march 13, 1865, for gallant
and meritorious service in the battles of Cedar Mountain and Manassas,
Virginia; honorably mustered out of volunteer service january 16, 1866;
lieutenant-colonel Third cavalry july 28, 1866; retired december 15, 1870;
died january 29, 1875. *Ibid.*, I, 835.

287 John Porter Hatch. New York. Brevet-second-lieutenant Third infantry

tenant [D.M.] Frost, quartermaster of the regiment. Major [James] Belger [288] is chief quartermaster.

MAY 10. The regiment was put in motion by Major-general Twiggs [289] at six o'clock and marched five miles,

july 1, 1845; transferred to Mounted Riflemen july 17, 1846; second-lieutenant april 18, 1847; brevet-first-lieutenant august 20, 1847, for gallant and meritorious conduct in the battles of Contreras and Churubusco, Mexico; captain september 13, 1847, for gallant and meritorius conduct in the battle of Chapultepec, Mexico; regimental adjutant november 1, 1847, to may 1, 1850; first-lieutenant june 30, 1851; captain october 13, 1860; brigadier-general of volunteers september 28, 1861; major august 30, 1862, for gallant and meritorious service in the battle of Manassas, Virginia; lieutenant-colonel september 14, 1862, for gallant and meritorious service in the battle of South mountain, Maryland; major Fourth cavalry october 27, 1863; colonel march 13, 1865, for gallant and meritorious service during the war; brigadier-general march 13, 1865, for gallant and meritorious service in the field during the war and major-general of volunteers march 13, 1865, for gallant and meritorious service during the war; honorably mustered out of volunteer service january 15, 1866; lieutenant-colonel Fifth cavalry january 15, 1873; transferred to Fourth cavalry april 10, 1873; colonel Second cavalry june 26, 1881; retired january 9, 1886; awarded medal of honor october 28, 1893, for distinguished gallantry in the battle of South mountain, Maryland, where he was severely wounded while leading one of his brigades in the attack under a severe fire from the enemy while serving as brigadier-general of volunteers commanding division; died april 12, 1901. *Ibid.,* I, 511.

[288] James Belger. New York. Army. Private, corporal, sergeant, and sergeant-major Second infantry november 7, 1832 to october 15, 1838; second-lieutenant Sixth infantry october 15, 1838; first-lieutenant february 27, 1843; regimental adjutant february 1, 1840 to january 1, 1846; captain assistant quartermaster june 18, 1846; brevet-major may 30, 1848, for meritorious conduct particularly in the performance of his duty in the prosecution of the war with Mexico; major quartermaster august 3, 1861; colonel assistant aide-de-camp july 11, 1862; dismissed november 30, 1863; major quartermaster march 3, 1871; retired june 19, 1879; died december 10, 1891. *Ibid.,* I, 207.

In addition to the above the following were with the regiment: Brevet-major Philip Kearny, Captain A. J. Lindsay, Brevet-captains Gordon Granger and Thomas Claiborne; First-lieutenants Charles L. Denman, Julian May, Thomas G. Rhett, James Stuart; Second-lieutenants Innis N. Palmer, J. McL. Addison, George McLane, W. E. Jones, George W. Howland, C. E. Ervine; Surgeons Israel Moses, Charles H. Smith; and civilians George Gibbs, William Henry Tappan, Alden H. Steele, J. D. Haines. Bancroft, *History of Oregon,* II, 81 footnote; Tannatt to Prosser, february 5, 1899.

[289] David Emanuel Twiggs. Georgia. Captain Eighth infantry march 12, 1812; major Twenty-eighth infantry september 21, 1814; honorably discharged june 15, 1815; reinstated as captain Eighth infantry december 2, 1815

the principal object being to obtain a start. For the benefit of those to whom the order of the day on a cavalry march is as unknown as it was to myself, I give it here.

Reveille sounds at three a.m. and the roll is called, immediately after which follows the stable call, when the horses are cleaned and their pickets changed. At a quarter before five is the sick call, and at five the general gives the signal to strike tents and pack the wagons; at half past five boots and saddles, at five-fifty to horse, and at six advance. On arriving at camp guard is mounted and the horses picketed outside. An hour before sundown they are again cleaned, watered, and picketed inside the camp. At sundown the retreat is sounded, the roll called, sentinels posted, and at dark the countersign is given out.

The order of march is first, the advance guard; second, the pioneers; third, the regiment; fourth, regimental train; fifth, supply train, and sixth, the rear guard.

Today we had a specimen of the vexations of beginners. One of our mules was missing at daybreak, and leaving the wagon to remain until afternoon I rode into town to search for it. After a fruitless hunt I returned and reached camp late in the evening. Our new camp was called Camp Sally B.

FRIDAY, MAY 11. This day we passed in camp, all be-

with brevet of major from september 21, 1814; transferred to First infantry december 14, 1821; major may 14, 1825; lieutenant-colonel Fourth infantry july 15, 1831; colonel Second dragoons june 8, 1836; brigadier-general june 30, 1846; brevet-major-general september 23, 1846, for gallant and meritorious conduct in the several conflicts at Monterrey, Mexico; recognized by resolution of congress march 2, 1847, and the presentation of a sword "in testimony of the high sense entertained by congress of his gallantry and good conduct in storming Monterrey"; dismissed march 1, 1861, major-general Confederate army, 1861-1862; died july 15, 1862. Heitman, *Historical register*, I, 976.

ing engaged in the numberless preparations for the journey, adjusting baggage in the wagons, and finishing all those minor arrangements that never are finished till necessity calls for them. A morning's amusement is afforded, at least to those who do not share in its annoyances, by the constant escape of mules and horses from their picket ropes. They are fastened out to graze, when not on actual march, by lariats some thirty or forty feet long, secured to the ground by a wooden pin, and not a night passes but some of them contrive to get loose and leave the camp. Most of the mules being still unbroken, and many of the muleteers also, and the horses being unaccustomed to their vocation, a daily chase on the part of the wagonmasters [ensues], which generally ends in the whole being brought in. Then the harnessing brings another scene of confusion, the mules kicking, plunging, and running off on every possible opportunity. All these matters will soon however adjust themselves.

MAY 12. The camp broke up at seven a.m. Our private troubles were not yet at an end, another of our mules having been taken by accident with the train. [This was] an annoyance for which, however, we soon found compensation in a better one left in its place. The vexations of a stranger on a march, when unaccustomed to the details of its arrangements and forced to make himself a general camp nuisance by asking questions of everyone, are no small ones at the time, but will soon become matters of amusement. One teamster, a Dutchman, is innocent of all knowledge, even of harnessing his mules. He seems however honest and willing. One other man, an Irishman hired as horse-keeper and general assistant, knows as little of his business, but he is equally good tempered and more intelligent. In these respects, therefore, we are well off, but until they shall be broken in we have everything to teach, and the lesson to learn first ourselves. We have been treated with the utmost kindness and patience on all sides, and are particularly indebted to Mr. J. F——,[290] the regimental sutler, and to his brother for every assistance.

Our route this day led through a beautifully wooded country with rolling hills. The trail [was] generally good until about noon, when a halt was ordered, the head of the column having reached a bad descent where a road had to be cut. Here was a brook of excellent water. The pass was difficult, but we escaped without accident, recrossed the brook and encamped about half-past four o'clock, the camp extending from east to west [and] fronting south on the brook. In the rear of headquarters was a high rolling hill, affording a fine view of the camp and surrounding country, which was singularly beautiful, the hollows, and especially the hills, being clothed with timber. The soil is deep, black mould, exceedingly rich, but light and changed rapidly into mud or dust by the weather. For this reason the rolling prairie is less fitted for cultivation than for grazing, for if broken by the plow the soil would be soon washed into the bottom. The hills are here in regular ridges, often of a grave-like outline with tables on the tops. Ledges of water-worn limestone occasionally crop out from the sides and fallen masses disposed in rows present a singular aspect from below.

Large masses of coarse red quartzose rock occur here and there, and pebbles of the same mineral are often intermixed with those of limestone rock, which is in this place. The trees are less advanced than a week ago at St. Louis and are just budding out. Beautiful flowers, many of forms familiar at the east, bloom amidst the grass, which though short is plentiful. It is not however

---

290 Probably J. Frost. If so the brother would be William Frost, agent for the regimental train.

sufficiently matured to afford healthy nutriment to our animals, [which are] accustomed to dry feed and grain, and an admixture of the old grass is sought for always in selecting a camp ground. Although upon Indian territory, the country being that assigned to the Kickapoos,[291] etc., the diminution of these tribes and the disappearance of grain render the burning of the grass much less universal. A consequence is the increase of timber, which in a few years will doubtless clothe much of the land. Our guide, one long accustomed to western life and a man of much observation, states that within his recollection the timber had increased whenever the practice of burning was discontinued. Our camp was named after the daughter of an officer, Camp Frederica.[292] The advance this day was about fifteen miles.

SUNDAY, MAY 13. Camp broke at seven a. m. Our march was about fifteen miles. The character of the country was the same as heretofore, and exceedingly picturesque. Our course during the day was generally northwest. About a mile out we had a last view of the Missouri river, some three miles to the right. Encamped some six miles from the river on excellent ground and with [an] abundance of fresh water. The road during the day was generally excellent, but with one very bad pass. During the ride a wolf was seen, some grey plover shot, and in camp a fine specimen of the swallow-tail hawk, *falco furcatus,* was seen. During the night we had a heavy thunderstorm with hail and high wind.

291 These Indians, whose prehistoric homes were about the Wisconsin and Fox rivers, drifted southward to the Sangamon and Wabash rivers, where they were followers of Tecumseh and fought under Black Hawk. Under the treaty of october 24, 1832, they were given a reservation extending sixty miles west and twenty miles north of Fort Leavenworth on the west side of the Missouri river. They surrendered the major portion of this reservation to the government in 1854. Connelley, *Kansas and Kansans,* I, 264-65.

292 In honor of Frederica Jones, ten-year-old daughter of Captain Llewellyn Jones. Swift, "Personal memoirs."

The supply train, owing to detention in passing the ravine, did not reach camp.

MONDAY, MAY 14. The camp did not break up until late, owing to the detention of the train. We passed several bad hollows or sloughs [which were] rendered soft by the rain of last night and advanced only four miles. The ground selected was a low and small village [*sic*], with grass and good water, but a steep descent. The camping ground, I may here mention, is selected by the guide, who precedes the column with a small escort and fixes upon a suitable spot at about the distance intended for the day's march. The first requisites are of course good grass and water, and finally wood for the camp fires. Of the latter very little is indeed necessary, a few sticks furnishing sufficient for a mess. Some of the officer's messes are provided with portable sheet-iron stoves, but the fires are usually made in a small hole to protect them from the fresh wind of the prairie.

TUESDAY, MAY 15. The camp broke up at seven [o'clock]. The road [was] still somewhat broken. At about six miles out we reached Wolf creek, a small stream running toward the Missouri [river]. The passage was here very bad, with a steep winding hill to ascend afterward. These passages, [crossed] with considerable labor and anxiety, furnish at the same time much excitement and even amusement. As each team approaches in turn, the wheels are locked, the mules led down the hill, and then, the chain being taken off, amidst a storm of blows, curses, and shouts, are run up the opposite side. With unbroken or unmatched teams, as ours are at present, this is a matter of no small difficulty, the wheel mules often refusing to draw or hold back as required, the forward ones kicking out of their traces or plunging from side to side, sometimes getting the wagon stalled in the mud [and] at others running in imminent dan-

ger of upsetting on the bank. Occasionally a pole or
axle breaks and the whole train is stopped for the time.
The forge comes up, extra poles are obtained and put
in, and the shouting and whipping commence. To one
unaccustomed to mules it is a matter of wonderment
that they are not oftener ruined. The little wretches
involve themselves in most inexplicable ways in their
chains and harness, plunging, kicking, and falling on
one another with a vicious perseverance that would kill
a train of horses, and generally with as little injury to
themselves as if they were of hammered iron. The duties
of the wagonmasters of [the] division and their sub-
ordinates are at these places harassing enough and de-
mand no little patience and presence of mind.

All those brooks which have given us so much trouble
could have been avoided, had the trail been run a few
miles farther west of the Missouri river.

About three miles from Wolf creek the [Fort] Leavenworth [road] strikes into the great trail from St. Joseph, now the most traveled of all the routes. The town
of St. Joseph, one of the principal outfitting towns in
western Missouri, has been created entirely by the business of the emigrants and is of so late an origin that its
very name is not given on the maps.[293] We have begun
to encounter the emigrant trains in numbers, winding
slowly along with their white-topped wagons and trains
of oxen and mules. In passing over this district, than
which few can be more beautiful, the eye wanders in
search of the familiar farmhouse and the barn, built

---

293 St. Joseph dates from 1826, when Joseph Robidou, trapper and Indian
trader, opened a post a short distance above the present city on Roy's branch.
In 1830 he moved to Blacksnake hills, now the heart of the city. In 1843
"Blacksnake hills," as the place was known until that year when the name
was changed, had a population of five hundred. It became a county seat in
1846 with a population of nine hundred thirty-six. In 1849 its population
was nineteen hundred and a year later three thousand four hundred sixty.

upon some little knoll by the brookside, that greets the
eye in our eastern landscape. I often found myself
almost cheated into the belief that the canvas covers of
some emigrant train, seen in the distance, were the fixed
residence of the white man. But no smoke except that
of the campfire rises here. The Indian himself is un-
seen, and so peaceful is all around, that the weapon
which every man carries seemed a useless plaything.

Our route was intersected or joined by a number of
smaller trails, some of them the perhaps immemorial
war paths of Indians. Others [were] distinguished by
their wheel marks as the roads made by emigrants from
distant points on the Missouri. I noticed today, and frequently afterward, circular spots or rings on the prairie
where the old grass remained unburnt in the midst of
an extent of fresh verdure. These the guide explained
as places where horses had been picketed the previous
year, or where a corral had been formed. We found a
good camping ground about a mile southeast from the
road, some twelve miles from the Missouri, and fourteen or fifteen from our starting point. The descent into
it [was] bad, but [it] contained good water and [was]
well protected. The evening was passed till a late hour
round a campfire, and enlivened with merry chat and
songs.

WEDNESDAY, MAY 16. It being deemed advisable to
rest the animals, the camp did not move today. I went
on with Mr. Glendery [Glenday], the guide, and a
party to seek a position for the next. We rode perhaps
sixteen or eighteen miles. The trail, which is here very
broad and beaten like a turnpike, was covered with
emigrant parties, who continued passing at intervals
during the day. These parties vary much in numbers
and much in the appearance of the individuals and the
apparent completeness of their outfit – some being in

excellent order [and] others hardly removed from destitution. I noticed that but few women or children accompanied them. They are chiefly made up from single towns or districts, less often of combined parties, and as yet they are not banded in large companies. Most of their wagons are drawn by oxen, from three to seven yoke to a team. It is hardly necessary to say that they are bound for California, and I learn that the most extravagant hopes animate most of them. Bitter disappointment is perhaps in store for all; distress and death for many most certainly. At points along the road we saw frequent cards and notes stuck on the top of sticks containing information to friends behind. The grass along the road is now almost eaten, and good camping grounds in its vicinity for so large a body of men as ours are scarce. The wood is also here less abundant, though patches of it show on either side in the bottoms. It should be noticed that the route is carried wherever practicable along the summit of the dividing ridges between the streams on account of a more level and drier track, [thus] avoiding the smaller ravines and swales. We are therefore often obliged to diverge for some distance. The turf on the prairie is several inches in thickness, very tenacious, singularly smooth in surface, and unless softened by recent rain affords a good road anywhere. This therefore seldom gives us much trouble. The country for some extent beyond this is well watered, and we rarely travel three or four miles without meeting places which would be suitable [camping places] in ordinary times.

We passed today a few sloughs, but the road generally was better, being drier. The sloughs are formed by the settling of the water in the swales or depressions leading into the ravines, which in turn empty into the streams. The turf once broken, the whole is converted, by passing in wet weather, into a tenacious and deep bed of mud, through which the wagons are drawn with difficulty, as they sometimes sink to the axles. Ours are very heavy at present and detentions frequently occur.

On the right of the road we had occasional glimpses during the day of the high and wooded banks of the Missouri, now at a considerable distance. We returned early in the afternoon, having selected the ground for next day's encampment. At night we had more rain, and the howling of the prairie wolves made a doleful accompaniment to the storm.

THURSDAY, MAY 17. Broke up at seven [o'clock]. We found the road good except the crossings, and reached camp at an early hour without accident. The ground was a good one, situated to the left of the road, about sixteen miles from the last. In the evening some of us went to bathe in the brook, which was no small gratification after a week's toil. One of the men caught a striped prairie squirrel, a female with young.

FRIDAY, MAY 18. Camp moved at six [o'clock], the regular hour for moving being resumed. I again went forward with the guide to select a position for the night. We passed a number of emigrant trains, some of which had now become old acquaintances. Two or three meetings constitute such on the prairie, and hearty salutations were exchanged as we went on. There are odd characters and odd vehicles among them too. Every profession and every class in society are represented, and every mode of conveyance from the Conestoga wagon and its lumbering oxen, and the light draft mule-team, to the saddle horse. We even saw a doctor's buggy with a bell-pull fastened to the hinder axle. The route today grows more monotonous, the divides longer, and the timbered streams more distant from the road and of less frequent occurrence. On either side we saw ves-

tiges of campfires, but all [made by] whites, for the
Indians are now mostly at their villages engaged in
planting corn. A practiced eye readily distinguishes the
fire made by an Indian from that of the emigrant or
even the hunter. The white man lights his wood in the
center of the sticks; the Indian always at the end, moving it up as it burns. The scarcity of wood in the prairie
has taught him this lesson of economy. We passed today
two bad sloughs on the opposite sides of a hill, and after
five hours' march selected a camp to the left of the road,
some twenty miles from that of last night. It had been
previously occupied and the grass was thin, but the
situation [was] good and water plent[iful]. The trees
in this bottom, as in most of those we have visited, were
sour elm and scrub white oak. I strolled with my gun
up the stream, but shot nothing. The birds particularly
noticed today were the turkey buzzard, common crow,
buffalo birds (the cow bunting of the east), doves, small
woodpeckers, and a number of the sylviae, upon which
I could not waste shot. The yellow-throated blackbird
was also constantly seen in the flocks of the buffalo bird.
Flowering plants were numerous, but none of them
[were] of rare varieties.

To this camp was given the name of Camp Mary.[294]
We passed another merry evening at the tent of an officer, to whom a benevolent Irishman had given a bottle
of ancient whiskey on condition that it should be drunk
beyond the bounds of civilization, and heard the next
morning's reveille with our usual regret.

There was another thunderstorm during the night,
fully justifying, in our opinion, the anathemas which
our guide passed upon this district, [which is] said to
be particularly subject to heavy rains.

[294] In honor of Mary, daughter of Brevet-major Charles F. Ruff. Ruff to
Davenport, n.d.

SATURDAY, MAY 19. A slight fall of rain occurred early this morning. Our course today lay nearly due west over the tops of long ridges. A heavy shower with hail fell about ten – the sky clearing off at noon and exhibiting the exquisite valley of the Great Nemaha. The approach to this stream on either side of the road is beautiful, the banks of the ravines being covered with wood. The river itself is small, notwithstanding its name, being at this time only some twenty feet wide and about a foot deep. The general course is here north-west, but its bed is very winding. The banks are high, disclosing horizontal strata of fossiliferous limestone, some of the inclosed shells preserving the nacre. I noticed also a number of recent shells in the mud of the bottom, but found no live specimens to preserve for identification. The pioneers had here constructed a tolerable road and we passed safely. The passage itself was highly picturesque, and I spent a pleasant hour or two in watering the teams and reading the various inscriptions which the Pilgrims of the West had left upon the trees announcing their arrival at this point of their long journey. Ascending the opposite bank we found a pretty and level plain, from which again arose the spurs of another dividing ridge. Here stood the newly-made grave of an emigrant marked by a rude headboard, with his name and the date of his death affixed on a scrap of paper. His search for the gold of the Sacramento had been soon ended. How will it be with the rest? About five miles farther on, and some twenty from our last place, we found our camp, which was named Almira. Strolling around the hills, I picked up some fragments of the lily-like stems of a zoophyte, and noticed an abundance of quartz pebbles and large boulders, one of which was split as if by lightning. The evening we again passed round the campfire of an officer, and the scene that our party exhibited was one not to be forgotten. The night was blackness itself; a wind such as blows only on the prairie or on the sea roared around us, a blazing fire was built under an enormous mass of red quartz rock, [and] around it lay on their blankets some twenty men in the rude costume of the march — our old guide among them. On its top stood some half dozen others leading the chorus which thundered from beneath to the good old song of "Benny Havens, O!"[295] As the firelight danced on their faces I could not but recall the pictures of Salvator[296] and regret that the inspiration of such a pencil was wanting here.

SUNDAY, MAY 20. Again went in advance with our guide, leaving camp a little before six [o'clock]. About five miles out struck a branch of the Nemaha [river, where] there were two crossings that needed repair. It has been a matter of regret all along that the government did not send a body of pioneers a month previous to prepare the road between [Fort] Leavenworth and Fort Kearny by throwing bridges over the most difficult places, or marking out roads that might avoid them. The expense would have been trifling in comparison to the immense advantage both to the emigrants and ourselves. In most cases sufficient wood could be found for the purpose in the immediate neighborhood, and in others a few wagonloads of brush, easily procured within a mile or two or carried along from one place to another would have saved hours of delay and often the breakage of wagons. The crossings rarely need mending for more than twenty feet, and a number of the worst could have been turned by a circuitous march of a short distance. These we had of course no time to explore.

295 Written by Lieutenant O'Brien.

296 Salvator Rosa (1615-1673), an Italian painter, etcher, satirical poet, musical composer, and chief master of the Neapolitan school of painting. He painted historical subjects, landscapes, marine views, and battle scenes.

As it is, we have been of great service to the emigrants who follow us. I could not but pity some whom we occasionally met on the road, with their wagons broken and no means of repairing them. The regiment was unprovided with materials beyond their own immediate wants, and though our forges have been kindly employed in many cases for their relief, our march is necessarily too hurried to delay a moment. It is, however, gratifying to observe that the emigrants are generally kind to one another, as well as that their conduct for the most part is exceedingly courteous and orderly. A few companies, we hear, have earned themselves bad names, but all that we have met have been as well behaved and well bred as [those] one would meet on a country road in the old states. Many are, in fact, led by men of high standing and composed of the most substantial class of the community. [It is a] pity that such should leave the comforts of civilized life to endure the sufferings that must await them before they reach the Utopia of the West.

This morning we again encountered heavy showers. The camp was selected to the right of the road, with good water, but wood scarce. This last item, the least important in our own calculations is, I observe, one of the most in that of the emigrants. "How far is it to timber?" is a question often asked of us as we return from our morning scout.

MONDAY, MAY 21. We have now reached the dividing ridges of the waters running directly eastward to the Missouri and those running more southerly into the Kansas or Kaw, which empties into that river below our own starting point, our general course having been at first much to the north and west. Since crossing the Great Nemaha we have kept more westerly, following the ridge between that stream and the Little Nemaha,

and we are now approaching the Big Blue. Leaving
camp a little before six [o'clock] I overtook the guide,
and at a quarter before nine reached a small branch
or ravine running about westward. Here we found a
very bad passage, but it was fortunately turned by the
pioneers who followed. At ten [o'clock] we struck the
valley of the Big Blue itself. Crossing the river the
guide selected a camp about a mile beyond to the left
and with the rear to the road. We then returned to wit-
ness the passage of the column. The river was at this
time about twenty-five yards wide, and up to our saddle
girths at the ford, with steep banks some twenty feet
high. The bottom [was] hard and covered with pebbles
of flint, quartz, and red jasper. The spurs approaching
the valley are terraced with great regularity, strata of
limestone and blue flint appearing on their edges. The
highest of these terraces, it may be observed, are often
more fertile than the second tables, from which the soil
is generally washed. In the bed of the river were quite
extensive bars of quartzose sand. Its banks were lined
with sour elm, maples, cottonwood, and willows, with
an undergrowth of seringa and other shrubs. The scene
of the crossing afforded the usual amusement, the mules
being most unwilling to take to the water, and often
obliging the teamsters to rush through up to their mid-
dles. All however passed in safety. Our camp here was
called Camp on the Big Blue. A short distance from it
was a beautifully wooded bend of the river in which
we bathed. In the evening we had another squall of rain.
Our general course during the day had been to the south
of west, and the viameter, now for the first time used,
and which was attached to the forge, gave sixteen miles
as the distance traveled.

TUESDAY, MAY 22. [The] column moved this day
only eight and a quarter miles by the viameter and

camped a short distance to the right of the road, the mules needing rest. Grass excellent, the water [was] not so good, [but] enough however [was] found in pools. We now pass the graves of emigrants daily along the road, their inscriptions generally giving cholera or dysentery as the cause of their death, and on inquiring [we find that] almost every company has lost one or two members. [We] noticed cows frequently yoked in the teams with bulls and oxen. They are said to draw very well, but their milk must be unwholesome. The ox-teams keep very well up with the train, making fifteen miles on an average per day. In some respects they are preferable to mules, as they improve in condition so long as the grass holds good, are more easily tended, and less liable to escape. When, however, the grass is more exhausted I apprehend that they will suffer much. We are now on the war grounds, and although we have literally not seen an Indian since leaving Camp Sumner, greater precautions are deemed necessary, and for the first time we form a corral. This is made by enclosing a space within the wagons and tents, into which the animals are driven at night. The emigrants are nightly losing horses and mules, but whether from carelessness or theft it is difficult to tell. There is a report that buffalo have been seen today by one of the companies, but it is doubted. Our camp is called Camp Ann.[297] During the night another shower fell.

WEDNESDAY, MAY 23. A heavy shower early in the morning. The country is now losing its character of rolling prairie proper, as it is near Fort Leavenworth,

---

297 In honor of Annie Elizabeth Dougherty Ruff, wife of Brevet-major Charles F. Ruff. Mrs. Ruff and her youngest daughter Margaret spent the winter of 1848-1849 at Fort Kearny, leaving her other daughter, Mary, with her grandmother at Liberty, Missouri. Early in the spring Mrs. Ruff in company with her father, Major John Dougherty, her brother, Lewis Bissell Dougherty, Captain Stewart Van Vliet, and an escort returned to Liberty for Mary. Ruff to Davenport, n.d.

the ridges becoming longer [and] the ravines of water less frequent. We met none until one mile before camp, where was one running to the westward. The great trail from Independence [298] joined ours shortly after leaving camp of last night. The junction is said to be [about] one hundred twenty-three miles from Fort Kearny. During the day an antelope was shot by one of the rear guard. Some of the hills passed were very barren and covered with quartz gravel. Where this red quartz, so often found in this district, occurs in place, I have never seen mentioned, and there is no surface rock by means of which the direction of its movement can be ascertained from the diluvial scratches. A range of hills, seen to the left, is supposed to bound the valley of the Little Blue which we are approaching. We marched twenty-five miles by the viameter and encamped half a mile to the right of the road on the Little Sandy [creek], [299] about one hundred ten miles from [Fort] Kearny and one hundred eighty-six from [Fort] Leavenworth. Camp fronts due west. The night was overcast with rain.

THURSDAY, MAY 24. Left camp as usual in advance. At a quarter before nine [o'clock we] passed a gully which the pioneers, who had come on, halted to fill. At nine [o'clock] we passed a small branch running into the Little Blue [which was] fed by springs at no great distance. The bottom [was] hard and [the] crossing pretty good. The guide allows from three to four miles an hour as the rate of his horse's walking, according to the state of the roads, and our distances are calculated accordingly in fixing the day's march. At half-past eleven [o'clock] we selected our camping ground about

[298] Near the junction of the Big Sandy creek and Little Blue river in Jefferson county, Nebraska.

[299] A tributary to the Big Sandy creek in northwestern Jefferson county, Nebraska.

a mile to the left of the road and facing south on Big
Sandy [creek], another tributary of the Little Blue
[river, which was] about ten or twelve feet wide and
rapid. Its banks [are] of granite sand and gravel, with
pebbles of agate and jasper, some of which are very
good specimens. Our course today has again been to the
north of west. The viameter gave twenty-one and one-
quarter miles, [which was] rather over our estimate.
The country during the ride [was] about the same as of
late, except that in some places the terraces are deeply
cut into by rain, which before has not been observed.
The banks disclosed are light colored and sandy. The
road runs upon very long divides and is as fine as possible, with the exception of a few swales. [The] sky was
overcast at noon and [there was] lightning to the northwest. [We] first noticed the prickly pear in this bottom.
Soon after arriving in camp we had a small stampede,
some thirty horses starting at the sound of a gun (mine,
by the way) and running several miles before they could
be stopped. Another heavy storm tonight.

FRIDAY, MAY 25. In consequence of the storm the departure of the column was delayed until eight o'clock,
and I rode forward with the guide at seven o'clock.
Our course was generally north-northwest and west. At
eight-forty [o'clock we] crossed the stream we had encamped on and found sandy flats along its banks and
the sand bluffs to the left. At eleven and twelve o'clock
[we] crossed branches or ravines leading to the Little
Blue river, and at twelve forty-five o'clock reached that
river itself. It lies in a deep bottom, from one-eighth to
one-quarter of a mile wide, and the approach is not
noticeable until gaining the summit of the hill over-
looking it. The river itself is beautifully fringed with
trees, among which the cottonwood predominates. We
found the bottom in the immediate vicinity of the road

much pastured by the emigrant trains, some of which were already halted. The sites for camping grounds are excellent, and having chosen one at a short distance we rode back. The regiment had, however, been already forced to halt some five or six miles back. The position was to the left of the road, about a quarter of a mile from it, with the rear and one side covered by a channel containing pools of good water. We find the buffalo grass, as it is called, now becoming common. It grows in small detached clumps, very thick and short, and curled. Along the road we now find frequent buffalo skulls and elk horns, the remains of races that have already well nigh disappeared from this region.

Today [we] met one party of emigrants returning. Their cattle had stampeded to the amount of sixty head, and the company in consequence broke up. They had counted five hundred forty wagons passing since the morning before. I noticed some trithorn acacias on the bank of the stream, and among the birds the red-headed woodpecker. Plover are very plent[iful] and tame, as they are now hatching. Some of the emigrants reported that they had seen wild turkeys near our camp of last night, and the guide states that they, as well as the honey bee, precede by short distances the advance of the whites and are not known beyond the mountains. Some of the gentlemen are cooking the stems of the young milkweed and of Solomon's-seal instead of asparagus and find them excellent. The camp is named Camp Lily. The night cold and rainy.

SATURDAY, MAY 26. We marched today some fifteen miles on a course varying a point or two either side of west. The trail does not pass the Little Blue [river], but continues up its right bank. Our camp was selected on the left side of the road, with its rear to the river. We found the stream rapid and swollen with the late rains. The banks were high and of light sandy soil, the timber as usual cottonwood, willow, and a few ash. Most of the ravines we have passed are filled or lined with sand-banks, washed from the adjacent hills. The black mould which covers the latter is constantly carried into the bottoms and is there very deep. I have had no opportunity of making any accurate observation, but so far as could be noticed in passing, [it was] often to the depth of four or five feet. The day was cold and cloudy but cleared towards evening.

Today we lost a soldier by cholera, the second only since our march commenced. He was a private named Caldwell,[300] a man of an excellent character and [his death was] much regretted by his officers. His funeral took place in the evening after retreat. I followed the procession to the spot selected for his grave, the head of a small ravine in the rear of the camp and shaded by large cottonwood trees. He was buried in his blanket, the camp furnishing no material for a coffin. The burial service was read over him by one officer, the dust and ashes scattered, and the first shovelful of earth thrown in by another. As the last rays of the sun glanced athwart the turf the crack of the rifle paid him the soldier's tribute. The band struck up a lively air as it returned, and he was left in that wild solitude without even the silent companionship of other dead around him. Never had the gloom of death struck me more forcibly. There is a consolation in lying down to one's last sleep amidst kindred and friends, or even where some eye shall now and then light upon the sod that covers us, but to lie there, with the howl of the wolf or the prairie wind alone to break the silence that broods over this green waste, is death indeed. A pretty child,

300 Patrick Caldwell, farrier of company F. Monthly returns, Mounted Riflemen, may 1849.

the daughter of an officer, had stood by my side, looking curiously on. She now pulled my hand, and we turned away to pick the flowers that grew around us, and I forgot in their freshness the blight that another day would bring to them also.

SUNDAY, MAY 27. Orders were issued late last evening for an officer with an escort to proceed to Fort Kearny in advance of the regiment. Three or four idlers like myself volunteered to accompany this party, and we started this morning at six [o'clock]. The first part of our route lay along the valley of the river, thence leaving it [we] passed over a large and level table and again returned to the bottom. Several antelopes were seen during the morning but we had no time to chase them. At noon we halted for an hour to rest and resumed our route. The only event of the day was a fruitless chase after some persons whose suspicious conduct led us to believe them either deserters or hostile Indians. We observed however a very perfect mirage. A number of emigrant wagons in the distance were perfectly reflected as if in water, but singularly, to me at least, some trees which intervened between them presented no reflection whatever. At seven o'clock, after making as we calculated over forty miles and having taken our last leave of the Blue river, we encamped upon a ravine to the left of the road, affording good pasturage but only very bad water in holes and no wood whatever. This we named Camp Kitty. We had taken a light wagon with our blankets, a tent, and two days' rations. Our party consisted of six, with six soldiers as an escort. Our horses were soon picketed, the tent pitched, and after a rough but welcome supper, we posted our guard and retired to rest. Each of us with a soldier, by turns kept watch, and for the first time I bore the responsibility of a sentinel on guard. There was little danger from Indians or anything else, and as I smoked my pipe and contemplated the new moon, the only sound that I heard was the occasional cry of the prairie wolf or the chirrup of some waking bird.

MONDAY, MAY 28. The gentleman having the morning watch blew a reveille through his hand at three in the morning. A handful of dry twigs picked up by one of the party furnished us a cup of hot coffee, and at half-past four we were again in the saddle. Shortly after leaving the camp we passed a large company of emigrants and crossed the ravine into which our branch led. Here we found the water deep, but stagnant and excessively muddy. Thence riding over long curves of highland, we crossed at half-past six [o'clock] a full stream running eastward, with water cool and tolerably clear. Neither of these are mentioned by Fremont, and we afterwards ascertained that they, as well as others which we have crossed before, are only occasionally full. The roads both yesterday and today were greatly cut up by emigrant teams, and we passed numerous sloughs. At nine o'clock we came in sight of a long ridge of sand-hills bordering the valley of the Platte. Crossing first a wide plain we passed the hills which are but scantily covered with vegetation, and at eleven [o'clock] reached the bottom, [which was] here two or three miles wide. The river itself is exceedingly wide, filled with islands of cottonwood [and] so shallow and filled with bars that not even a canoe can navigate it. We found the bottom, which is a dead level, eaten bare by the emigrant teams which actually whitened the trail as far as the eye could reach, [and] the whole plain was dotted for miles with oxen and mules. The rains had filled every old buffalo wallow and swale with water, and the trains had diverged from the route on the river and kept nearer the bluffs. After a halt to rest our ani-

mals we pushed on and [at] about four o'clock reached
what is called Fort Kearny. Here we were most hospitably received by the officers, and for the first time in
a month sat down under a roof and watched the smoke
of fire on a hearthstone.

TUESDAY, MAY 29. We are all too glad to rest ourselves to seek other amusement than sleep or lounging.
I [here] take advantage of the time to transcribe the
rough notes I have been able to make on the road, and
to add something respecting the post itself. Fort Kearny,
first called Fort Childs, was established under the act
creating forts on the Oregon route in 1846-47. The first
troops sent here were a battalion of mounted Missour-
ians known as the Oregon battalion, who encamped at
the place during the summer of 1847 and erected the
walls of the long adobe building and the turf walls of
a few others now used as officers quarters. The battalion
was marched back in the fall and disbanded, and the
post occupied in october by two companies of Mounted
Riflemen under Captain, now Brevet-major [Charles
F.] Ruff, who has since remained in command. The
buildings, such as they are, were completed by the
troops, and with a turf corral now constitute the "fort."
The situation is on the low flat bottom, about a third
of a mile from the Platte river, near the head of Grand
island, and fifteen from where the trail enters the valley.
A more unfortunate one in some respects could hardly
have been chosen. Entirely unprotected by trees or high
ground, its climate is excessively severe in winter and
in the spring the plain is rendered a marsh by the heavy
rains. Water can be obtained anywhere by digging to
the depth of four or five feet. It is cold and palatable at
first, but has a taste of sulphur after standing in the holes
for some time. No wood is to be had except the soft
cottonwood found on the islands of the Platte, which is

brought up with difficulty and not fit for building when
obtained. The original design was to form an inclosure
of pickets, inclosing the building and an area of about
four acres, with blockhouses on the diagonal corners
containing each four guns. The number of these is however reduced to two each. The pickets and blockhouses
are expected to be built of cottonwood, and the whole
is to keep in awe a broken tribe of Pawnees, [which is]
fast disappearing under their wars with the Sioux and
whose nearest village is now one hundred twenty-five
miles distant. The establishment, including the expenses
of the Missouri battalion, cannot have cost less than half
a million of dollars. The turf buildings are already so
dilapidated as to be almost uninhabitable in wet weather. Were any substantial aid contemplated to the emigrants by retaining this post there might be wisdom in
so doing, but so far as keeping the Indians in awe is concerned, a moving camp of dragoons during the summer
months would be far more serviceable.

It is due the officers stationed here, and more particularly to Captain Van Vliet,[301] the quartermaster, to say
that every attention and kindness which they can per-
sonally afford the emigrants has been cheerfully rendered. The scene at the office during the time we have
stopped here has been most amusing. Men are coming

---

[301] Stewart Van Vliet. New York. Second-lieutenant Third artillery july 1,
1840; first-lieutenant november 19, 1843; regimental quartermaster march
28 to june 1847; captain december 1853, which he vacated same date;
captain assistant quartermaster june 4, 1847; major quartermaster august
3, 1861; brigadier-general of volunteers september 23, 1861, which expired
july 17, 1862; brevet-lieutenant-colonel and brigadier-general october 28,
1864, for faithful and meritorious service during the war; brigadier-general
of volunteers march 13, 1865; major-general march 13, 1865, for faithful and
distinguished service in the Q. M. D. during the war and major-general of volunteers march 13, 1865, for faithful and meritorious service during the war;
lieutenant-colonel deputy quartermaster general july 29, 1866; honorably
mustered out of volunteer service september 1, 1866; colonel assistant quartermaster general june 6, 1872; retired january 22, 1881; died march 28,
1901. Heitman, *Historical register,* I, 984.

in at every moment bringing letters for the states, [which are] dispatched from here twice a month by a government express, making thousands of inquiries on every conceivable subject, offering to sell or to buy everything under the sun, and asking for every sort of assistance and information.

The condition of many of the emigrants already forbodes the disasters that await them. Numbers of them, finding their teams overloaded or insufficient, have thrown away portions of their provisions or used their bacon as fuel to cook with, [and] others have thrown out stools, stoves, etc. Some few have either abandoned their wagons or cut them up to make pack-saddles. Others, [being] wiser, have gone home again. It is amusing enough to see men carrying on their shoulders or their saddles, in a country where there is now neither game nor enemy, the long, heavy rifles of the west and their holsters filled with pistols – each one a marching ordnance department. We see them every day roaming about the country, miles to the right or left, looking, I presume, for buffalo or deer. The practice will probably be continued until a few are snapped [up] by some of the more western tribes. Government, I learn today, has with wise liberality directed that the commissary shall hold a surplus of provisions for the relief of emigrants broken down and returning to the states.

The number of wagons which have passed here up to tonight amounts to nearly four thousand. Allowing four persons to a team, which is less than the average, at least sixteen thousand men have already reached this point and probably half as many more are on their way. This does not include [trains] moving on the north side of the river from Council Bluffs. [These are] composed principally of Mormons, who may amount in all to ten thousand.

WEDNESDAY, MAY 30. Very heavy storm last night. The command of this post has devolved on Lieutenant-colonel [B. L. E.] Bonneville, who arrived yesterday with [Captain William H. T.] Walker's[302] company of the Sixth infantry under the immediate command of Lieutenant [Levi C.] Bootes.[303] Major [R. H.] Chilton[304] with his company of dragoons arrived on the twenty-third, and Lieutenant Davis with [Lieutenant-colonel Clifton] Wharton's[305] company on the twenty-

302 William Henry Talbot Walker. Georgia. Brevet-second-lieutenant Sixth infantry july 1, 1837; second-lieutenant july 31, 1837; brevet-first-lieutenant december 25, 1837, for gallant and good conduct in the war against the Florida Indians; first-lieutenant february 1, 1838; first-lieutenant Sixth infantry november 18, 1840, to rank from february 1, 1838; captain november 7, 1845; brevet-major august 20, 1847, for gallant and meritorious conduct in the battles of Contreras and Churubusco, Mexico; lieutenant-colonel september 8, 1847, for gallant and meritorious conduct in the battle of Molino del Rey, Mexico; major Tenth infantry march 3, 1855; resigned december 20, 1860; major-general Confederate army, 1861-1864; killed july 22, 1864, in action near Atlanta, Georgia. Ibid., I, 997.

303 Levi Clark Bootes. District of Columbia. Private and sergeant Mounted Riflemen june 19, 1846 to july 25, 1848; brevet-second-lieutenant Sixth infantry june 28, 1848; second-lieutenant september 28, 1848; first-lieutenant june 9, 1853; captain june 5, 1860; brevet-major july 1, 1862, for gallant and meritorious service in the battle of Malvern Hill, Virginia; lieutenant-colonel december 13, 1862, for gallant and meritorious service in the battles of Fredericksburg, Virginia and Gettysburg, Pennsylvania; major infantry september 20, 1863; transferred to Twenty-sixth infantry september 21, 1866; unassigned march 15, 1869; assigned to Twentieth infantry december 15, 1870; lieutenant-colonel Twenty-fifth infantry january 1, 1871; retired october 7, 1874; died april 18, 1896. Ibid., I, 230-31.

304 Robert Hall Chilton. Virginia. Second-lieutenant First dragoons july 1, 1837; first-lieutenant february 21, 1842; captain assistant quartermaster may 11 to december 6, 1846; captain First dragoons december 6, 1846; brevet-major february 23, 1847, for gallant and meritorious conduct in the battle of Buena Vista, Mexico; major paymaster july 25, 1854; resigned april 29, 1861; brigadier-general Confederate army 1861-1865; died february 18, 1879. Ibid., I, 299.

305 Clifton Wharton. Pennsylvania. Second-lieutenant light artillery october 28, 1818; transferred to First artillery june 1, 1821; transferred to Third artillery august 16, 1821; first-lieutenant july 6, 1825; transferred to Sixth infantry march 24, 1826; captain assistant quartermaster may 19, 1826 to october 6, 1830; captain Sixth infantry april 22, 1830; transferred to First dragoons march 4, 1833; major july 4, 1836; lieutenant-colonel First dragoons june 30, 1846; died july 13, 1847. Powell, List of officers, 666.

eighth, so that the post is now full. Major Simonson with the Bear river command passed here on the twenty-third, and Major Sanderson with that for Fort Laramie on the twenty-sixth.

THURSDAY, MAY 31. The weather again rainy this morning. The regiment came up today and encamped a mile or two from the fort. They have got along without serious accident, but found the road very heavy. Lieutenant-colonel [Osborne] Cross [306] has arrived with orders to relieve Major Belger in command of our supply train on reaching Fort Laramie.[307] The regiment is in good health and spirits.

---

[306] Cross was not promoted to the rank of lieutenant-colonel until february 26, 1863.

[307] Gibbs was in error here. Cross relieved Belger at Fort Kearny.

March from Fort Kearny to Fort Laramie

(The annexed continuation of Mr. Gibbs's journal came to us endorsed as follows by the postmaster of St. Louis, Missouri:

"Recovered from the wreck of the steamer *Algoma,* which was burned at the wharf at St. Louis on the morning of the twenty-ninth of july 1849. Said boat had a large California mail, a large portion of which was consumed. JOHN M. WIMER, P.M.)

Fort Laramie, June 25, 1849.

FORT KEARNY, FRIDAY, JUNE 1. The regiment moved a couple of miles to fresh grass, as we had to await the arrival of the beef cattle, and encamped fronting and about a mile distant from the Platte, with a swale of water on the left and front. We found near the road two or three emigrants, who had concluded to abandon their journey and SETTLE. They had pitched their tent for a permanent location, plowed several acres of ground, and were about to put in a crop. This day orders were issued that the command be divided into three [divisions] for greater facility in moving as well as [to make it] easier to obtain suitable camp grounds. The first consists of Tucker's company K and Porter's F, under Major Tucker; the second of Ruff's I and Jones's D, under Major Crittenden; and the third of Backenstos's H and Van Buren's A, under Brevet-lieutenant-colonel Backenstos. The whole are, of course, under the command of Colonel Loring, who with his staff proceeds with the first. The supply train of Major Cross is equally divided. They are to be encamped within a short distance of one another, according to circumstances.

SATURDAY, JUNE 2. The first squadron marched at noon, the others following. Camped about ten miles in advance, near the [Platte] river, headquarters facing east, with right to the road and left to a swale of water. Grass excellent. The other squadrons about half an hour apart. Camp Nebraska.

SUNDAY, JUNE 3. Marched twelve and a half miles and encamped under the bluffs near a ravine, at the head of which stands a large ash tree. The ground near the river [did] not afford forage, a circumstance always to be regretted on account of the water. We found here great quantities of mushrooms encircling old buffalo stamping grounds. From one spot I picked a bucketful, some weighing nearly a pound. Although of fine appearance and odor, they proved tough and indigestible. Plover, heretofore abundant, have now become scarce in the bottom, the rains having driven them to the hills. Noticed several curlews. Weather fine and most beautiful, the sun sinking behind a fringe of trees on a distant point. [It was] cloudless, with a sky melting in even tints from blue and pale green to purple and gold. In general I have been disappointed with the atmospheric effects of the west. The features of the landscape furnish none of those bold contrasts of light and shadow which ruder countries afford. The clouds rarely if ever are as gorgeous in their hues, and the want of trees scattering and breaking the level rays is always felt. Still, the skies are pure and deep colored, and the masses of the thunderstorm, of almost everyday occurrence in this valley, are grand as they must ever be.

MONDAY, JUNE 4. Marched about ten miles and encamped, with left to the Platte and headquarters to the eastward. The hills on the south side today approach nearer to the river. The Platte is, I imagine, alone among rivers. Straight and swift, shallow and muddy, it is unfit for navigation, bad to ford, destitute of fish, too dirty to bathe in, and too thick to drink, at least until custom habituates one to it. Rivaling in length and breadth what are called great rivers even in our own land, running with a current equal to the East river at Hell Gate, draining a country in extent one-fourth the continent, an Indian canoe cannot even float upon its broad waters. Excepting for quicksands and occasional holes a horse may wade it without wetting his saddle girths, even where, as here, it is a mile in width. Where cut up with islands, as is often the case, it extends to double or treble [that distance], and in one place to seven miles wide from shore to shore. It is easily swollen by rains, running almost on a level with its banks, and often above much of its valley, and, I have reason to suspect, periodically affected according to distance by the daily melting snows in the mountains. Timber is rarely found upon its banks, although the islands are generally covered with willow and cottonwood. Ash trees are found only upon the ravines which come down from the bluffs. The islands are not the least remarkable feature in the scenery. [Being] low and narrow, they are often of great length. Grand island, which terminates near Fort Kearny, is one hundred fifty miles long.

A considerable part of the day's march lay over a table-land elevated some twenty feet above that which intervened between it and the river. At about two hours out we passed Plum creek, a ravine with steep banks, known to emigrants as a land mark. Today we passed the first prairie dog village, lying to the left on the higher level. The roads now unite, as the ground is more elevated, heretofore there having been two, one on the river bank [and] the other, used in wet weather, under the bluffs. The weather [was] fine, with wind from the east. Another man died of cholera. He had been on duty in the morning and died after two hours illness. [We] received newspapers giving accounts of the New York riots.[308] Camp Ellen.

TUESDAY, JUNE 5. Marched twelve miles [and] camped on the river with [the] rear to it. Colonel Loring, with Captain Hatch and the guide, forded it on foot to ascertain if a passage were practicable, but found the bottom too uncertain. The Platte today leaves the bluffs on the south side and runs towards the other with bad swales between it and the road. [The] grass [was] good, but much of the low ground had been recently burnt over. [I] noticed the common red-winged blackbird, ring-necked plover, and some curlews. Animal life of any kind but domestic is of so rare occurrence [here] as to be remarked.

Information was received from emigrants on the other side [of the river] that only about two hundred wagons were in front on that road and that the Mormons would not leave Council Bluffs until the fifteenth of june. They were supposed to have at least five thousand wagons. These emigrants had found the old Pawnee village abandoned.[309] And about one thousand were said to be on the Loup fork between the two deserted villages. These were rumored to have murdered one

308 On may 10, 1849, the admirers of Edwin Forrest stormed the Astor Place opera house when Macready, the English actor, undertook to give a performance. So keen was the rivalry between the two actors and so determined were Forrest's friends that the Englishman should not perform that a serious riot was staged. The militia which was called out to restore order was attacked by the mob. Twenty-two lives were lost in the affair. *Dictionary of American biography,* 529-31.

309 During the winter of 1848-1849 the Pawnees were destitute and many of them starved to death at their old village seventy-five miles below Fort Kearny. They abandoned this one and began a new one at the mouth of the Saline river some eighty miles nearer the frontiers of Missouri. Nebraska state historical society *publications,* xx, 194.

person, but did not molest them. In the evening Captain
Gordon Granger reached camp from Forts Leavenworth and Kearny. He had measured the distance between those two points by an odometer and fixed it at
three hundred twenty-five miles. It was reported that
eight Pawnees had been killed by the emigrants in a
fight, with a loss of only two wounded.[310]

WEDNESDAY, JUNE 6. We had rain with vivid lightning during the night, [the] morning [was] overcast,
and a very heavy shower from the west-southwest a
little after noon. The lightning was very brilliant,
and I noticed distinctly return flashes from the earth.
Marched only about ten miles and camped again on the
river, and with rear to it. It runs here about its general
course, a little north of west. The road is at a short distance from the edge of the first table. We saw today, for
the first time, the remains of a buffalo killed this spring.

THURSDAY, JUNE 7. A messenger arrived this evening with the welcome news that our beef cattle, nearly
five hundred head, had reached Fort Kearny and were
on the way. Marched about twelve and one-half miles,
found that no camping ground could be got near the
river at that distance, and selected one under the bluffs.
The road here leaves the river considerably, owing to
the marshy and uneven ground. The first timber on the
main shore since we left Fort Kearny occurs here, and
although the bottom is cut up by ravines and sloughs,
the emigrants, who always follow it, had pastured the
grass completely. The heavy rain of yesterday had
passed over the first half of today's march and left the

[310] On june 14 Stansbury said "a fight had taken place on the north side
of the Platte between the Indians and two parties of emigrants, in which
the former were defeated with the loss of their chief, five others killed, and
six wounded; the whites having one man wounded and a horse killed."
Exploration and survey, 27. The news of this affair was brought to Stansbury by Major Belger who, with an escort, was on his way to Fort Leavenworth.

ground slippery. Weather fine but hazy. The bluffs on the south bank daily become higher and more irregular and broken by ravines. Several buffalo [were] seen to-day, and one of them killed by a man in the quarter-master's employment. It was a large bull, very fat, and the meat [was] hard and dry.

FRIDAY, JUNE 8. Another heavy thunderstorm occurred during the night. This morning was overcast and threatening, but the day [was] fine. The camp moved but six miles. I rode with some others into the bluffs in search of buffalo, but saw none nor any signs of them. The two seen yesterday were evidently lost bulls, which had wandered off from the main body. The bulls, it is said, never keep with [the] cows, which remain to-gether, but are scattered about from half a mile to two or three days' march on either side. We penetrated some twelve or fifteen miles into the hills to the dividing ridge between the waters of the Platte and those running towards the Arkansas. The bluffs, it is said, extend at this point about as far to the southward as to the northward of the line, [then they] subside into the rolling prairie, which ends only with that river. From the dividing ridge long spurs stretch out toward the Platte. [They are] deeply cut by ravines on three sides, and between them are valleys with steep banks shaded often with ash and red cedar and filled with deep and rich grass. We saw no running water, but found one clear pool on the summit of a hill and a slough in a hollow from which we watered our horses. Many of the lateral valleys among those hills are exceedingly beautiful. The flowers which we found in the open prairies grew among them in profusion. Dwarf cherry and plum trees, currant bushes, and grape vines formed the under-brush. The wild rose, now just in bloom, gave out its perfume, and the music of singing birds rose from the thicket as we lay down on the turf to rest ourselves and refresh our horses. Our route lay for the most part over the hills, as we wished to examine the country and particularly to search for buffalo. In proceeding, we followed generally the parts worn by these animals in passing between the Platte and the south. These trails are about the width of a country footpath, and where the nature of the land permits it six or eight abreast. They are far more straight than those worn by domestic animals, the buffalo proceeding in files with the utmost regularity and directness to his object, unless the country be broken. His path is always chosen by the hunter as the surest and speediest route.

We found today but little game. A few wolves, an antelope, and some curlews were all that we even saw, and these [were] so wild that we could not reach them with our rifles. A pair of curlews had evidently formed a nest in one hollow, and I was amused at the courage with which they attacked and beat off a large hawk that approached it. We met in the interior of the hills a party of emigrants on foot who had evidently lost their way. They mistook us for Indians, and after some manoeuvering left a wooded ravine where they were perfectly safe from attack and mounted a bare hill. On our approach, Glenday being in advance, they all presented their rifles at him and would have probably fired had he not called to them. The consequences, had we been Indians, may easily be imagined. They excused their terror by telling us a long fable of one of their party having been attacked by Pawnees the night before. According to their account he had killed two in his defense, but he had not waited to take their scalps, an indispensable requisite to the credibility of an Indian story. These scared gentlemen afterwards reported that they had scared five of the regulars. Our camp tonight was under the bluffs.

SATURDAY, JUNE 9. The beef cattle have at last arrived. We marched eighteen and three-quarters miles and camped to the right of the road, and between it and a swale of running water. During the march we crossed several ravines extending from the hills to the Platte [river], on some of which the ash trees follow down. [This was] an unusual circumstance. About twelve miles from the old camp we passed the end of the high bluffs. Here [they are] at their greatest elevation and [are] known as [O']Fallon's bluffs. I noticed at the extremity of this ridge, for the first time, blocks and fragments of stone, if [they] can be so called, appearing to be composed of clay, lime, and sand, considerably indurated. A little farther on the same rock appeared in places in horizontal strata. From [O']Fallon's bluff the ridge on the south side subsides into rolling ground. On one of the ravines we found encamped a party, chiefly of Cherokee Indians, going to California. They were ill with cholera and three had already died. One man died yesterday in the second division of the regiment, and three more were sick today. The appearance of cholera invariably follows the camping among the bluffs, as the soldiers cannot be prevented from drinking the water of the swales and wells.[311] No suspicion of contagion exists. It is sometimes impossible to find grass or [camping] ground near the river, but we avoid leaving it when practicable. The water of the Platte, muddy as it is, seems to be perfectly wholesome, and by use becomes even agreeable.

SUNDAY, JUNE 10. Today we pass on the left of the low ridges into which the bluffs have now subsided, and which it is said extend to the Arkansas. A band of five buffalo bulls were seen in the bottom, between the road and the river, [which] turned up toward the train.

---

[311] The emigrants frequently dug shallow wells in preference to using the muddy water of the Platte river.

Then a most exciting chase commenced, several officers joining in, and a detail of men being also sent out. The whole were shortly killed, two of them by officers with their revolvers [and] the others massacred by the crowd. I found myself in at the death of one of them, shot by Captain R[hett] after a sharp chase, which ended with a savage charge of the victim. He was in fine condition and bore a magnificent scalp and mane. Glenday butchered him after the prairie fashion and returned loaded with meat. We noticed that our horses entered on the chase with as great excitement as ourselves, but could not be got up to the dead animal without trouble.

Some seventeen miles from the last camp we reached the lower passage of the south branch of the Platte. The division takes place a little below our camp of last night, but the forks separate so gradually, and the main stream is so filled with islands, [that] the exact point is not easily noticed. Just above this crossing commences the dividing ridge. [It is a range of] hills of the same rolling form as the others and composed like them of clay and sand, but still more barren. The ridge on the left side of the South fork here approaches the river directly. We moved along it about seven miles farther, determined to take an upper crossing, as we found this one bad, the banks being deeply mired by heavy rains and the continued passage of emigrants. Our camp was pitched in a hollow, with front to the river.

MONDAY, JUNE 11. A tremendous thunderstorm occurred during the night. The flashes [were] so brilliant and continuous that the intervening darkness seemed the exception to the ordinary condition of things. The movement was delayed till seven [o'clock] to allow the tents to dry. A few miles above the bluffs again recede from the river, leaving a level bottom on this side. We

camped about fifteen and three-quarters miles from the
last, to the right of the road with front to a slough of
water, the river not being easily approached. Here we
were met by a party of Sioux from a village camped on
the other side of the river. The village itself moved on,
leaving us a large delegation headed by Bull Tail, an
old Indian, in a costume half military, half savage,
wearing a pair of epaulettes, and decorated with a
medal. The flag of peace, bearing two calumets crossed
with a red and white hand united, was hung in the
midst. On the arrival of the officers a talk was held, the
pipe smoked, and some presents of bacon and tobacco
offered and accepted with huge satisfaction. The har-
mony of the meeting was, however, soon interrupted by
the arrest of a horse belonging to the regiment brought
in by an Indian, and which an officer had taken from
him. The talk was broken off, the presents abandoned,
and the greater part of the assembly retired in high
dudgeon. The whole difficulty arose from the want of
an interpreter, none having been provided by the government to any of the tribes on the route. Our guide
spoke only the language of the Crows. Indeed, in respect to any negotiations with the Indians, no provision
whatever had been made [and] no presents furnished.
[This is] an indispensable requisite on occasion of meeting with parties whose good will towards the emigrants
it is desirable to conciliate. On a representation of the
facts being made to Colonel Loring, that there was no
probability the Indian had himself stolen the horse but
obtained it from some deserter, that the regimental
mark was unknown to them, and that prairie law as well
as equity in such cases allowed the Indian to retain an
animal, he directed Mr. Glenday, the guide, to return
to the camp with the head chief and negotiate on the
subject. Wishing to see the village, I gladly took the

opportunity to accompany them. The procession consisted of ourselves and four Indians, led by old Bull Tail himself. [He was] mounted, much to his satisfaction, on the disputed animal, [and sat] excessively straight with an aspect of amused dignity. We forded the river, here about three-quarters of a mile wide, and reached the village, which had moved up about ten miles, a little before sunset. Our arrival [was] announced by loud cries, [and] we found the owner of the horse and others had started out for the purpose of making reprisals on the whites. They were, however, immediately recalled. Proceeding to the head chief's lodge, the horse was delivered up in due form, to the marked delight of the tribe. Glenday was taken to the lodge of the war chief, where he was entertained, and I was seated in the midst of another party of about a dozen to renew the ceremony of smoking. This finished, I dined formally with Bull Tail and his family. The dinner consisted of dried buffalo meat and the *pomme blanche,* and was concluded with a cup of coffee and a pie. It was served with excessive ceremony, the youngest wife cooking it, the eldest fingering it to see that it was properly prepared, Bull Tail then tasting it and passing me the dish. He afterwards exhibited to me, with evident satisfaction, a broken umbrella and a pocket handkerchief, treasures which his intercourse with the whites had procured him. His costume of state had been laid aside immediately after entering the lodge and he sat nearly in his natural dress.

During the evening Captain L— and Mr. W— arrived and were received with due hospitality. Our horses were picketed out by the squaws, our saddles and arms put into their possession, and we were invited to stroll through the village. It consisted of perhaps one hundred fifty lodges, most of them containing four or five men each, besides women and children without number and more dogs than I supposed to exist. We spent the night there at the two principal lodges and returned to camp at sunrise.

TUESDAY, JUNE 12. Heavy rain had again fallen in the night. We reached camp at breakfast and started for the next crossing, ten and one-half miles distant. The forenoon was spent in trying the ford, the troops being sent across [first]. It was found practicable but very inconvenient, as the route was crooked and the bottom uneven. The horses were therefore recalled and we camped in the vicinity, the three divisions being all near together. Colonel Loring, with the guide, Major Cross, and Lieutenant Frost went forward to explore the upper crossing and concluded to pass at Kearny's ford.[312] The Sioux village had moved up opposite, and in the afternoon the principal men came over again. At night another thunderstorm.

WEDNESDAY, JUNE 13. We moved forward about twelve miles to the upper ford, situated one hundred sixty-five miles from Fort Laramie. While the train was coming up some of us rode on about a mile farther to examine an Indian burial lodge which stood on the plain not far from the river. It was the ordinary lodge of a chief carefully closed and pinned down, with a tattered American flag hanging to the poles. On looking through a hole we saw dimly what we supposed to be the body, wrapped in a robe and fastened to the earth, and above it a small scaffold on which was his property.

The train crossed without difficulty or other accident

312 On june 6, 1845, Colonel S. W. Kearny, en route to South pass on his summer campaign to the Rocky mountains, crossed the South Platte at approximately the one hundred second meridan. This would be about seven miles below Big Spring, Nebraska, at the "California" or "upper crossing." Copies of Kearny's report were no doubt being carried by members of the regiment. Hence "Kearny's ford." Kearny, "Report of a summer campaign," june 6.

than the loss of a couple of mules. The water varied in depth, but nowhere came above the beds of the wagons. In making these fords care should be taken, where it becomes necessary to cross from one sandbar to another, to pass down, instead of upstream, as the easiest slope is thereby secured on the ascent. Our actual time of crossing was about two hours. We found the bank on the north side rising into bluffs of sand and clay, the ascent gradual, and on reaching the top, a table-land with gentle hollows in which lay water. We camped tonight near the fork. The South fork of the Platte, it may be mentioned here, resembles in its character the main stream, while the North fork is deeper and less muddy.

THURSDAY, JUNE 14. The camp moved at twelve o'clock, for the purpose of obtaining fresh grass. We ascended the hills and encamped about nine miles from the last place in a swale. The only accessible water was from rain in the hollows. Here we found the grass short but very good. At night heavy rain with thunder.

FRIDAY, JUNE 15. About four miles from camp we reached the commencement of the approach to Ash hollow. A large winding passage through the hills, which are here cut up in every direction by rains, ends in a precipitous descent of considerable difficulty. The sides of the bluffs exhibit strata of indurated clay, and the bottoms are filled with silicious sand and gravel. Gravel trails have been opened down this place and ox-teams pass without much risk, but mule-teams require to be eased down with a rope. The command descended without accident. The scenery of Ash hollow was a delightful change from the general monotony of the valley. Precipitous bluffs today arose on each side, the strata standing out in bold relief, while the stream that flows through it was shaded here and there by numerous clumps of the tree from which it takes its name. Emerging from this valley we reached the North fork, a stream much deeper and more narrow than the South fork and with clearer water. Similar ranges of precipitous clay bluffs extend on the left side. On the opposite [side] are ranges of low and rounded hills, said to be filled with pools of water. The hills on the left side soon receded from the river, leaving a marshy plain between it and the road. We marched today sixteen miles, being about seven miles and a half beyond the valley and making the width between the forks at the passage fifteen and one-half miles. On the road we found a note addressed to the commanding officer, recommending to his care a maniac, who had escaped from an emigrant train. Colonel Loring secured the man and had him taken care of, with the intention of conveying him on to [Fort] Laramie. His charity was further appealed to this evening on behalf of a woman, whose husband and two daughters had died on the route, and who was left with her team, a sick son-in-law and some younger children without assistance. Extra teamsters were furnished to convey her to the fort. Our camp tonight was in the plain between the road and the river. I noticed the appearance in the bluffs of conglomerate rocks formed of the same material as the strata before noticed. Some large masses had fallen down, and the inclosed pebbles were identical with the cement.

SATURDAY, JUNE 16. The bluffs opposite the camp present a singularly castellated appearance. The road today [was] very sandy, and [we] found several ravines coming from the hills with beds of sand and gravel, one of them of considerable size, to which, in default of another name, we gave that of Minnow brook. Beyond the point of hills [next] to this stream the bluffs sink again into low rolling ridges, similar to those on the opposite bank of the river. Some of those we passed today have been very picturesque, the tops assuming the forms of chimneys, towns, etc. The distance made was seventeen and three-quarters miles. [The] weather [was] unpleasantly warm.

SUNDAY, JUNE 17. Marched twenty-one and one-half miles. Weather very warm, and [the] road in some places [was] heavy, though better than yesterday. Camped with right to the river on good grass. Two noted landmarks, the Courthouse and Chimney rock, are in sight of our camp.

MONDAY, JUNE 18. The camp moved as usual. Two or three of us rode into the bluffs to visit the Courthouse, or as it is often called, Solitary tower. After a far longer ride than we anticipated, we were astonished on reaching it at its immense size. The buttes which constitute this singular hill have been evidently a spur from the end of the chain of high bluffs of which Chimney rock, here distant fourteen miles, is an offshoot. Formed of the concrete already mentioned, they have been gradually absorbed by the heavy rains of this valley till they have taken their present shape. From the point of the road where we first saw them they presented the exact appearance of a square building surmounted by a dome. Farther on the shape varies and the tower stands out distinct from the remaining mass. On a near approach we found the former to be a huge circular mound rising perpendicularly from a sloping base. The latter, which is a few hundred yards farther west, is ragged and rises like a cone to a still greater height. The summit has been variously estimated at from six to seven hundred feet above the level of the Platte. The larger of the two only is practicable in ascent. We climbed up nearly to its top, but the wind which blew a hurricane deterred us from passing a point where the footing was insecure.

As it was, we had a fine view of the surrounding country and the valley of the Platte. There can hardly be said to be danger in the descent, except in wet weather, as the feet do not slip upon the dry clay. The bluffs of which these constitute a part stand some miles back from the river, with ridges of low hills and the bottom intervening. There lies between our last camp and the Courthouse a lateral valley, in the midst of which is the broad and sandy bed of a river known as Dry creek. Round the south side and under its walls winds a stream of excellent water, coming from the west and here turning north to the Platte. It has eaten its way deep into the hill, the side next the base of the tower being some fifty feet perpendicular. On every side deep ravines are also furrowed in the clay, from the rock down to the plain. We could see from here other hills in the course of being isolated from their ranges and cut down in like manner. The geological processes at work among those buttes are in fact of the highest interest. Owing to the yielding nature of the material, they go on with great rapidity as compared with other formations. The observer will find the cutting down of main and lateral valleys, the separation of continuous chains into peaks, the gradual destruction of the peaks by carrying down the material into the valleys, and the raising of the valleys into low bottoms going on within the reach of his eye with a distinctness he cannot misunderstand. I should have mentioned that under the clay bank overhanging the stream beneath the Courthouse, and on a level with the water's edge, I noticed a layer of vegetable matter visible for a depth of two feet. [This was] similar to that which overlies brown coal and probably indicative of its existence.

Descending the Courthouse we found our horses quietly feeding in a ravine, and rode on towards camp.

I could not help reflecting upon the change which had come over this scene within a short year, its extraordinary causes and probable results. There were two of us, an artist from Boston [313] and an ex-lawyer from New York, hunting the picturesque among the hills of the North fork of the Platte river with only one pistol between us, and that probably beyond discharging – miles distant from the great road, encountering only an occasional emigrant, and yet as free from danger as if we had been in Suffolk county [314] or among the hills of Bergen. The country we were riding over was the war ground of the Sioux, where twelve months since men went only armed and in bodies sufficient to insure protection. The explanation was the line of white wagons which covered yonder road – the end who is to foretell?

Tired and hungry, for we had been out twelve hours with neither food nor drink except water, we charged into an emigrant camp and asked for some refreshment. Here too was a matter of wonder. In the midst of half a dozen wagons two women were cooking pancakes over a fire, a boy was churning butter, and men were splitting wood that they had brought in their wagons or fetching water from the river. They were emigrants from Connecticut via Ohio, and as I tumbled off my horse and emptied a can of buttermilk I laughed heartily at the luxuries they were enjoying, and which the army seldom sees. We found camp pitched on the river bank, twenty and one-half miles from the last, on good grass.

TUESDAY, JUNE 19. Mr. T[appan] and I again left the road to visit the famous Chimney rock, taking another long ride before we reached it, for the distance at which objects are seen upon these plains is immense. On arriving at the rock, formed of the same indurated

313 William Henry Tappan. See introduction pages 27-29.
314 On Long island, New York.

clay as the bluffs, we ascended the cone to the commencement of the Chimney itself. The view from here
was a fine one, disclosing many other points of similar
but less developed forms. The Chimney has undergone
much dilapidation within the memory of travelers,
and a deep fissure from the top threatens no distant
ruin. Around its base we found a stratum of much
whiter material than the rest, probably containing a
surplus of lime, and a seam was also visible near the
top. These strata extended at about the same level
through all the adjacent hills. On the sides of the cone
we found the yucca just coming into bloom and everywhere the yellow cactus. We have now been some days
in the country of the artemisia or bitter sage.

Leaving the rock we followed the camp, now a long
distance in advance. About fifteen miles beyond the rock
the road leaves the river and turns to the south of the
high range known as Scott's bluffs. We found the camps
all together opposite to it, to the left of the road and in
the wide plain which extends from these to a range of
bluffs on the south side. Everywhere objects of interest
now present themselves. The bluffs for the first time
are covered with red cedar, heretofore found only in
ravines, and the valley throughout its whole extent is
covered with dry branches and trunks, evidently drift-
wood. Mr. Fremont's theory is that these must have
been washed down from the Black hills, but their distance is so great that I should have been disposed to
question it, thinking it more probable that they either
grew on the spot or came from the adjacent bluffs,
were it not that they are everywhere intermingled with
cones of the pine tree which nowhere occurs in this
region. The soil of this region is everywhere thin, but
the grass is good in the bottoms. A circumstance somewhat amusing but for its annoyance occurred today.

When the guide, accompanied by some officers, selected the camp ground, a fine stream of water was running down from the hill. As the very thing wanted, they fixed on a spot adjoining it, but when after pitching camp they returned to it, they were astonished to see it suddenly stop. The explanation soon suggested itself. A thunderstorm, which we had seen from a distance, had deluged the hills and the supply was copious for a time only. We went pretty much without water that night. The distance traveled today was about seventeen miles by leaving the river, and six and a half more to camp. A man died today of cholera, under circumstances which clearly indicated its origin in his case, as we had abundant evidence it had in others. He was seen drinking copiously of swale water during the march. Two hours after he was attacked with the disease and at night was buried. The water of the Platte valley, whether from the surface or from wells, seems invariably fatal, while that of the river, if drunk in moderation, has no bad consequences. The character of the salts which are seen efflorescing on the surface remains for analysis to discover.

WEDNESDAY, JUNE 20. Mr. T[appan] and myself again remained behind to sketch the bluffs. The valley enclosed between them seems about eight miles long and from five to six wide. It is surrounded on every side by precipitous hills [which] assume castellated forms, and is by far the most beautiful in point of scenery that we have met in the Platte country. After spending an hour or two among the hills we rode on, regretting that our time would not permit us to ascend them to enjoy the view of the Platte, of which we had already a glimpse. Near the head of the valley we encountered a brook of running water, up which we rode for two or three miles, the banks becoming higher and the ravine filled with ash trees and underbrush of roses, currents, and plums. On ascending toward the road we saw a little beyond us an Indian lodge, and riding towards it, to our astonishment, a log cabin. We amused ourselves with speculating whether some emigrant, tired of his journey, could here have established a "grocery" and on the probabilities of finding spruce beer and cakes under Scott's bluffs. It turned out to be the "fort" of an Indian trader, who with his half-breed family had settled himself here, posted up a sign "Tinware, by A. Rubidue," [315] and occupied himself by doing blacksmith work for the emigrants in the interval of the trading seasons. As an appropriate memento I have posted up an enameled visiting card in the blacksmith shop. After sheltering ourselves from a passing thunderstorm we rode on. Emerging from the valley to the high ground beyond we caught the first view of Laramie's peak, bearing nearly due west, and of other points in the range of the Black hills. The high bluffs on our left now bear away to the southward, and we come upon rolling prairie again. It deserves to be mentioned that the same strata of white clay and lime, referred to in speaking of Chimney rock and other points, ran continuously around the bluffs of the valley just passed, suggesting the idea that it has been excavated throughout its whole extent from a higher level in the same manner as the narrow ravines. We passed the ravines, one of which proved to be a bend of Horse creek, and found that the regiment had crossed the main stream and camped on the road between that and the river. The distance traveled was

---

315 Undoubtedly Antoine, and not Basil Robidou, as has been said. The post was established in 1848 and destroyed by the Arapahos about 1852. *Nebraska history magazine,* xv, 38. Stansbury found a "temporary" blacksmith's shop and "grocery" in one building. The stock of the latter consisted principally of articles bought from the emigrants. The forge was rented to emigrants for seventy-five cents per hour. *Exploration and survey,* 52.

nineteen and one-half miles. The camp was named by Colonel Loring, Camp Taylor.

THURSDAY, JUNE 21. A few miles beyond the last camp we saw the sandstone formation on the right of the road noticed by Mr. Fremont, and farther on the same in the low bluffs which approach it to the left. The country today was very uninteresting, with sand-hills on both sides of the river. The road, however, [was] generally good. We camped nineteen and one-half miles beyond the last in a bottom near the river and to the right of the road. The grass on the main [road] was very much exhausted but good on an island opposite where we pastured the animals. Glenday and myself attempted to ford the main branch on foot, but found it too deep and rapid. Pebbles of jasper and agate are here abundant and some of them of fine quality, and the sand thrown up by the ants everywhere is granitic. Ash trees fringe the river at this point and [are] often of large size, but emigrants and Indians have committed sad waste among them. Weather oppressive.

FRIDAY, JUNE 22. Marched sixteen and one-half miles, reaching Fort Laramie. Finding the grass destroyed by the emigrants in its immediate vicinity [we] camped a mile or two above on the left bank of Laramie's river without crossing. We found Major Sanderson's command, consisting at present of company E only, already arrived and encamped on this side of the creek opposite the trading-fort. Major S[anderson], with [Lieutenant Daniel P.] Woodbury of the engineers, had proceeded some forty or fifty miles up the Platte to select the site of the new fort but we were most hospitably welcomed by Captains Duncan and McLane. The situation of this trading-post is well known from Fremont's report. Hardly anything could be more forlorn or destitute of interest. The regiment, however, found excellent grass on the river in a pleasant spot fringed with trees where the facilities for bathing and washing our clothes were equally welcome. Laramie's river is a cool, rapid, and tolerably clear stream, fordable easily in several places, and containing several varieties of fish. The hills in its immediate vicinity are barren and covered with quartz and agate pebbles and sand. The timber on its banks consists of ash and willow.

In the afternoon we had [an] amusing scene at the lower encampment. A corporal who had been sent out to find some missing horses brought in two, and with them an emigrant in whose possession he had found them. The company to which the man belonged had been pointed out to him as one of bad character, but no proof existed on which to found a conviction of horse stealing, nor was the arrest directed by any authority. Some of the younger officers and citizens traveling with the regiment determined, however, to make some fun out of the affair and organized a drumhead court-martial on their own account. A judge-advocate, the most noted wag in the regiment, was appointed on behalf of the government and a citizen as counsel for the defense. The contest was carried on with due vehemence and personality, the prisoner of course convicted, and sentence of death passed upon him with awful solemnity by the president. Fifteen minutes were allowed him for preparation, at the end of which time he was taken with a lariat rope round his neck to a tree for execution. There a friendly officer interposed, attracted the attention of the guard, cast off the rope and told him to run as his last chance of life. The man, who was half dead with terror and had exhausted himself with tears and supplications, forthwith took to the water, dashed across [the river] amidst a volley of balls fired in every other direction but his, and ran for the hills with the speed of a greyhound. A more complete imposition was never practiced, and probably a more deserved punishment never inflicted, but the transaction was entirely without the knowledge of Colonel Loring and was censured extremely by him.

SATURDAY, JUNE 23 AND SUNDAY, 24. The command remained at their encampment to rest their animals, wash up, and prepare for the march through the Black hills on which we now enter. Orders had been given out to cut and dry a quantity of grass in anticipation of scarcity on the route, but Major Sanderson had returned with information that abundance exists for a distance of seventy-five miles above here on a route not followed by emigrants. We proceed tomorrow, therefore, at the usual hour. The only change in the disposition of the command is that Captain Rhett remains here and Captain [Mc]Lane proceeds with us.

We are now advanced one-third of the distance between Fort Leavenworth and the Pacific, and so far without any serious detention or other casualty than the loss of a few men by death and desertion. The carrying through in safety of so large a body at such a time, over so great a distance, is a work of the highest responsibility. We have as yet no reason to fear its successful accomplishment, and certainly none to doubt it, if a sense of that responsibility and an anxiety to sustain it on the part of those concerned can ensure it. As regards the emigrants, of whom information will be everywhere desirable, I regret to say that the forebodings entertained at an early period are fast becoming fulfilled. A great proportion indeed are persons of high character and ample means, but even these frequently suffer from the loss or giving out of their animals and are forced to abandon a part of their wagons. Other companies, not well assorted, have broken up from disagreement or broken down from weakness. Few, comparatively, have turned back indeed, but they are proceeding under circumstances which must be highly disastrous. The road is lined with broken wagons and abandoned provisions, and as destitution increases, so will robberies. The mortality from cholera has been considerable, but by no means as great as anticipated.

FORT LARAMIE, MONDAY, JUNE 25. I hope to be able to write you again from Fort Plat[te].[316] The regiment has crossed the creek and is under way.

This letter goes by special express sent by Major Sanderson under charge of Captain Perry. A charge of two cents a letter is made to defray the expenses, and though open but a week, over three hundred dollars are already received.

G.G.

---

[316] Probably built in the fall of 1840 or spring of 1841 by L. P. Lupton on the west bank of the Platte about three-fourths of a mile above the mouth of the Laramie river. Its walls were of adobes four feet thick and twenty feet high, enclosing an area two hundred fifty feet in length and two hundred wide. It was sold to Sybille, Adams and company, 1842, and was abandoned in 1845. Hafen and Young, *Fort Laramie*, 67-94.

Official Report of
Colonel William Wing Loring

Report of Colonel Loring

Headquarters, Regiment Mounted Riflemen,
Oregon City, Oregon, October 15, 1849.

COLONEL: I have the honor to state that, as previously reported, my command, consisting of five companies of the regiment of Mounted Riflemen, one hundred seventy-one wagons, Brevet-major [James] Belger, assistant quartermaster in charge of the supply train, and Lieutenant D. M. Frost, regimental quartermaster of the regimental train, marched from Camp Sumner near Fort Leavenworth may 10, 1849 (the remaining four companies of the regiment, as previously advised, having been directed to establish posts at Fort Laramie, and Bear river or Fort Hall).

[I] reached Fort Kearny on the Platte river, three hundred ten miles from Fort Leavenworth, may 31.

In consequence of the recent rains, later than usual, the road in places had become almost impassable, the streams much swollen, [and] many of them had to be bridged, occasioning delay in the march. Our animals were in a weak state, many of them unbroken, the wagons overloaded and poorly equipped, [and] in part driven by soldiers and inexperienced citizens. [This] made the commencement of the march a very arduous one. The road is over a rolling prairie country, [but] by following the ridges and bridging the streams a much better road can be made.

During the march the cholera made its appearance. By timely aid and proper precaution on the part of the surgeons its spread was prevented.

Company I, under command of Brevet-major Ruff, joined the command at this post; Major Cross, quartermaster, reported for duty and relieved Major Belger as chief quartermaster.

It being impossible to proceed with the train so heavily loaded, I directed that a portion of the extra supplies, which could best be dispensed with, should be left at Fort Kearny.

Up to this time the command had marched entire, but finding it difficult from the nature of the country for so large a command to find pasturage and encampments at any one place, and learning of the immense emigration that was in advance (at least forty thousand animals), I determined to move from here in three divisions.

In this order the march was resumed on june third; Brevet-major Tucker in command of the first, Major Crittenden of the second, and Brevet-lieutenant-colonel Backenstos of the third division. The divisions marched from three to five miles apart, with myself retaining the command and supervision of the whole.

[We] arrived at the upper crossing of the Platte river (South fork), four hundred seventy-seven miles from Fort Leavenworth on the thirteenth of june. A crossing was effected the same day. It is a rapid, turbid stream, one thousand ninety yards wide, very difficult to ford, its bed of quicksand continually shifting. The road, which courses along the Platte from Fort Kearny to this crossing, a distance of one hundred sixty-seven miles, is the best on the route and is covered with the finest pasturage.

Striking across the dividing ridge, a distance of fifteen and one-half miles, we again reached the level bottom of the Platte (North fork), and continuing along the river arrived at Fort Laramie on the twenty-second of june, six hundred twenty-five miles from Fort Leavenworth.

During the march in the Platte bottom the cholera again visited us, and for a time was somewhat prevalent. On approaching the mountains it disappeared entirely. On the twentieth of june Major Crittenden was relieved from the charge of the Second division and Brevet-major Ruff was placed in command.

Fort Laramie is situated on Laramie river, near its mouth, and as far as our observation extended, in a country nearly destitute of timber and with no lands that are susceptible of cultivation. Horseshoe creek, thirty-five miles, and Deer creek, one hundred one miles beyond (both affluents of the Platte) will be found to possess advantages for a military post. The lands are good with great abundance of pasturage and timber.

After a short halt for preparation [we] marched [on the] twenty-fifth of june and reached the crossing of the North fork of the Platte on the second of july, seven hundred sixty-three miles from Fort Leavenworth.

The road, after crossing the Laramie river, ascends the Black hills. Many of them [are] precipitous in their descent, with numerous streams and ravines cutting through them, making the road in places extremely difficult of passage. In consequence of the general sterility of the soil the country is ordinarily scarce of pasturage. The emigration that was before us had swept the country adjacent to the road of what little there had been, reducing us frequently, after reaching our encampment at night, to the necessity of sending our animals from three to ten miles, searching [for] grazing upon mountain streams and into ravines. It is laborious, but by adopting this course, pasturage may always be found.

The North fork of the Platte at the crossing is about

one hundred fifty yards wide, [but] we were not able to obtain the exact width [since] it is a rapid mountain stream. The unusual rains and snow had so swollen it that we were compelled to ferry, which in consequence of very inadequate means was a dangerous service. I would recommend that future expeditions be provided with boats or pontoons for ferrying wagons, not only for use at this stream, but at others on the route. The cottonwood is the only timber found near them and will not answer for rafts.

The first and second divisions crossed at the upper crossing on the fourth and fifth, and the third division fifteen miles below on the sixth of july.

From this point I was obliged, in consequence of the scarcity of grass, to increase the distance between the divisions to from ten to fifteen miles, making occasional halts (where grazing could be found in sufficient quantity) to consolidate the command [and] for the purpose of examining the condition of the train, resting the animals, and equalizing the loads. The equalization was rendered necessary by the ordinary consumption of provisions and the failure of many of the mules.

[We] marched from the upper crossing on the fifth, sixth, and seventh of july, and arrived at the South pass on the sixteenth. Soon after leaving the North fork the road passes through an alkaline region, which continues to Independence rock, fifty-one miles, the water greatly affecting our animals. Near the road and not far from Independence rock, large quantities of bicarbonate of potassa [potassium], nearly pure, may be gathered. After striking the Sweetwater at Independence rock the country improves and the pasturage is better, although the same alkaline substance continues. We continued on this river seventy-five miles, frequently crossing it, and finally left it a short distance from the

South pass. The distance from Fort Leavenworth to the pass is nine hundred twenty miles.

Before reaching the South pass [and] while encamped on the Sweetwater near Independence rock, july eighth, a reward of two hundred dollars ($200) was offered for the apprehension of deserters (as previously reported). This became necessary for the safety of the command, and for the reasons stated in the notice issued, appended and marked "A". Many had already deserted, and I had certain information that large numbers were to follow. Every exertion had been made to avert it, [and] frequent pursuit and all other means had been resorted to without avail. Upon publishing the notice desertions immediately ceased, and although we passed several roads leading to California few or no attempts were made.

[We] passed South pass and arrived at Green river on the nineteenth of july. This river is similar to the North fork of the Platte [which] compelled the command to ferry.

[We] left Green river on the twenty-first of july and arrived at Fort Hall on the fourth, fifth, and sixth of august, twelve hundred forty miles from Fort Leavenworth.

The route taken was that by Fort Bridger. It is nearly forty miles farther than the one known as Sublette's cut-off, and is well supplied with water and pasturage. On the other route there is said to be a scarcity of water. The road to California by the way of the Salt lake turns off at Fort Bridger.

After leaving Fort Bridger we ascended several hills somewhat precipitous and dangerous for wagons. These continued until we struck the Big Muddy river, eighteen miles [distant]. [We] continued up the Big Muddy to its source [and] crossed the "dividing ridge between the waters of the Pacific and the waters of the Great Basin." Its ascent is gradual and [the] descent into the Bear river valley [is] easy. At its base the road becomes circuitous and dangerous for wagons. With some trouble the command encamped in the valley of Bear river. This valley is, as represented, one of the few spots on the route where a temporary repose may be had. The portion of the valley through which we marched is from three to five miles wide, bordered on either side by high mountains. Judging from the extreme cold experienced here in july (having had frost and ice during the night), the winters must be severe, [and] snow is said to fall to a very great depth. Colonel Fremont makes the altitude five thousand eight hundred forty feet. Portneuf [river] valley in which Fort Hall is situated is extensive, the soil better for cultivation [than that on Bear river], with comparatively a mild winter. Colonel Fremont makes its altitude four thousand five hundred feet.

There will no doubt be a better and nearer road to Oregon and California by the way of Cache valley or the Salt lake. In that event the Cache valley or the Salt lake will be the most desirable points for the establishment of a post.

It is the general opinion of all acquainted with this country that a much shorter road can be found to Oregon and California by the way of Mary or Humboldt river, than the one now traveled. That to Oregon [crosses] the Cascade mountains between Mount Pitt and where the Hamath [Klamath] river passes through the mountains.

After a delay of two days in the valley we continued our march, following the course of Bear river eighty-four and three-fourths miles [to] where the second road to California turns off, thence across a ridge fifty-four miles to an encampment near Fort Hall.

At Fort Bridger an express met me with information that Lieutenant Hawkins of the Rifles had started from Oregon, by the way of the Willamette valley and the southern route, also advising the expedition to take that route. Not meeting Lieutenant Hawkins as expected at Fort Hall and all information of the southern route that could be obtained being of an uncertain character, the proximity of the road to the mines and other reasons determined me to select the upper route, the one originally intended. An express was sent to Lieutenant Hawkins (as previously reported) advising him of my movements.

For reasons which the accompanying letter marked "B" will fully explain, I relieved Brevet-major J. S. Simonson from command of the cantonment near Fort Hall, and placed Brevet-lieutenant-colonel Porter in command. I also made an exchange of their respective companies ordering company G to join my command and move with it to Oregon and detaching company F for duty at Fort Hall.

The train having been here sufficiently reduced, I divided the command into two divisions; Brevet-major Tucker, commanding [the] first and Brevet-lieutenant-colonel Backenstos, [the] second division. They marched from Fort Hall the seventh and eighth of august respectively, and arrived at the crossing of Snake river, or Lewis fork of the Columbia, on the seventeenth, one thousand four hundred twenty-one miles from Fort Leavenworth.

The road soon after leaving Fort Hall strikes Snake river and continues along it nearly the whole distance to the crossing, one hundred seventy-seven miles, passing through the most desolate country we had seen on the march. [The] roads [were] rocky and hilly, [with] scarcely pasturage sufficient to sustain our animals, and at times not sufficient water.

An attempt was made to ford the river, but finding it impracticable I was forced to order the command to continue the march on the southern side.

[We] left the crossing on the twentieth and arrived at Fort Boise, the second crossing on Snake river, on the twenty-ninth, one thousand five hundred forty [-three] miles from Fort Leavenworth.

The road was very difficult and the country a waste. The mules became much weakened for want of food, and the horses entirely unfit for service, many of them having died upon the road. The country from Fort Hall to Fort Boise is too well described by Fremont when he says of it, "grass can only be found at the marked camping places and barely sufficient to keep strong animals from starvation."

The train having become so much weakened [and] to guard against contingencies, I sent an express to Oregon, requesting transportation to be sent to the Dalles of the Columbia river for the command and its baggage, expecting the train to cross the Cascade mountains lightly loaded. [I] also required supplies to be sent to meet the probable wants of the command.

[We] camped on the thirtieth at Malheur creek, fifteen and one-half miles from Fort Boise, where the command halted temporarily to arrange the train. The command was here dismounted, and the horses driven the remainder of the march. Five companies with their baggage and provisions were placed in advance, the remainder of the train, the weakest horses, and one company followed by easy marches under command of Brevet-lieutenant-colonel Backenstos.

From this place the road ascends high and precipitous hills, passing through gorges and crossing numerous mountain streams. The country [was] much improved, and the pasturage better. [We] reached the Grand[e] Rond[e] the eighth and tenth of september, [having traveled] one hundred twenty-three miles from Fort Boise. The [Grande] Rond[e] we found the most inviting locality, both as to country and pasturage we had seen.

We here met several chiefs of the Cayuse and Nez Percé Indians [and] found them friendly and intelligent. The Cayuse Indians live in the country bordering the Umatilla and lying between that and the Blue mountains. Having extensive plains of fine pasturage, they own numerous bands of horses, many of them quite as large as the ordinary American horse, and said to be remarkable for their endurance. In the absence of American horses they would answer for cavalry, and may be had very reasonably.

Left Grand[e] Rond[e] on the tenth and thirteenth and arrived at the Dalles of the Columbia on the twenty-second and twenty-sixth of september, one thousand eight hundred seventy-seven and one-half miles from Fort Leavenworth.

Before leaving the Grand[e] Rond[e] Major Cross, quartermaster, with an escort under Lieutenant Lindsay, was directed to proceed to the Dalles for the purpose of facilitating movements after the command should reach that point.

From the Grand[e] Rond[e] we ascended the Blue mountains, [and] found less difficulty in crossing them than had been anticipated. After four days' march [we] entered the valley of the Umatilla river [and] continued along this stream, crossing it repeatedly until within a short distance of the Columbia river.

We arrived at the Columbia on the sixteenth of september, one hundred six and one-half miles from the Grand[e] Rond[e], [and] continued down the Columbia to the Dalles, ninety-eight miles, fording Deschutes river at a bar near its mouth. This portion of the route varies from heavy and shifting sand to high and precipitous hills, with great scarcity of wood and pasturage, making the travel exceeding difficult.

Upon reaching the Dalles I found the transportation expected had reached there, but not enough for the whole command, [neither could] a sufficiency be obtained in Oregon.

The usual rainy season being near, I deemed it prudent to reach the final destination of the command at as early a day as possible. I accordingly directed Major Tucker with one hundred men to proceed by the trail on the north side of the Columbia to Fort Vancouver. The train lightly loaded, under the direction of Lieutenant Frost, [was directed] to be taken across the Cascade mountains [and] the horses in two detachments with sufficient guards to cross the mountains in charge of Captain[s] Van Buren and McLane.

The remainder of the command with the baggage was transported by way of the Columbia and Willamette rivers to Oregon City. Major Tucker with his command arrived at Fort Vancouver on the thirtieth of september, [and] the headquarters of the regiment on the second of october. The command arrived in Oregon City on the eighth and ninth of october. That portion sent over the mountains have since reached this city.

In crossing the Cascade mountains every exertion was made to get through safely. It will be recollected that this is the most difficult range of the whole route. Besides the natural obstructions of a mountainous road, only passed with great labor, the mountains had been for days enveloped in a dense smoke. Fires were still burning, [and] falling trees [were continually] blocking up the road and impeding the movement of the train. In consequence of the density of the smoke and scarcity of pasturage (there being little or no grass for four days) numbers of the animals were lost. The accompanying statement marked "C" will show the number started with from Fort Leavenworth and the number that reached this city.

During the march numerous bands of Indians were seen [and] many visited our encampments on the Platte river, at Fort Bridger, Bear river, Fort Hall, and along the Snake, Umatilla, and Columbia rivers, all evincing the most friendly disposition.

It is gratifying to state that the expedition has reached its destination safely after one of the longest marches that has ever been made, a distance of over two thousand miles across a country – a large portion of which approaches a waste and much of it mountainous – where the command was compelled to feel its way along. The whole [is] a wilderness, at no point of which supplies of any description can be had. [There are] few spots at which a temporary repose can be found (and if there [were more] one season would not permit [taking advantage of them]). [We were constantly] encountering difficulties that no one can conceive except those who have experienced a journey across this continent, and made at a time when so great a number of persons were traversing the plains.

When it is taken into consideration that the regiment had just been recruited, that the outfit was certainly inadequate to such an undertaking, subjecting us to every inconvenience and want of comfort, that we were passing the roads leading to California and the mines at a time when thousands were traveling in that direction, and it was thought that the rank and file, unable to withstand the temptation, would leave, it will appear that the march has been one of trial and difficulty.

To Major Cross, chief quartermaster, is the command indebted for the untiring energy and ability with which he conducted its supplies. Lieutenant D. M. Frost, regimental quartermaster, in charge of the regimental train, Brevet-captain J. P. Hatch, adjutant, and assistant surgeons, I. Moses, and C. H. Smith, are entitled to my warmest thanks for their energy and ability in the performance of their duties.

Where every officer in the command felt anxious to do his duty it is difficult to make a distinction, [and] it may be said in a word that all are equally entitled to consideration.

To future expeditions I would respectfully suggest that they leave the settlements or Fort Leavenworth as early as the first of april, carrying twenty days forage. By the time the forage is consumed grass will be found in sufficient quantities in the Platte bottom, and the distance to Fort Laramie will be accomplished with ease.

During the march from Fort Laramie to Oregon City there is little or no rain. This, added to the dryness of the atmosphere, with no dew, very soon parches up and destroys the nourishing qualities of the pasturage, [but] this difficulty, which is seriously felt by the middle of august, is avoided to a great extent by an early start. Have light and strongly-made wagons, six good mules to each team, and not over fifteen hundred pounds to the wagon. Boats [should be carried] for crossing wagons over streams, [since] those you cross are rapid mountain rivers [which are] dangerous without proper preparations, and the crossing of them is frequently attended with loss of life.

By adopting the above course an expedition to Oregon or California may be made in four months.

Accompanying this is a table of distances, kept by Doctor Moses, senior surgeon of the expedition, also reports of Major Cross, and Lieutenant Frost, showing the state of the trains.

With the experience we have gained in crossing the mountains we might possibly improve, certain it is that we have endeavored to do our duty.

> With respect, I have the honor to be,
> your obedient servant,
> W. W. LORING, Brevet-colonel, U.S.A.
> Commanding Oregon expedition.

Colonel William G. Freeman,
Adjutant-general, Headquarters, U.S. Army.

> Official: Irwin McDowell,
> Assistant adjutant-general.

Headquarters of the army,
New York, feb. 14, 1850.

Journal of Distances
travelled by the Regiment of Mounted Rifles during a march from Fort Leavenworth, Mo. to the Dalles of the Columbia, in the Summer of 1849 [317]

			MILES	
May	10th	Regiment marched from their Camp "Sumner" near Fort Leavenworth, making their first camp from that place	8	
"	12	To Small stream	9	17
"	13	" " creek	15	32
"	14	" " "	15	47
"	15	" " "	12	59
"	17	" Camp, water ¼ mile distant	15	74
"	18	" " near a creek	20	94
"	19	" " four miles beyond the Nemahaa	20	114
"	20	" " beyond Big Vermillion	24	138
"	21	" " on branch of Blue	16½	154½
"	22	" "	8	162½
"	23	" "	24	186½
"	24	" " on Big Sandy	21	207½
"	25	" " on Dry branch (water scarce)	13	220½
"	26	" " on Little Blue	15	235½
"	27	" " do do	20	255½
"	28	" " beyond the Blue	20	275½
"	29	" "	16½	292
"	30	" " near Fort Kearny six miles	12	304
"	31	" " beyond Fort Kearny two miles	8	312

[317] Hitherto unpublished table of distances, kept by Dr. Israel Moses, from the original manuscript in the National archives, Washington, D.C.

				MILES	
June	1	To Camp		2.21	314.21
"	2	" "		9.76	323.97
"	3	" "		12.42	336.39
"	4	" "		14.64	351.03
"	5	" "		11.98	363.01
"	6	" "		10.87	373.88
"	7	" "		12.86	386.74
"	8	" "	Junction of N. & S. Forks of Platte River	6.21	392.95
"	9	" "	on a Branch	19.08	412.03
"	10	" "	Six miles above the Lower Crossing of S. Fork of Platte	25.07	437.10
"	11	" "		15.75	452.85
"	12	" "		11.81	464.66
"	13	" Crossing of South Fork of Platte, upper ford— 3271 ft. wide		13.31	477.97
"	14	" Camp beyond the Crossing		6.65	484.62
"	15	" "	on N. Fork of Platte	16.86	501.48
"	16	" "		17.75	519.23
"	17	" "		20.85	540.08
"	18	" "	3 miles east of Chimney Rock	21.30	561.38
"	19	" "	near Scott's Bluffs	23.51	584.89
"	20	" "	on Horse Creek	19.28	604.17
"	21	" "	on N. Fork of Platte	19.33	623.50
"	22	" "	one & a half miles beyond Fort Laramie	15.50	639.00

From Fort Kearny to Fort Laramie, 327½ Miles.

"	25th	To Camp beyond "Bitter Cottonwood Creek"		21.74	660.74
"	26	" "	on Horse-shoe Creek near Heber's Spring	14.20	674.94
"	27	" "	Among the Hills	19.52	694.46
"	28	" "	On Spring branch	21.08	715.54
"	29	" "	Deer Creek	26.62	742.16
"	30	" "	Crooked Muddy Creek	10.	752.16
July	2d	" "	Crossing of N. Fork of Platte at Mormon ferry	11.75	763.91

					MILES	
July	5	To Camp		near Marsh & Spring (Mineral)	18.63	782.54
"	6	"	"	near Willow Spring (on Spring 3 miles beyond)	18.85	801.39
"	7	"	"	On Sweet Water—2 miles from Independence Rock	15.08	816.47
"	8	"	"	on Sweet Water	7.32	823.79
"	10	"	"	do	10.5	834.29
"	11	"	"	Branch of do	18.75	853.04
"	12	"	"	Morass where ice was found at the depth of 12 in.	16.5	869.54
"	13	"	"	on Sweet Water	16.25	885.79
"	15	"	"	on stream, 9 miles from South Pass	25.	910.79
"	16	"	"	Spring branch (9 mi. beyond is Sublette's cut off)	16.25	927.04
"	17	"	"	on Sandy (Little) (13 miles back is Sublette's cut off)	20.75	947.79
"	18	"	"	on Big Sandy	11.25	959.04
"	19	"	"	Green River Ferry	23.	982.04
"	21	"	"	on Black's Fork	20.5	1002.54
"	22	"	"	on Muddy	18.966	1021.506
"	23	"	"	on Black's Fork, two miles from Fort Bridger	15.07	1036.576
"	24	"	"	on Big Muddy	18.695	1055.271
"	25	"	"	on do	16.948	1072.219
"	26	"	"	on Bear River	25.527	1097.746
"	29	"	"	on Spring branch	23.447	1121.193
"	30	"	"	at Foot of Big Hill, two miles from Smith's Trading house	17.09	1138.283
"	31	"	"	on "Camp Spring"	18.22	1156.503
Augt.	1	"	"	on Bear River, 2 miles beyond Soda Springs The California Road by way of G. S. Lake turns off 4 miles beyond.	21.923	1178.426
"	2	"	"	On Portneuf	23.351	1201.777

					MILES	
Augt.	3	To Camp	on Rock branch	15.	1216.777
"	4	" "	four miles from Fort Hall	22.846	1239.623
"	7	" "	beyond crossing of Port-neuf	12.789	1252.412
"	8	" "	on Snake River bottom, near a spring	13.75	1266.162
"	9	" "	on Snake River	14.20	1280.362
"	10	" "	on Raft River	15.	1295.362
"	11	" "	on Snake River	25.44	1320.802
"	12	" "	on do do	13.817	1334.619
"	13	" "	on Rock Creek	16.116	1350.735
"	14	" "	on do do where it runs in a very deep cañon	14.424	1365.159
"	15	" "	on Shute or Salmon Fall Creek	23.	1388.159
"	16	" "	on Snake River, on bluffs	19.5	1407.659
"	17	" "	at first Crossing of Snake River	13.292	1420.951
"	20	" "	on Dry Branch	6.816	1427.767
"	21	" "	on Snake River	12.205	1439.972
"	23	" "	" "	20.194	1460.166
"	24	" "	Catharine Creek	11.715	1471.881
"	25	" "	on Snake River	21.946	1493.827
"	26	" "	Small Creek	6.461	1500.288
"	27	" "	Snake River	13.92	1514.208
"	28	" "	do	14.4	1528.608
"	29	" "	near Fort Boiseé at 2d Crossing of Snake	14.244	1542.852
"	30	" "	on Malhern River	15.515	1558.367
Sept.	3	" "	on Birch Creek	22.308	1580.675
"	4	" "	" Burnt River	9.192	1589.867
"	5	" "	do do	11.355	1601.222
"	6	" "	on Spring branch of Burnt River	13.515	1614.737
"	7	" "	Spring branch in a mountain gorge	10.373	1625.110
"	8	" "	on Slough of Powder River	17.59	1642.7
"	9	" "	Second Fork of Powder River	13.66	1656.36

				MILES	
Sept.	10	To Camp	in Grand Rond	16.50	1672.86
"	11	" "	on branch of Rond River	7.25	1680.11
"	13	" "	in Blue Mountains	12.	1692.11
"	14	" "	Lee's near some springs of water	16.647	1708.757
"	15	" "	at base of Blue Mts. on branch of Umatillah	14.604	1723.361
"	16	" "	at Crossing of the Umatillah	13.948	1737.309
"	17	" "	on plain. Water ½ mile distant	12.71	1750.019
"	18	" "	on Umatillah	16.	1766.019
"	19	" "	on the Columbia	13.523	1779.542
"	20	" "	do do	16.213	1795.755
"	21	" "	on Creek, ¼ mile from River	12.502	1808.257
"	22	" "	on Columbia	14.871	1823.128
"	23	" "	do	12.	1835.128
"	24	" "	on John Day's River	5.373	1840.501
"	25	" "	on Columbia	17.265	1857.766
"	26	" "	at Dalles. 10 miles back after crossing a creek, the main road over the Cascade Mts. turns towards the left.	19.646	1877.412
"	29	" "	on Spring branch N.E. from Mt. Hood	6.75	1884.162
"	30	" "	on 1st branch of Chute's River. The road here strikes the main road, where it comes from Dalles Creek	9.21	1893.372
Oct.	1	" "	near an Indian Village, on a large branch of Chute Creek	15.41	1908.782
"	2	" "	on small branch of Chute Creek	12.06	1920.842
"	4	" "	on Sand Creek	15.	1935.842
"	5	" "	on Sandy, passing a dividing ridge	8.75	1944.592

					MILES	
Oct.	6	To Camp	on second prairie	7.	1951.592
"	8	" "	on Sandy, having crossed it four times	13.75	1965.342
"	9	" "	on Fern Prairie, water in springs	14.	1979.342
"	10	" "	at opening on the woods (no water)	13.50	1992.842
"	11	" "	at Foster's Farm, being the first house met with on the road	4.	1996.842
"	13	" Oregon City		20.	2016.842

Head Quarters of the Army,   Official:
New York, Feb. 15, 1850.   IRWIN McDOWELL
                                                    Asst. Adjt. Genl.

Bibliography

ADAMS, ZU. "Biography of John Brown Dunbar," in Kansas state historical society collections, x.

AMERICAN STATE PAPERS, military affairs (Washington, 1858-61) III, IV, V, VII.

APPLETON's Cyclopaedia of American biography (New York, 1888-89) 6 vols.

BALLENGER, THOMAS LEE. Around Tahlequah council fires (Muskogee, Oklahoma, 1935).

BANCROFT, HUBERT HOWE. History of Nevada, Colorado, and Wyoming (San Francisco, 1890).

——— History of the northwest coast (San Francisco, 1884) 2 vols.

——— History of Oregon (San Francisco, 1888) 2 vols.

——— History of Washington, Idaho, and Montana (San Francisco, 1890).

BELSHAW, MARIA PARSONS. "Diary, 1853," in Oregon historical society quarterly, XXXIII.

BENNETT, COLONEL C. R. Letter to editor, january 27, 1939. MS.

BOARDMAN, JOHN. "Journal, 1843," in Utah historical quarterly, II.

BONNEY, W. P. Letter to editor, march 24, 1939. MS.

BROWN, JENNIE BROUGHTON. Fort Hall on the Oregon trail (Caldwell, Idaho, 1932).

BROWN, JOHN EVANS. "Memorial of an American gold-seeker," in Journal of American history (New Haven) II.

BRYANT, EDWIN. Rocky mountain adventures (New York, 1888).

——— What I saw in California (New York, 1848).

BUSHNELL, DAVID I. jr. Drawings of George Gibbs in the far northwest (Smithsonian miscellaneous collections, XCVII, no. 8).

BUSHYHEAD, DENNIS W. Autobiography. MS. (John Ross manuscripts and papers, Phillips collection, University of Oklahoma).

BUSHYHEAD, ELOISE BUTLER. Statement to Grant Foreman, quoted by him in letter to editor, january 23, 1939. MS.

BUTLER, E. H. Taylor and his generals (Philadelphia, 1847).

CLARK, BENNETT C. "Diary of a journey from Missouri to California, 1849," in Missouri historical review (Columbia) XXIII.

CLEMSON, JOHN G. Letter to editor, march 9, 1939. MS.

CLAYTON, W. The latter-day saints emigrants' guide (St. Louis, 1848); reprinted by A. William Lund (Salt Lake City, n.d.).

CRAWFORD, G. W. Letter to commanding officer, Mounted Riflemen, march 28, 1849. MS. (Old records section, archives and claims division, Washington quartermaster depot, Fort Meyer, Virginia).

CROSS, MAJOR OSBORNE. Letters to General Thomas S. Jesup, june 14, 24, august 8, 1849; to Lieutenant F. S. K. Russell, august 8, 1849; to Brevet-captain J. P. Hatch, september 1, 14, october 11, 1849; to James B. Leech, september 9, 1849; to Captain Rufus Ingalls, september 23, 1849; to Lieutenant D. M. Frost, september 27, october 12, 1849. MSS. (Old records section, archives and claims division, Washington quartermaster depot, Fort Meyer, Virginia).

—— File in Pension bureau records. MSS. (National archives, Washington, D.C.)

DEIBERT, RALPH C. History of the third United States cavalry (Philadelphia, n.d.).

DELANO, A. Life on the plains and among the diggings (New York, 1857).

DICTIONARY of American biography (New York, 1933) VI, X, XI, XX.

DOUGHERTY, LEWIS BISSELL. "Experiences on the Oregon trail," as told to Ethel M. Withers, in Missouri historical review, XXIV.

DRUM, GENERAL RICHARD C. "Reminiscences of the Indian fight at Ash hollow," in Nebraska state historical society publications, XVI.

EGAN, HOWARD R. Pioneering the west, 1846 to 1878, edited by W. M. Egan (Richmond, Utah, 1917).

ELLIOT, T. C. "Richard (Captain Johnny) Grant," in Oregon historical society quarterly, XXXVI.

FAIRCHILD, LUCIUS. California letters, edited by Joseph Schafer (Madison, Wisconsin, 1931).

FIELDING, MANTLE. Dictionary of American painters, sculptors, and engravers (Philadelphia, privately printed, 1926).

FOREMAN, GRANT. Letter to editor, march 23, 1939. MS.

FREMONT, JOHN C. Report of the exploring expedition to the Rocky mountains in the year 1842 (Washington, 1845).

FRONTIER GUARDIAN (Kanesville, Iowa) june 27, 1849.

FROST, LIEUTENANT D. M. Letter to Major Osborne Cross, october 26, 1849; to Colonel W. W. Loring, may 30, 1850; to General

Thomas S. Jesup, november 16, 1851; estimate of supplies, january 11, 1849. MSS. (Old records section, archives and claims division, Washington quartermaster depot, Fort Meyer, Virginia).

GHENT, W. J. Road to Oregon (New York, 1929).

GREENE, ALBERT R. "Bugle calls in the desert," in Kansas City (Missouri) journal, november 28, 1915.

HAFEN, LEROY R. "Cherokee gold-seekers in Colorado, 1849-1850," in Colorado magazine (Denver) XV.

———— The overland mail (Cleveland, the Arthur H. Clark company, 1926).

———— and F. M. Young. Fort Laramie (Glendale, the Arthur H. Clark company, 1938).

HUGHES-HALLET, EMILIE S. VON. Letter, n.d.; copy supplied by John G. Clemson. MS.

HATCH, BREVET-CAPTAIN J. P. Letter to Brevet-lieutenant-colonel Andrew Porter, april 28, 1850. MS. (National archives, war department records, office of adjutant-general, document files).

HATHEWAY, BREVET-MAJOR J. S. Letter to General R. Jones, november 5, 1848. MS. (National archives, war department records, office of adjutant-general, document files).

HAWKINS, LIEUTENANT GEORGE R. Letter to Brevet-lieutenant-colonel Andrew Porter, february 24, 1850. MS. (National archives, war department records, office of adjutant-general, document files).

HEADLEY, JOEL T. The great riots of New York, 1712-1873 (New York, 1873).

HEITMAN, FRANCIS B. Historical register and dictionary of the United States army (Washington, 1903) 2 vols.

HENDERSON, PAUL. Map of the Oregon trail. MS.

———— Letter to editor, december 31, 1938.

HULBERT, ARCHER BUTLER. Forty-niners (Boston, 1931).

———— Crown collection of American maps, series III (Denver public library, Denver, Colorado).

INGERSOLL, CHESTER. Overland to California in 1847 (Chicago, 1937).

IRVING, WASHINGTON. Adventures of Captain Bonneville (London, 1855) 3 vols.

———— Astoria (New York, 1868).

JAMES, MARQUIS. "That was New York," in The New Yorker (New York) december 3, 1938.

JONES, GENERAL R. Circular letter, july 14, 1848; letter to W. L. Marcy, july 18, 1848. MSS. (National archives, war department records, office of adjutant-general, document files).

KEARNY, COLONEL S. W. Report of a summer campaign to the Rocky mountains in 1845 (Washington, 1845).

KEPLER, FRED J. G. Letter to editor, february 23, 1939. MS.

LANE, JOSEPH. Letter to James W. Nesmith, march 5, 1850. MS. (Oregon state historical society).

LAUT, AGNES C. The overland trail (New York, 1929).

LORING, BREVET-COLONEL WILLIAM W. Letters to General R. Jones, january 12 (L-13), 13 (L-16), 15 (L-43), february 2 (L-43), 8 (L-47), may 10 (L-144), 19 (L-151), 31 (L-168), june 4 (L-171), 8 (L-185), 22 (L-200), 25 (L-205), july 22 (L-260), august 7 (L-251), december 18 (L-314), 1849, january 8 (L-64), 16 (L-66), june 30 (L-243), november 12 (L-246), 1850; to Colonel L. Thomas, june 24, 1849 (L-201); to Colonel W. G. Freeman, october 15, 1849 (L-307), january 8 (L-64), march 6 (L-89), april 28 (L-166), 1850; to Major Winslow F. Sanderson, december 18, 1849 (L-314); to Major-general Persifor F. Smith, january 16, 1850 (L-66, 67); to adjutant-general, march 28, 1850 (L-96); proclamation, july 8, 1849 (L-315); to General D. E. Twiggs, january 12, 1849 (L-13). MSS. (National archives, war department records, office of adjutant-general, document files).

LUND, A. WILLIAM. Letter to editor, february 1, 1940. MS.

LUNT, GEORGE. Letter to G. W. Crawford, march 21, 1849. MS. (National archives, records of secretary of war).

MACKAY, COLONEL AENEAS. Letters to General Thomas S. Jesup, april 11, 15, may 17, july 5, 1849. MSS. (Old records section, archives and claims division, Washington quartermaster depot, Fort Meyer, Virginia).

MONTHLY RETURNS, regiment of Mounted Riflemen. MSS. (National archives, war department records, office of adjutant-general, document files).

MORRIS, CAPTAIN R. M. Letter to Major S. S. Tucker, july 26, 1850. MS. (National archives, war department records, office of adjutant-general document files).

MOSES, DR. ISRAEL. Table of distances and letter, november 4, 1849. MS. (Old records section, archives and claims division, Washington quartermaster depot, Fort Meyer, Virginia).

NEBRASKA state historical society publications, XX, XXI.

OREGON SPECTATOR (Oregon City), november 1, december 13, 27, 1849, february 21, march 7, april 4, 18, may 2, 1850.

PACKWOOD, WILLIAM H. "Reminiscences," in Oregon historical society quarterly, XVI.

PARKMAN, FRANCIS. The Oregon trail (Boston, 1925).

PLANK, PRYOR. "The Iowa, Sac, and Fox Indian mission and its missionaries, Rev. Samuel Irvin and his wife," in Kansas state historical society collections, X.

PORTER, BREVET-LIEUTENANT-COLONEL ANDREW. Letter to Captain J. P. Hatch, february 24, 1850. MS. (National archives, war department records, office of adjutant-general, document files).

POWELL, COLONEL W. H. List of officers of the army of the United States from 1779 to 1900 (New York, 1901).

READ, GEORGE WILLIS. A pioneer of 1850, edited by Georgia W. Read (Boston, 1927).

ROBERTS, EDWARD. Shoshone and other western wonders (New York, 1888).

RUFF, ANNIE DOUGHERTY. Letter to Mrs. Ethel Ramsay Davenport, n.d. MS. (Private collection of Mrs. Davenport, New Hope, Pennsylvania).

RUFF, BREVET-MAJOR CHARLES F. Letter to Colonel Nathaniel Ford, february 26, 1850. MS. (Oregon historical society).

SABIN, EDWIN L. Kit Carson days (New York, 1935) 2 vols.

SERVICE RECORD, Lieutenant Joseph Cross, U.S. naval academy. MS.

SHEPARD, GEORGE. Diary of a journey from Waukegan, Illinois, to Hangtown, California, in 1850. MS. (Collection of Mrs. B. T. McClave, McClave, Colorado).

SMITH, WILLIAM E. "The Oregon trail through Pottawatomie county, Kansas," in Kansas state historical society collections, XVII.

SOUTHWEST historical series V: Southern trails to California, edited by R. P. Bieber (Glendale, the Arthur H. Clark company, 1937).

SPAULDING, OLIVER LYMAN. The United States army in war and peace (New York, 1937).

STANSBURY, CAPTAIN HOWARD. Exploration and survey of the great Salt lake valley of Utah (Washington, 1853).

STEELE, ALDEN H. With the rifle regiment. MS. (Bancroft library, University of California).

STEVENS, JOHN A. Memorial to George Gibbs (New York, 1873).

SWIFT, MAJOR-GENERAL EBEN. Personal memoirs. MS. (Collection of Colonel Eben Swift jr., Fort Sam Houston, Texas).

TALBOT, THEODORE. Journals of 1843 and 1849-52, edited by Charles H. Carey (Portland, Oregon, 1931).

TANNATT, MRS. T. R. "Letter to Colonel W. F. Prosser, january 25, 1899," in Washington historian (Tacoma) I.

TAPPAN, CHARLES. Letter to Philip Greely jr., march 19, 1849. MS. (National archives, records of secretary of war).

TAPPAN, DANIEL L. Tappan-Toppan genealogy (Arlington, Mass., 1915).

TAPPAN, WILLIAM HENRY. Letter to Acting-governor C. H. Mason, june 19, 1854. MS. (National archives, department of interior records, office of Indian affairs, Washington superintendency).

—— "Letter to Colonel W. F. Prosser, february 12, 1898," in Washington historian (Tacoma) I.

—— Letters to Dr. Alden H. Steele, october 8, november 30, 1852. MSS. (Oregon historical society).

—— Letter to Charles Tappan, february 15, 1849. MS. (National archives, records of secretary of war).

TILDEN, ANITA S. Letter to editor, february 15, 1940. MS.

TURNER, LIEUTENANT HENRY S. Journal of an expedition performed in 1845 (Washington, 1845).

TWIGGS, MAJOR-GENERAL D. E. Order no. 8, february 9, 1849. MS. (Old records section, archives and claims division, Washington quartermaster depot, Fort Meyer, Virginia).

U.S. HOUSE. 28 cong., 2 sess., no. 2, 132c.

—— 29 cong., 2 sess., no. 4, 68d.

—— 30 cong., 2 sess., no. 1, 184, 193-97, 204-208.

—— 31 cong., 2 sess., no. 1, 126-231.

U.S. SENATE. 27 cong., 2 sess., no. 1, 78, 92.

—— 29 cong., 1 sess., no. 1, 220d.

—— 30 cong., 1 sess., no. 1, 78-79, 96d, 282-84, 303-306, appendix, 74-77.

—— 31 cong., 2 sess., no. 1, pt. 2, 77-78, 128-231, 284-89.

—— 34 cong., 3 sess., no. 5, pt. 2, 172.

VICTOR, FRANCES FULLER. All over Oregon and Washington (San Francisco, 1872).

WAR OF THE REBELLION, a compilation of official records of the union and confederate armies (Washington, 1880-1901) series I, VII, XXV, XLVII.

WATKINS, ALBERT. "History of Fort Kearny," in Nebraska state historical society publications, XVI.

WHARTON, MAJOR CLIFFTON. "Expedition of, in 1844," in Kansas state historical society collections, XVI.

WHEATON, PERCY A. Letters to editor, february 4, march 2, 1940. MSS.

WHITE, ELIJAH. Thrilling adventures (New York, 1859).

WINTHROP, ROBERT. Letter to G. W. Crawford, april 6, 1849. MS. (National archives, records of secretary of war).

WISLIZENUS, F. A. A journey to the Rocky mountains, 1839 (St. Louis, 1912).

YOUNG, F. G. "The Oregon trail," in Oregon historical society quarterly, XVI.

Index

on frontier, 18; at Jefferson barracks, 18n; where stationed, 18-19; in Seminole war, 19; in Mexican war, 19; at Fort Leavenworth, 19; Twiggs transferred to, 278n

First regiment Missouri Volunteers: 248n

Fish: location, 181, 212, 325; *see also* Trout, Salmon

Fitzpatrick, Thomas: 52n

Five Crows: Indian chief, 230n

Five-mile creek: 234n

Five-mile rapids: 101n

Flathead Indians: 263, *see* Salish Indians

Flour-mill: of Hudson's Bay company, 264

Flowers: seen, 280, 309

Fontenelle's fork: 144

Forest fire: 167

Forge, traveling: 81

Forrest, Edwin: 307n

Fort Boise: history, 199n; described, 206; country, 216; distance from Fort Leavenworth, 338

Fort Bridger: deserters brought in, 129; distance from Big Muddy river, 335; route compared, 355; two divisions go by, 335

Fort Childs: 14; *see also* Fort Kearny

Fort Crawford: 19

Fort Gaines: 43n

Fort Hall: built, 101n; distance from Independence rock, 126; Hawkins at, 129n; main road by, 130n; two companies at, 166; described, 170; distance from Fort Leavenworth, 172, 335; distance from Fort Vancouver, 172; distance from Bear river, 337

Fort John: 52n

Fort Kearny: name changed to, 14; Riflemen at, 17, 55; described, 55-56, 299; buildings in *1848*, 57n; Bonneville at, 60n; number of emigrants passing, 79, 301; Mrs. Ruff at, 292n; distance from Oregon

trail, 293; cost, 300; distance from Fort Leavenworth, 308, 331; distance from Little Sandy creek, 393

Fort Laramie: Gibbs sends journal from, 25; history, 52n; garrison, 56n; Husband in charge, 78n; council of *1845* near, 83n; mutinying teamster taken to, 94; description, 98; distance from Fort Leavenworth, 98, 333; Sanderson at, 98n; Moore at, 98n; Duncan at, 98n; Rhett at, 98n; Roberts at, 99n; company C at, 99n; company D Sixth infantry at, 99n; Bootes at, 99n; distance from Fort Kearny, 99; situation, 324, 333; third of distance to Pacific ocean, 326

Fort Leavenworth: Oregon battalion mustered in, 14; history, 33n; Gibbs at, 275; distance from Fort Kearny, 308; time to start from, 342; distance from Little Sandy creek, 393

Fort McHenry: 13

Fort Meyer: 22

Fort Morgan: 43n

Fort Nez Perce: 239n

Fort Nisqually: 271

Fort Pike: 18

Fort Platte: 327

Fort Scott: 19, 74n

Fort Smith: 60n

Fort Snelling: 19

Fort Steilacoom: 26

Fort Vancouver: headquarters removed to, 22; history, 104n; ninety miles from Dalles, 265; Tucker's command at, 265n; situation, 266

Fort Walla Walla: Tappan at, 29; Cayuse Indian mission near, 230n; troops might move from, 239

Fort William: 52n; *see* Fort Laramie

Fort Winnebago: 19

Fort Wood: 18

Foulke, Pvt. Aeneas: 74n

Fourth cavalry: 277n

Fourth infantry: 18, 182, 278n

vided, 63, 66, 172, 304-305; difficulties, 66-67; on South fork, 79; overhauled, 99, 126, 166, 167, 212; no bell, 113; left at Malheur river, 211; disorder, 250; crossing streams, 282-83; of emigrants described, 284-85; condition, 331, 338; crossing Cascade mountains, 247n, 251, 340

Tribes of Washington and Northwestern Oregon: 26

Trinity river: 26

Trout: location, 181, 183, 221

Tucker, Capt. Stephen S: at Chapultepec, 15; establishes post, 22; biography, 104n; command, 167n, 337; on Columbia river, 255, 340

Tulsa (Wyo.): 143n

Turkeys: seen, 295

Twiggs, Gen. David E: command, 14, 16; at Fort Leavenworth, 16-17; puts regiment in motion, 277; biography, 277n

Twin Falls (Idaho): 184n

UMATILLA river: Cross reached, 226; burial ground on, 229; Indians on, 230n

Umatilla valley: described, 223; range for stock, 226

Umpqua river: 21

Unfortunate river: 210; *see* Malheur river

Union Pacific railroad: 223n

Upper crossing: Riflemen cross at, 85, 86-87, 315-16, 333; distance from Fort Laramie, 315; distance from Fort Kearny, 332

Upper falls: 248

U. S. Army, Pacific division: 17, 20

U. S. Board of geographic names: 36n

U. S. Geological survey: 122n

Ute Indians: 150n

VALE (Ore.): 211n

Valverde (New Mex.): 142n, 276n

Van Buren, Capt. Michael E: 16; biography, 251

Van Vliet: Capt. Stewart: 292n; biography, 300; quartermaster, 300

Vasquez, Louis: 129n

Vaughn, Bailey: 261n

Vegetables: grow, 269

Vera Cruz: campaign against, 14; Riflemen at, 15; Cross at, 19

Verdigris river: 73n

Viameter: used, 291

Vinton, Major D. H: 269n

Volcanic: signs, 156; three buttes, 161; fragments, 177; action, 178, 230; formation, 187, 230; rock, 236

WABASH river: 281n

Wagonhound creek: 108n

Wagonmaster: responsible to agent, 66; discharges carbine, 212

Wagons: number in train, 16, 179, 331; for officers' families, 35n; number of mules to, 36, 86, 342; broken, 39, 50, 51, 94, 137, 154; appearance, 42; number on road, 42n, 52, 53, 55, 79, 295, 307; speed, 46; corralled, 66; number under wagonmaster, 66; descent into Ash hollow, 89n; left behind, 99, 101-102; 251; ferried, 110, 143; wheels calked, 138; capsized, 193; loads, 212, 213, 301, 342; carry stores at portage, 262; drawn by oxen, 285; seen in mirage, 297

Waiilatpu: 230

Walker, Lt. J. G: 15

Walker, John: 261n

Walker, William H. T: company, 302; biography, 302n

Walla Walla Indians: 232

Walla Walla fork: 234, 239

Walla Walla river: 239

Wallowa mountains: 222n

Walnut creek: 39n

Walnut trees: 44

Warm spring: 103n

Warren, Major G. W: 270n

Wasatch range: 156

Wascopam mission: 233n; *see* Old Mission